The
Wild Man
from
Sugar Creek

The
Wild Man
from
Sugar Creek

The Political Career of
Eugene Talmadge

WILLIAM ANDERSON

LOUISIANA STATE UNIVERSITY PRESS

Baton Rouge

ISBN 0–8071–0088–9 (cloth)
ISBN 0–8071–0170–2 (paper)
Library of Congress Catalog Card Number 74–82002
Copyright © 1975 by Louisiana State University Press
All rights reserved
Manufactured in the United States of America
Printed by Moran Industries, Inc.
Designed by Albert Crochet
August 1975 printing

for my
Mother and Daddy

"The poor dirt farmer ain't got but three friends on this earth: God Almighty, Sears Roebuck, and Gene Talmadge."

—EUGENE TALMADGE

Contents

Illustrations

Preface

It was a time of culmination: when the seed, thought dead, broke ground; when the world came to Georgia and her dormant mind began mirroring the sparkle of a million new bits of information. It was a time of profound change in a changeless land. It was the 1930s, and the significance of the period is the significance of the politics of Eugene Talmadge. He was the antithesis of the new time, but the personification of its heritage. Immovable in the sudden rush of history, he became typecast for his regressive politics as a backwater southern demagogue, a ranting antique who represented all that had been wrong with traditional southern economics and morality. He has been largely dismissed as inconsequential in the history of that period, an annoying obstacle to the thrust of destiny. His role in the scheme of that time has been cemented in the American mind by too many oversimplifying books and movies. He was long ago relegated to a kind; his was the mold from which demagogic stereotypes were made for Central Casting: mention the name and the mind's motion picture flicks on our man strutting across the turpentine-oozing pine planking, under a sweltering sun, raking the air like a runaway windmill, hair askew (carefully grown that way), suit somehow whiter and brighter than those of the boys in the crowd, and yet correctly rumpled to show he was no fashion plate, just one of us. The words pour out like daggers from a crazed tent preacher scourging the souls of the overalled tobacco-stained gathering. The crowd was also delivered from Central, all gnarled and burned by the weather and the plow handle, cow manure on the boots, grass stains on the knees of the just-cleaned overalls, bad posture; a slump, gift of the plow, white shirt sleeves rolled up, burned neck, bad teeth, dull-eyed except that now before the rage of the speaker there is a fanatical roundness to them. We know these people are not bright or they wouldn't be standing there howling like moonstruck dogs, and they would not dress that way and talk with that drawl. We have already seen Gene Talmadge and his gang of wool-hat boys while we were eating popcorn. It was a grade B picture show, and it reinforced our resentment of southern demagogues and the ragtag band of down-and-outers that yelped after them. Gene Talmadge has been done before, and we have him nicely filed away under "redneck racist." Why do him over? Because we have not done him right. Because in our communications makeup where we by necessity categorize, we have categorized the flesh from him and his kind, and his times have been lost. We have skeletonized because it is easier to remember history that way, and Georgians and others have erred in the interpretation of themselves because of that propensity.

It is difficult to write of a man like Gene Talmadge because he dealt in a politics of crisis and of style and, quite often, of theater. His career as a Georgia politician lasted twenty years—from 1926 to 1946—and in that span he either dominated or haunted the political structure as few men have done in any state's history. His impact was such that he polarized Georgia's voters as few men had in her history. In the tradition of the frontiersman, he felt the best way was the shortest, least complicated way. And his method of operation ran counter to the complex times. He wanted Georgians to remain true to their heritage in a time of iconoclasm. He wanted them to remain cultural isolationists when Dixie was being eroded like sand castles at high tide.

He was the champion of the mythical little man, of the have-nots, the dejected, the mentally awash, the orphans of the rural life propelled by the depression to the doorstep of the city, alone, uncertain, afraid. Yet his politics didn't do much for the little man other than provide him with a teether while he attempted to cope with the urbanizing world. Perhaps Talmadge's legacy was the crutch he afforded, the security of the past that made the way into the future a little easier. He was a root, a rock, a certainty, while the future fragmented the past into a meaningless jumble.

It does not take much searching to discover the scarcity of documented political history on the Talmadge period. Oral interviews had to serve as a basis for his biography.

The voices who spoke intimately with the man have now grown hoary with age, their days on the stage forgotten by most but themselves. Surprisingly, many of those intimates are now alive—or were alive when I started work on this book. Their memories form the flesh of the man and were my primary source in understanding just who Gene Talmadge was. Their remembrances are vivid, though often in disagreement. He was so volatile and controversial that he struck a schizophrenic stance, and it has been difficult to balance conflicting views of the man.

Tom Linder, Henry Spurlin, Hugh Howell, Lamar Murdaugh, John Whitley, Chip Robert, J. C. Corley, and James Peters, members of the inner circle at various times, were alive with memories of their days with Talmadge. Of them none drew closer to the man than Spurlin. As a seventeen-year-old state militiaman, he came to Talmadge's attention in 1934 during the textile union upheavals, and was practically adopted by the governor, entering into most of his confidences until the day Talmadge died. Spurlin served as chauffeur, valet, messenger, adviser, manipulator, liaison man with political organizers, and trusted friend. Spurlin was the only man allowed to write checks on Gene's bank account, the only man who paid himself out of the account on his own signature. Spurlin said, with deep affection, "No man knew the Governor better than I. And I loved him like he was my father." Spurlin's detailed knowledge spanned 1934 to 1946.

Tom Linder more or less sanctioned Talmadge's entry into state politics in 1926, when, as a legislator, he obtained the cooperation of many of the state's politicos in backing the unknown Talmadge. His accounts of those early days were vivid and enhanced with a surprising overview of the Talmadge years. Attorney Hugh Howell started with Gene in 1926, and he remained a trusted loyalist until Talmadge crushed their friendship by refusing to appoint Howell his successor in 1936. Howell served as chairman of the state Democratic party in 1935 and 1936 when the state party was bitterly split over supporting Roosevelt. Through Howell, Talmadge maintained tight control until both men were ousted by the Roosevelt juggernaut in the summer of 1936.

Lamar Murdaugh was the primary source for Talmadge's initial forays into local politics. Murdaugh lent the struggling Talmadge the use of his law office and became an early adviser. His knowledge of that early period proved crucial to an understanding of the intense frustrations Talmadge suffered as he attempted to break into politics, and the value of Murdaugh's words became evident when he was found to be the only surviving confidant of that era.

Probably no man spanned the entire Talmadge career as did his close personal friend and constant companion, the road builder John Whitley. Gene used to escape to the Whitley fishing camp in LaGrange to relieve the pressures of office. A rare view of the relaxed Talmadge was obtained from Whitley and his wife Sarah. They remember him well and fondly, having spent many, many hours swapping stories, fishing and hunting, sharing intimacies, and laughing at Gene's self-deprecating jokes and Whitley's famous yarns.

Lawrence "Chip" Robert was Atlanta Establishment. He knew Talmadge from the businessman's point of view, and, ironically, he was a close friend of FDR, serving as his assistant secretary of the treasury. Robert reflected well on the terrible split in the state party and how it was partially caused by a stubborn FDR. The anguish of Georgia Democrats at that time was very colorfully portrayed by Mr. Robert.

J. C. Corley, a Forsyth farmer, lived next to the old Talmadge land all his life and remembered riding on Gene's boyhood pony. The two men renewed their childhood friendship in the 1930s when Corley became a grassroots organizer, driver, messenger, and general helper for the governor. He was what Gene called "one of the boys," that transitory group of common people who served Gene at various times in various capacities, sharing the closest of secrets for one term in office before returning to their farms or law practices. Corley knew Talmadge the farmer also, for he oversaw Talmadge's cattle herd on the Forsyth farm in 1939.

James Peters, Manchester banker and legislator, was a key source for the political Talmadge. His retrieval of names and events was computerlike. Peters was an organizer and strategist for Talmadge and was particularly close to him in the 1940 election and the term that followed. His behind-the-scene glimpses of the turbulent University of Georgia crises disclose the tremendous pressures Talmadge encountered in the most fateful decision of his career.

Three who knew the Talmadge family personally and for long periods were Lucy Cameron, whose husband was a key Talmadge adviser; Bethel Harbin, the ordinary for the McRae courthouse who was present at the early Talmadge battles there; and Duncan Clegg, justice of the peace in McRae, a man who rode with Gene in 1918 in his first attempt at state office. Their accounts were firsthand and intimate.

Some of the rarer information, received through an interview, came from former state treasurer George Hamilton. His bitter confrontation with Talmadge in 1936 over Gene's takeover of the treasury has been recounted here for the first time.

Members of the governor's office staff included Elsie Ray, Matilda Jackson, and Talmadge's executive secretary, Carlton Mobley. Mr. Mobley was most helpful in describing the office atmosphere and operations. He also gave the governor's side of the controversial pardons procedure and treasury crisis. Others who gave insight into brief periods were C. Abt and Bill Kitchens of Mount Vernon who knew Gene as a fiery, struggling young lawyer, a year out of school; H. J. Anderson,

Gene's barber; and Atlanta reporters Ed Bridges, M. L. St. John, and Lamar Ball.

Members of the Talmadge family included his indomitable wife, "Miss Mitt"; his son, Senator Herman Talmadge, and his wife Betty; Gene's son-in-law William Kimbrough; and his older sister Marylynne. Miss Mitt was reluctant to dwell on the past, though she did graciously describe the days when Gene was courting her. She also discussed widely separated periods of particular stress on her husband. Their son Herman and his wife Betty were very kind in responding to my questions and provided both overview and detail to the latter Talmadge years—from a personal as well as political viewpoint. Mr. Kimbrough was a member of the Talmadge family during the latter part of Gene's career, and his insight was excellent. Talmadge's sister Marylynne, being older than her brother, was able to provide glimpses of his now almost unknown childhood.

Because of Talmadge's controversial nature, I limited my interviews to those surviving friends and relatives closest to him. I found that the further from his inner circle I moved, the less accurate became the accounts.

Talmadge opponents Ellis Arnall and James Carmichael provided disappointingly little, either because of reluctance or infirmity. Conversely, political kingpin Roy Harris was most helpful in reliving his association with Talmadge.

The best written materials on Talmadge consist of four theses: A. Dixon Adair's "Eugene Talmadge of Georgia," Mary Glass Crook's "The Platform Pledges of Governor Eugene Talmadge and Resulting Statutes," Sarah McCulloh Lemmon's "The Public Career of Eugene Talmadge: 1926–1936," and Willis Sutton's "The Talmadge Campaigns: A Sociological Analysis of Political Power." All are well researched and excellent aids, particularly Lemmon's and Sutton's. An attempt was made at a popular biography—*Red Galluses* by Al Henson, but it was so biased in Gene's favor that the Talmadge family has dismissed it as without worth.

Both family and friends assert that "Gene just didn't write much." He relied on personal contact to an enormous degree in every facet of his life. There are, therefore, very few papers existing on any part of his life. Senator Talmadge stated that at the end of each term, correspondence was either thrown away or burned. About all the family appeared to have kept were scrapbooks filled mainly with clippings, most of which were thrown away after being ruined by rainwater in the basement of the McRae home. The Georgia Archives contain the bulk of what remains of any personal or official papers, and that isn't much. His executive minutes contain a small amount of very good information; but I found more in Talmadge's correspondence during the election of 1938 and a valuable storehouse in the minutes of the Board of Regents of the University of Georgia.

To understand Talmadge is to understand Georgia's history prior to 1900, particularly before the Civil War, for his total being was rooted there. This necessitated a wide and general study of Georgia and southern history, of economics and men. Among the most useful sources were George B. Tindall's *The Emergence of the New South*, R. P. Brooks's *History of Georgia*, William Bacon's *A History of Georgia*, E. Merton Coulter's *Georgia: A Short History*, W. J. Cash's *Mind of the South*, Ulrich Bonnell Phillips' *American Negro Slavery*, V. O. Key's *Southern Politics in State and Nation*, Howard W. Odum's *Southern Regions of the United States*, Willard Range's *A Century of Georgia Agriculture*, Richard Hofstadter's *Age of Reform*, Roland M. Harper's *Development of Agriculture in Georgia*, and Absalon H. Chappell's *Miscellanies of Georgia*. Also carefully covered were most of the books and papers on James Jackson, George Troup, Alexander Stephens, Joe Brown, Henry Grady, and, most diligently, Tom Watson. These men were the giants of their respective eras, and much of Georgia's past may be traced through their personal histories.

In 1942 a young college student named John Helm Maclean started writing his senior thesis on Eugene Talmadge. His notes and outlines promised a very thorough work in the offing, and some of the correspondence he conducted with men who knew Talmadge intimately proved exceptionally revealing on the politics of the day. Maclean never finished his work. He was drafted and died in World War II. His materials are in the Georgia Historical Society.

The dismaying lack of known extant correspondence from or to Talmadge limited the number of libraries used. Emory University, the University of North Carolina, the Roosevelt Library in Hyde Park, the National Archives, the University of Georgia, and the Georgia Archives filled most of my needs. The flesh of this work is primarily from oral interviews.

Special thanks are given to George Core and Ken Cherry whose intelligence, gracious advice, and faith came to mean a lot to me personally and to the fruition of this book.

WILLIAM ANDERSON

The
Wild Man
from
Sugar Creek

1

How and Where
It All Began

Times had gotten hard. They were never real good in the twenties. The land was used up or washed out, and the boll weevil got what grew. I was a fertilizer salesman. It was one of the few jobs a country boy could work at that didn't want to farm. Since just about the whole state was dirt farmer, I figured there would be money in that many people needin' the same thing. I was also in the legislature, but there was no money in that. Being from Vidalia, I sold a lot in the McRae area, and early that spring—'25 or '26, I don't recall—I had driven into Montgomery County to sell the boys that were doing their spring plowing. It had rained a lot and the creeks were swollen so I had to leave my car and take a path I didn't normally go. I'd sell 'em in the house, but it was easier to catch 'em out between the plow handles, and I came up on one fellow who didn't want any, but said there was a Talmadge over the way who was plowing that day and might buy. I walked down the road and came to this fresh-plowed field. Out in the middle sat this farmer on one of his plow handles pouring dirt out of one of his boots. He had been plowing up old corn stalks and hogs and chickens were rootin' and peckin' all around him lookin' for worms and bugs that had been turned up. It was hot that day. He was tired. Said he had a nigger who had a mule he paid wages to, but he hadn't showed up. He had a two-mule farm. But that day it was just him and that mule. We talked awhile. He didn't want no fertilizer. I think I told him I was in the legislature and since I had been pushin' for reforms in the fertilizer business, some of the boys got me to try to find somebody to run against old J. J. Brown, the agriculture commissioner. I wasn't having much luck since everybody was afraid of J. J. He had become a powerful man, and he was in with the fertilizer people who were selling the farmer fertilizer with rock and dirt in it, and he wouldn't let us pass legislation to stop them.

A few nights later Talmadge and a lawyer friend came to my house. Talmadge said he thought he was the man to beat Brown. We talked a long while. I said I'd back him if he wanted to do it. I didn't know much about him, or where he'd come from.

TOM LINDER[1]

Strung to the world by a mudhole of a road that twisted like a dying snake to Macon—Forsyth, Georgia, was raw frontier: notched-up log

1

shacks, crazy-sawed wooden houses. Oxen pulled whatever men couldn't; horses were scarce and prized. The air rang by day with the rifle crack of axes splitting hardwood, and the nights glowed with huge fires that rendered the cut oak to ashes, signaling the birth of another dream. Another dirt poor Carolina or Virginia family—eager to chop down, clear off, saw, nail, plow up, and plant—had been witness to fortunes in the making as they trudged across the broad state, and they leaned into the Forsyth soil like a man who has sunk it all on a one-shot chance.

It had first been the far point of civilization, and then it had become a between place. Officially born with the Indian Springs Treaty of 1821, Forsyth had before that been a tiny trading village on the western Georgia border where the Indians were in sullen retreat and the cotton plant was beginning to side up to the ancient American wilderness. Forsyth's growth following the treaty had spurted it to a surprising maturity, for after the area was an official part of the state, Georgians began moving there in droves, bringing in established culture with them. By 1827 a visitor noted Forsyth's advancement had come so far "that there was no room for further progress except in clearing more land and gradually substituting fine framed and painted houses" for the log cabins.[2]

In dry times the dust that lay on the Forsyth roads became the color of a woman's rouge and almost as fine. It smoked from wagon wheels and mule hooves and painted the vine and broomsage hard by its side. The ways into and out of town were brick hard in dry times and mudwashes after rains. The roads sloped at the edges where they washed like an old woman's face. The only good sure road was the railroad that, when built, went down to Macon and later on up to Atlanta. That made Forsyth a good between-place.

The roads and the building did not come easily, but whites and blacks have been on the place for 150 years now and have worked it so much that no part of it has not known the weight of a heel or hoof. Little of it has not felt the chopping slice of a hoe or the splitting thrust of a plow or been dampened by the sweat from a back or face. It lies just above the midpoint where the southern flatlands begin to rumple up like the soft wrinkles on a sheet; where the swells indicate that the northern hill country has begun its slow, long rise to the Blue Ridge and Appalachian ranges. It is erratic land, not angular or sharp, but decidedly more hill than flat. The town itself spreads along one of the rounded ridges that move like aimless snakes between the shallow waters of the Towaliga River and Little Tobesofkee Creek—streams that do not water so much as they drain, that move apologetically as the land allows, and that do not erode the land as much as they once did.

The land does not look particularly fertile when its dirt lies exposed; but it is, and for a century and a half it has supported livestock and produced millions of dollars' worth of such foodstuffs as corn, wheat, oats, small grains, apples, peaches, melons, potatoes, berries, and upland cotton. The shrub, vine, and grass that spring from it grow thickly along the water courses, where they rush at the creek bottoms and worm along with the damp ground so that from a hill the course of the creek could easily be followed by the dark green foliage snaking above it.

Fields are now safe for birds and rabbits to nest in the broomsage and briar, or they can scurry through the only monuments to man's passing —the old houses that lean in long collapses to the waiting earth. Their boards, wizened with the thousand tendrils of the honeysuckle, disappear beneath exploding rushes of vine and briar that appear to feed on the rotting planks. The farms and the houses are silent except during storms when the wind lurches under the tin roofings and the metal clangs a mad, harsh death knell.

The original yeoman immigrants were forced into an isolated existence from the outset. They were frontiersmen who, as they surrounded themselves with more and more arable land, sealed their lives in a time vacuum and became the adolescent society that never grew up. They concreted themselves into eternal frontiersmanship which created a "rampant... almost suicidal individualism."[3] It also made them staunch conservatives, primitively religious seekers of the simple solution, provincial, limited in their foresight, unimaginative, ignorant of the outside world, suspicious, chatty, quick to laugh and quick to shoot, and uninterested in government. They were men born to the land; men whose life cycles were governed by the plants they grew, and primarily by the one plant, cotton. They rose and fell with the sun; plowed, planted, and harvested with the seasons. There was a great naturalness to their lives, a harmony, a smooth, unending flow of life and event from year to year where change stabbed out like an obstruction to man and his cotton. It appeared to be a perfect marriage of man and nature, and yet it became a tragedy for the former, primarily because of the singlemindedness demanded by growing and maintaining primarily one plant.

The farmer had forests to clear, and land to plow and plant, and little help with which to do it. He had arrived on foot or in an oxcart with little more than the clothes on his back, and the task of surviving and of chasing the dreams of wealth that had brought him there quickly obsessed his mind and his time, so that governments and other places came to matter little to him. His vision became restricted by the cyclic demands of the cotton plant, and its dictates constricted and bound his habits and his perspective.

Forsyth became a cotton town, because the area grew the crop well and because it was located between the trade city of Macon and the rail center of Atlanta. The success attracted and kept business-conscious farmers, and their values and attitudes brought excellent schools and many churches to the area. Forsyth became known for its educational facilities, its dozens of cotton gins, and its sound middle class and merchant group, all devoted to the business of cotton.

Today Forsyth is a small town whose industry died some time back, and whose concepts of destiny faded with the plant it was built upon. But the roots of the people living there now go back to that destiny; their thoughts and philosophies continue to seek a certain nourishment in that time, though the abrasions of technology and societal movement have wrought their altering influences. New costumes clothe the actors, and there is a touch of the outside world in the talk, but the stage is the same, and there is a timelessness about the characters.

Tom Talmadge had seen it all on a trip through the state, on the way home to New Jersey, after chasing all over Florida with Andrew Jackson; he had seen the cotton sweeping in from the sea, the great empty tracts of wilderness waiting for the plow. And he saw, as thousands had seen and heard, that opportunity lay in the Georgia state and that it could be found in the growing of only one crop. There appeared to be a great simplicity about it all: a little land; a mule or ox and a wood plow; a hoe and an ax; cotton seed; a black, maybe; and a little cash or credit. The black wasn't essential, if you had a healthy family; but if most didn't have a black when Tom and his wife Jemimah Padelford pulled up, most were wanting one. Because the farmer was desperately needing labor, and the black was symbol.

When Talmadge arrived in Georgia (probably in early 1822), he entered the state at the busy trade center of Augusta. He was part of the mass migration that swept into Georgia and the lower South with the opening up of Indian lands and the birth of the cotton culture. The streets of Augusta teemed with families hopeful but weary after long journeys over bad roads; their only common denominator was their hunger for land. The newly ceded western Georgia lands had sent speculators scurrying to the immigration cities, such as Augusta, ready to sell their free land grants or to buy someone else's. Talmadge bought 408 acres just to the west of the unincorporated Forsyth in the spring and late summer of 1822.[4] And then in November, he bought 202 more acres, soon after moving downriver to Savannah. The first 400 acres went for about a dollar apiece, but he got the second 200, located just north of Forsyth, for sixty-three cents an acre.[5] Shortly thereafter he moved out across Georgia to his new property and found that he liked the acreage north of Forsyth better than that to the west. He gave the western land lots to his daughter Hannah, who had remained in New Jersey, and to his son Edward, who was in Savannah.[6]

In 1824 Talmadge bought the 202 acres adjacent to his north-Forsyth property,[7] and here would mark the physical boundaries for the borning and raising of many of the Talmadge family. It is typical Monroe County land, rolling long and gracefully—branched, wooded in the hollows, good soil for the long-leaf cotton. A fairly flattened ridge dominated the property and along it the Talmadge house was built, a one-story place of boarding so crudely cut that it looked like log siding.[8] So flat was this ridge that when the rail line was run up to what would be Atlanta, its rails were laid over the ridge and almost over the Talmadge house.

Of their five children, only the Talmadges' second-born, Aaron, would have a long life. In hopes he would carry on the Talmadge name in the Forsyth area and continue the work in cotton his father had begun, he was given one-half of the 405 acres north of town for "natural love and affection" and one dollar.[9] Aaron did stay and farm, though he sold his acreage; and he saw Forsyth and his state grow into a total dependency on the plant that had brought his father to that place. He also saw the little town develop one of the finest school systems in the state, and this seemed to provide it with some breathing room above the cotton inundation. An indication of Aaron's intelligence and fortune was his only son's enrollment at the University of Georgia, a privilege enjoyed by only a few. The son, Thomas Remalgus Talmadge, was a bright young man who survived the economic and psychological deprivations of the Reconstruction period. Born in 1858, he grew up in the aftermath of the Civil War, became well educated, lived on his grandfather's land, and was one of the few who returned to cotton and made money at it. He found, however, that safer money lay in the ginning of the stuff, and he did both grow and gin. In a world of growing sophistication, he had followed the natural progression of the agricultural economy, from simple tilling and harvesting to processing and marketing. Born of cotton people, Tom Talmadge, the second, was probably not much different from his grandfather in his beliefs or attitudes.

It seems incredible that the cotton culture, from cotton gin invention to Civil War destruction, had taken only seventy-one years, and not really that long in its truly established timespan, and that the effect could be so completely ingrained in the third generation living in the industrializing 1880s. So surely did the heritage of the first cotton generation pass on that it became the T. R. Talmadges' inheritance in the new, unfolding southern fabric to emulate, redefine, mythologize, and glorify the Old Way. They became the curators of the legend, using the propped-up version as the basis for their revised political structure. But if the soul of Tom of the third generation belonged to his grandfather's time, his head had partially extricated itself from that bondage, allowing him to become what the ebullient Henry W. Grady would have termed a darling of the New South. Financially solid amid a time of mass squalor, a diversified farmer, an ambitious capitalist, well educated, public-service minded, a dabbler in local politics, a devotee of the Democratic party and believer in its omnipotent wisdom, not dogmatically opposed to a new idea, a member of everybody's board—he was the strong middle class the South desperately needed toward the end of the nineteenth century.

He married a Monticello beauty in 1881, Carrie Roberts, daughter of "the meanest man in Jasper County," an irascible lawyer, Eugene R. Roberts. Tom and Carrie made their home in the old Talmadge house on the north acreage, and the groom made plans to buy from his sisters their inherited portion of the remainder of the land. Children came quickly. The first was a girl, Marylynne; the second, a boy named Eugene after his mother's father.

Eugene Talmadge was born in 1884, in the small old Talmadge house that seemed forever to be in a collision course with every passing train. Cedar and oak shaded the house and the tracks to the front and cooled the smooth, rust-colored dirt roads. Cotton fields stretched toward Macon to the south and behind the house to the east. Born on September 23 in the last days of that lingering, uncertain month that clings tenaciously to summer's heat while giving its nights to the coming fall, Eugene had yellow jaundice early. The illness slowed his body as a child, though for only a brief period; and in that time his mind grew abnormally fast, aided by the best schooling the area offered. The Talmadge children would escape the stunting drudgery of sunup to sundown farm work that bound many Georgians in a birth-to-death work cycle. Old Tom had money. And he wasn't raising any farmhands. Eugene's first education came from a Mrs. Thweatt who taught in one of the best of dozens of tiny classrooms in the community. The elder Talmadge took Gene, as the family called him, and his older sister Marylynne in the family buggy on his way to the cotton gin company. The curriculum was not broad, but it was thoroughly applied.[10]

Tom Talmadge's fortunes steadily improved; by January, 1890, he was able to buy his sisters' quarter interests in the original Talmadge land.[11] He needed more cotton land, and a larger house was needed for the growing family. Shortly after the purchase of this land, he built a larger, more comfortable single-story wood house across the rail tracks and up the ridge rise directly west. He had one regular wage hand, and he hired pickers and planters as needed.[12]

Gene wasn't one of those pickers, although he later boasted that when it came to farm work he "wasn't off attending no wienie roast." A childhood friend remembered the only time he saw Gene Talmadge in a cotton field was when he was crossing it to go to the creek.[13] He had his chores. He knew the feel of a plow handle as it twisted through hard ground, jerking up over sod clumps, careening off rocks, and becoming stubbornly entangled in thick roots. He tried the plow as a boy, but his mind was recognizably his strong suit, and his father, who at one time or another was a member of all the major school boards in town, knew his son's future should not be in the fields.

One Gus Tyson, who grew up with Talmadge, later wrote, "Eugene Talmadge wore brogans until he was about grown. They were made in Barnesville and called Barnesville Brogans. . . . His father was a real dirt farmer. And when Eugene was attending school . . . he plowed at home on Saturdays." Tyson said he picked peaches with Gene for the first money the boy ever earned.[14]

Napoleon was Gene's first hero, and he baited family members and house guests by betting them he could quote passages from the volume of Napoleon's biography he constantly carried around. "I bet you don't think I can do it!" he would say until someone would answer that they didn't believe he could. A verbatim quotation would then issue forth, and its length and precision never failed to impress all who heard it.[15]

At twelve he was enrolled at the Hillard Institute for Boys. He was one of the few boys in school with his own pony and buggy.[16] A schoolmate remembers, "Gene had a good mind. He was very quick, and had a particularly good wit. He had a great deal of devilment in him, always playing jokes. He loved to start fights between the boys, and then sit on a fence rail and laugh while they battled it out for no reason. The only subject he was not good in was penmanship. But he really made a name for himself as a debater. Debates helped teachers grade the students and helped the students show off at the end of the quarters. Everybody's folks would come, and the boys would speak. Gene won about every speaking he was in."[17] Gene, in his usual self-deprecating manner, later told a friend, "The nigger boys I grew up around used to call me 'Lugene,' and more often, 'mean Lugene,' 'cause I was so damn mean." [18]

When the cotton harvests came to bloom, the roads that rose and fell with the Monroe County ridges were soon filled with creaking wagonloads of the area's money crop. Most farmers had no one to help bring in the crop but themselves and their families. Those of more substance hired Negroes on a day basis, and the larger farmers had sharecroppers and tenants to lean in that painful stoop over the rows with their huge sacks dragging with a heavy lifelessness behind. Once a wagon had been filled with bolls, it would be driven into Forsyth to be ginned. Forsyth, being a twenty-gin town, had plenty of competition for the farmer's product. Farmers often did not tell their drivers which particular gin to go to, and this prompted the mill owner to send boys out to road intersections to hail down the wagons and ask the drivers to go to their mill. Gene was "hired" by his father to man an intersection for the Southern Cotton Seed Oil Company, and the boy took great delight in riding out from the house early in the morning with his father and being let off with a ledger book to stand and wait for the wagons that would be coming all day. He would mark the name of the farmer who owned each wagon he hailed down and ask his father that night if those wagons had in fact stopped at his business. It made the boy so happy when his father said yes that Tom Talmadge usually said yes whether the wagon had stopped or not.[19]

For the Talmadge children, summertime meant a long visit to Atlanta by train, for the buggy ride was too strenuous. They visited their grandmother there and other city relatives, and often these relatives would go to the country where they would revel in the life of a big farm. On Sundays, during good weather, after church, the family would visit neighbors or have company, and if it were hot they would sit on the front porch peering out over their foot-packed grassless front yard to the dusty road beyond, intently watching the occasional passerby. Farming, prices, weather, and who was sick filled the soft, slow chatter. Discussing illnesses took up a great deal of these talkings. And politics. So many of the giants had recently passed: Bob Toombs, little Alex Stephens, the Cobbs, Hill, Brown, John B. Gordon, and Henry Grady. Now the man of the day was that hell raiser from McDuffie County, Tom Watson. Telling the dirt farmer and the blacks the Democratic party had done nothing for them; preaching Populism, trying to make them aware of what cotton, debt, politicians, and big business had done to them; what blind acquiescence to a one-party system had done to them. The first to arouse their political conscience, old Tom was a spellbinder.[20]

Mass entertainment was church, court day, circuses, and fairs with their agricultural exhibits and contests. Circuses were the most bizarre of the events punctuating the cyclic life of the area, and the Talmadge children would stand wide-eyed before the strange animals and people who brought Forsyth its rare glimpse of other worlds. Emotionalism was generally allowed to run free at revivals and at election time at big speakings. These were the days on which heroes were made. Oratory flourished, and the people roared their delight, with the poorest of the boys usually yelling the loudest. Gene Talmadge was a speech attender. His love of debate as a child drew him to most of Forsyth's speakings, but for only one man would he go out of his way—Tom Watson. Napoleon was the hero of his childhood; Watson became the spiritual leader of the young man. He was fascinated by Watson's fiery style, his understanding of the rural mind, and his electrifying manner in a speech.[21] Gene's college roommate, John Monaghan, remembered Gene getting so excited every time he talked about Watson that he would get out of his chair and pace the room as though he were on stage. He would always brag about how far he had walked to a Watson speech, and how the farmers stood in such awe of the man.

Important to the destiny of Gene Talmadge and every young Georgian of the time was the Democratic party. It was glorified as the party of resistance to the North during Reconstruction, the political unit that loosed the Yankee grip and allowed the South to resurrect its disenfranchisement of the Negro and to use that race as its whipping boy, the carrot that kept the poor whites in line. The party was the symbol of psychological recovery and as such enjoyed a dictatorial reign over governmental action and dogma. Its obsession with keeping the black man down and with observing the mythology of the Old Way made the party appear more a curator of that way and a brutal racist than a functioning governmental organization. It was a party of hindsight, and it served the Tom Talmadges with its inaction. Publicly it supported cotton and in doing so helped keep a large portion of the population in poverty. In fact it did more for the wealthy. The party served history and some of its leaders served themselves by bringing railroads to Georgia. The rails and the cotton mills appeared to be the party's only acknowledgment of the industrial age. Historian Ulrich Phillips blamed this governmental inaction on the natural response of a people whose lives were governed by a primitive one-crop economy and a moderate climate. He felt northern history was the adjustment of people to a changing and varied economy and environment. In the South there had been no adjustment, because of the numbing sameness.[22] Georgia was in the early 1900s very much agricultural, and very much cotton, and this meant few governmental services: little road construction, little manufacturing, unsophisticated approaches to finances and economics, and isolated people. And Gene Talmadge grew up within this cultural and political isolationism.

2

"She's a Real Skinner!"

He was lean as a twig, medium height, a very correct, starched, and pressed dresser with a high, board-stiff white collar capping a tight, solid dark suit—not a dandy, but a young man who knew the fashion of the day and could afford to enjoy it. His smooth, smallish face, slightly discolored by the childhood jaundice, was punctuated by piercing black eyes. He had a wide, thin mouth; the bottom lip and chin protruded slightly, giving a firm block-jawed appearance, though the face was not square or large, and the neck was rather thin. He looked well-bred and comfortable. And he was well-bred, but not comfortable, because he had just been graduated from the university after being Big Man on Campus—football manager, champion debater, Sigma Nu, Phi Beta Kappa—a charming, witty boy known for his quick mind and opinions.

Now in 1904 he found himself teaching at the Perry Rainey School in the tiny farm town of Auburn, Georgia. Nowhere. He knew he was there only because he didn't know what he wanted to do or be. He knew he didn't want to be a cotton farmer or ginner like his father, and other than farming there was not a whole lot more for an educated Georgia boy to do but go into business, and he was too impatient for apprenticeships or for being a teacher. He was doing that, and he was bored. He could be a lawyer; it was the profession of his heroes. There was intellect in it, and debate. So he left the stultifying Auburn and enrolled back in Athens as a law student.

While still in school he had enjoyed traveling over to Atlanta to visit his relatives, and he began to meet young ladies of the city at ice-cream parties. He became friends with an Atlanta boy, Chip Robert, who attended the new technical school, Georgia Tech. He could never understand why Robert would attend a technical school. He would ask, "Why in hell do you go to that school?" [1] Technology was a strange word in 1906.

11

Gene left Athens with a law degree in 1907 and found work with the blue-chip firm of Dorsey, Brewster, and Howell. Hating deed work, he seemed happiest around the capital city's legislators, the farmer-politicians of the day. The proximity to power, success, and money only served to fuel his frustrations, and his natural sharp humor and barbed sarcasm turned to a cynical and sour disposition. He was a very unhappy young man. Gene saw his father quite often around Atlanta, for the elder Talmadge had cultivated a number of influential friends at the state house. His son's obvious dejection caused Tom Talmadge to ask his friend, legislator William Peterson from Montgomery County, for help. "Bill, I've got a son out of college, smart, a good worker, but so Goddamn mean, I can't do anything with him!" Peterson replied, "I can straighten him out. Just give him to me." More to the point, a friend of Gene's asserts, "Gene was like a black sheep in his father's house. Old Tom and his family were kind of aristocratic acting, and Gene didn't mix with them. I don't think they wanted him around which is probably why he sent him off to Ailey." [2]

Tom's remedy was to send Gene down to the Peterson-run south Georgia village of Ailey, where Peterson's sister Carrie was living with a young widow. "Mr. Bill" didn't like the women living there alone and thought the well-bred young lawyer could hang out his shingle, be his own boss, and take a room in the house with the women. This would offer them protection and some additional income and at the same time allow Gene to room and board inexpensively while starting his own practice in a thriving cotton community. The idea intrigued Gene, and he left Atlanta on the train for his third attempt at making a living. He was told to find the telegraph operator at the Ailey depot upon arriving, for she was the young widow with a child who lived with his sister Carrie. Her name was Mattie Thurmond Peterson and she was from South Carolina.

Her nickname was "Mitt," and she didn't care for having this city slicker come to live with them. She was a country girl and city people were suspect. She let Carrie know—as was her way—that she didn't like the idea, and Carrie said that, as a compromise, Mitt could take a look at the young man when he got off the train and if she didn't like what she saw she could just tell him there would be no room. On the day of his arrival, Mitt saw a thin-necked man with slicked-down hair, dressed in a starched Sunday-go-to-meet'n outfit get off the train and come to her telegraph desk. He said he was Gene Talmadge and asked if she was Mitt Peterson. She had been nervously awaiting his arrival all day, and as soon as he introduced himself, she blurted out, "The rent'll be $13.50 a month and if you don't like it you can go back to Atlanta!" It was a whopping sum to be charging for the area, but Gene was there to stay, and said he would accept. A little stunned, she walked him from the depot, up the slight rise through Ailey, and to the large, well-kept Peterson home.[3]

When Gene wrote Mr. Bill saying he had arrived, was well quartered, and paying $13.50 a month rent, the legislator wrote back good naturedly that Gene would have to watch out for Mitt. "I'm sorry you didn't see Carrie first about the rent. You better watch Mitt. She's a real skinner!" [4] Indeed Gene found Mitt to be more than that. She was sassy, even more independent than he, a hard worker, and she had an infectious sense of humor that complimented the Talmadge wit. She was a country girl with simple tastes, but there was an almost out-of-place twinkle in her eye that gave her an air the young lawyer could not resist, and he and the telegraph operator soon fell in love.

Their courting was mostly on horseback. She was an excellent rider, and it was the one recreation that allowed them to get away from the house and from Ailey's wagging tongues. They rode the long cotton fields and picnicked under the pines at their edges. The summer's heat also made ice-cream making a favorite pastime, along with swinging on the broad front porch at dusk.

The relationship quickly progressed to the point that it seemed improper for Gene to remain in the Peterson home. Ailey was a very small town. Gene moved a few miles down the road to the community he had been working in, Mount Vernon. It was slightly larger than Ailey, the county seat and a cotton trading town, but still very small and isolated in the south Georgia piney woods. Gene had entered into a partnership of sorts with an older lawyer, a Colonel Underwood. Their office resembled a house and was located on the main street of town, only a short walk across the street to the strangely majestic courthouse. Gene boarded a few doors down from the office with a Mrs. Fox and her boy. He didn't like the child, and they were forever arguing. Their bickering culminated when Gene's red pony got out of its pen and Gene angrily accused the boy of intentionally freeing the animal. When the boy pleaded innocent, Gene glowered at him, "You lying little sonofabitch, I'm going to beat the hell out of you!" The boy ran terrified to his mother, who ordered the fiery young lawyer off her premises. The incident enhanced Gene's reputation around the area as being profane, quick-tempered, bull-headed, and arrogant. He is still remembered by one old man in Mount Vernon as "the meanest sonofabitch I ever met." [5]

When he wasn't handling cases around the courthouse, he seemed to be forever riding out of town to nearby Ailey on his small red pony. The two, and the girl they journeyed to see, became frequently discussed subjects around the town, but then it seemed that everything Gene Talmadge did caused discussion. He was not particularly popular, both because of his personality and because of cases he would handle. They were usually those that the established attorneys didn't care to take on— muggings and murders and the problems of the poor, who paid their legal fees in chickens, eggs, or milk. Gene would take any case. It was simply a matter of survival. He defended one Negro woman who was so poverty stricken that she gave him her four young boys as partial payment or perhaps because she could not afford to keep them. Gene took the boys in and fixed a place for them in the small barn behind a modest frame house he had moved into after Mrs. Fox ran him off. The boys did odd jobs around the house, and stories still circulate about how he used to beat the hell out of them when they disobeyed him. There is no proof that he kept them; but the rumor does persist. [6]

Mitt Peterson didn't think Gene Talmadge was quite as mean as some of the locals thought, for on September 12, 1909, she married him. "We didn't have no weddin'," Mrs. Talmadge remembers, "we just got married. Then we moved into his house in Mount Vernon." [7] Mitt's six-year-old son John, from her previous marriage, moved along with them.

The young couple lived in Mount Vernon for two years. "We didn't have nothin'," said his wife. "Gene wasn't makin' no money bein' a lawyer. He even tried to sell some mules for awhile. Times were real hard." Being lawyer for the poor of the community meant you got paid in produce, and you earned the scorn of the landowners and the other attorneys. And Talmadge got his belly full of this "root-hog-or-die" existence and began badgering his wife about moving twenty-three miles down the road to the town of McRae. His wife remembers, "My first husband had left a 2,000 acre farm in McRae, and Gene like to run me crazy talking about moving to McRae and farming." Mitt liked Mount Vernon and didn't want to move. "Neither one of us knew a damn thing about farming," she said. [8] When the argument stalemated, Gene told his wife, "Mitt, I've made up my mind. I'm moving to McRae and if you won't go with me I'll go by myself. I'll try to get up to Ailey and see you and John much as I can." [9] She relented.

He wrote Bill Peterson soon after arriving, "Bill, I haven't got a damn thing but my hat, trunk, a mule and a wagon, and a pint of Paul Jones Whiskey." But Mitt didn't recall his arriving with much more than the hat and the whiskey. "We were awfully poor. We moved into a little house in McRae that either Gene's daddy bought for us, or Gene got through a law case, I don't remember which. But we weren't there long before he was on to me again. 'Let's move to the farm. Let's move to the farm.' He was acting like he was dying to be a farmer. There was an old house out there we moved in and we weren't hardly in the place and started to plantin' before Gene decided he didn't want to be no farmer. You could say he liked being a farmer, but he didn't like farming. So I started learning how to run a farm from the old nigger farmers that lived around the place. Gene might have plowed a few rows behind a mule, but not many." [10]

The truth of the matter was that Gene Talmadge had failed to make much of a living in Mount Vernon, had gotten excited about the big profits in farming, then gotten out behind a mule in McRae and found out fast that the money wasn't worth the effort, and wandered almost aimlessly back into law. The man had obviously not found his place, was more or less living off what his wife was earning at the farm, and became a steady in the checker games that were forever going on under McRae's shade trees.[11]

3

"The Nigger
Who Came
to Town"

Georgia had uniquely thwarted the rush of history in 1876 by creating an addition to her primary electoral system which guaranteed rural domination of state politics. Called the county-unit system, or the Neill Primary Act (of 1917), it gave each county two votes for every representative it had in the general assembly. At the state Democratic convention these votes could void the popular vote. Six votes were given the 8 largest counties, four each to the next 30 in population, and two votes to the remaining 121. Obviously 3 tiny counties had the power to nullify the vote of giant Fulton County. The popular vote was, in effect, disfranchised. Also voided was the vote of minority groups who had fled to the cities. As Georgia entered the twentieth century the county-unit system became the cornerstone of her politics. While her economy began to slowly industrialize and her people to urbanize, the power in the state would remain steadfastly stagnant in the staunchly conservative multitude of counties. Georgia politics therefore became even more myopic, status-quo conscious, anti-reformist, and corrupt. Management of the system fell into the hands of the county politicians, each of whom demanded homage and promises at election time. They held their sway over local voters through numbered ballots, the secret ballot not being a state law. When they said they could deliver votes they meant it. By comparing a voter's name with his ballot number they knew who had followed their endorsements and who had not. The general punishment for not voting right was refusal to pave the road around a man's farm.[1]

This rural power source created a group of power-wielders known as the "courthouse gang" or ring. Composed of city and county officials, the newspaper editor, the sheriff, and county lawyers, the gang represented the common denominator of Georgia's power structure. Each gang had its own staying power, its own idiosyncratic ways of operating, of obtaining power and losing it. The gangs were highly egotistical affairs, usually loose-knit and of little duration. Members were the power brokers for the community. While serving in a useful political capacity, they also appeared to expend great energies in maneuverings and intrigue designed to maintain their cohesion and membership. These struggles appeared insignificant and ego-serving to an outside world, but to the gang and its aspirants, they were gargantuan battles for power, influence, and often money.

The gangs formed a complex association of power with the state's money sources in urban Atlanta that grew stronger during the first two decades of the century as technology moved into Georgia. These money sources revolved around Atlanta's three largest law firms which wielded enormous influence over state politics because of the corporations they represented. Spalding, MacDougall, Sibley, and Brock handled more major state corporations than any other firm; they were followed by Troutman and Arkwright, and the vestiges of the old Hoke Smith gubernatorial machine headed by Marion Smith. The law firms were the contacts for many of the communications between county boss and corporation head. The connection between rural power and urban money was threefold: Georgia Power, the railroads, and the oil companies.

The state's largest utility, Georgia Power, was evolving by the 1920s into the backbone of many small-town newspapers by running large institutional ads and paying for yearly contracts in advance. This curried favors at election time from the local editors for the men Georgia Power was backing. With substations scattered throughout Georgia, the company had its front men on the scene to pass the word about what Atlanta wanted.

Railroads had become the largest client for many small-town lawyers. They represented the rail companies for that portion of the lawyer's county that the lines passed through. Since 85 percent of the members of the general assembly were lawyers, and normally a key man in the courthouse gang was a lawyer, it figured that the railroads were getting good representation up and down the line. Rails were particularly good clients, since the auto was a little slow in coming to the state.

The law firms of Atlanta also represented the thousands of small oil and gas dealers and stations that were following the automobile into Georgia in the 1920s. These agents would meet annually in Atlanta, where a portion of what they heard was who the oil firms considered to be politicians friendly to all of their interests. An observer on the scene at that time wrote that the irony of the law firms controlling so many radical rural Democratic bosses was that they were all "hide-bound

Republicans at heart while working and often running the state's entire democratic political machine." Another wrote, "The Georgia boss succeeds to the degree that he can play off rural democracy against financial interests in the cities. His political power comes from the rural sections, but he must secure his funds in the city." [2]

The gang's members were usually elected officials or families "who owned the town." Lawyers were frequently the members, but their ascent to power was normally not as easy as that of the man elected to office. The sheriff, county commissioner, and judge were almost assured of their places, and the greatest fighting took place around these posts. Defeat at the polls usually meant banishment from the gang.

Despite its pettiness the gang did serve many purposes. Members of the courthouse gang represented the needs of their county as a lobby of sorts to the legislature, and would wheel and deal with great majesty, offering to "give" their county or "deliver" it to the politician who promised to serve the local needs. They controlled the county purse strings and the machinery for government. They were the county's voice, though much of what they did was done to keep themselves in power. They were a small, not so elite group, who, in a small county such as Ailey's Montgomery which was dominated by one family, enjoyed long tenure and served the wishes of the family. Here the gang was not a "gang" but more a subservient group of elected officials. The family in power usually got that way either by having been the first to settle the area or by being unquestionably the wealthiest.

There was no one strong man or family in McRae when Gene Talmadge arrived, but there existed one of the more hotly contested and continuous fights for control of the gang. McRae was small, but its power-seekers were deadly serious in their politicking. So tense was the situation when the skinny new lawyer came to town from Mount Vernon that he met instant hostility and rejection from those embroiled in the latest contest, and this included all of the town's attorneys. Gene was viewed by the lawyers as "the nigger who came to town," a derogatory way of describing an unwanted stranger. The combatants figured that if he was a lawyer, he was a potential power-seeker, and their suspicions were not long in justifying themselves. Talmadge had hardly unpacked his bags before he was hanging around the courthouse asking who were the members of the gang, and acting in his brusque manner as though he were going to take the place over.[3]

Gene was desperate for business. The town didn't need another lawyer, and the town attorneys fought tooth and nail his attempts to get started. They lost no opportunity to talk him and his abilities down, making it difficult for him to get any business other than the poorest and most unpopular cases. Every time he was seen in court he seemed to be defending someone for doing something the rest of the community disliked. But he could get no other work. He had no office, no library, and therefore was placed at an embarrassing disadvantage when he needed to look up the law. So unpopular did he become in town that he found it difficult to win a case before the jury. It became an exasperating and humiliating experience. Gene didn't help the situation by attempting to mollify his critics. Instead he aggravated them with his abrasive tongue and his bull-headed attitude.[4] He wouldn't play their games; he wouldn't kow-tow to the courthouse gang. If he appeared to have changed since leaving Ailey and Mount Vernon, he had not, for those communities were under the iron control of the Peterson family. That courthouse gang was subservient to the family, that same family which had afforded Gene his opportunity in the area. Not only would it have been ungrateful for him to have sought to destroy it politically, but also it would have been fruitless and stupid. McRae was a different story. It soon became obvious to him that the political structure there was highly volatile, transitory, and very responsive to elections. It offered him his first opportunity to "play at politics," and he leaped at the chance.

The initial failures in the McRae courthouse forced Gene once again to concentrate more of his energies into the farm. It was a large, fairly flat piece of land that rose slightly where the Talmadge house stood. The outbuildings and laborers' houses were scattered along the west side of the rise, facing McRae five miles away. It was in the Scotland community, a voting district composed of cotton farms. All of the old Peterson land worth cultivating had been cleared long ago, so that the only hardwoods remaining were those left for shade around the buildings. Pine stands poked their thin persistent trunks through the broomsage in untended areas, and pecan trees flourished around the laborers' houses. Briar and vine thickets spun in their mad swirls at the ends of fields. The land stretched in long fields back to a small, meandering swamplike branch called Sugar Creek. The stream moves quietly around McRae, following the shallow dips in the earth. The waters are slow and dark. Trees pursue the creek's course and frequently grow within its waters, and where there is a particularly large depression, the waters sift out into a swampy pond. It is a soothing, flatland creek, whose name would become synonymous with the Talmadge farm.

The main house was one story, clapboard, and of average size. A porch ran its length, and a swing hung stiffly on one end. Wicker and wood rocking chairs were scattered along the plank flooring, their order and placement determined by the shade-angle of the trees in the front yard. The house had rather high ceilings, for cooling purposes, and was modestly furnished with two bedrooms, a living room, and a dining room and kitchen in the back. The size and design were those of the farmer who was not going hungry or sharecropping, but who was not getting rich either. He was the farmer who worked his fields, who spent his time between the plow handles, and had one or two blacks working for him. Gene did manage the books on his place and with Mitt bought its seed and machinery and mules. This farmer signed his name on the line at the bank to borrow the money to buy those things, and at harvest, he was the man who traded for the best price with the local cotton factor. If he showed a profit at year's end, he paid his hands in cash, bought shoes for his wife and children, and cloth for her to make them clothes. If, like Gene Talmadge, he were a lawyer, he had to invest in respectable looking clothes.

Mitt's home was her first responsibility and it reflected her simple tastes. Its windows were shuttered; its doorway screened and handworn. The thin whitewash that Gene painted on the exterior planking was soon tinged with a pale red from the dust in the yard and the road below. There was no grass around the front of the house. It had been worn down from the time the house was built by the passage of countless feet and hooves and wagon wheels. Two tree stumps remained just outside the picket fence that ran along the front of the house. Their roots flowed out over the ground like ancient veins; their acorns lay smashed and splinter-like around the base and hurt the childrens' bare feet when they stepped on them. Irregular barns and toolhouses and an outhouse stood just off to the right—their boards, warped by the rain, jutted and twisted from their moorings. Their earth floors were cluttered with simple machinery and plows, harnesses, sagging bags of seed and fertilizer. They seemed forever in a half-light with a mist of fine grain-dust hanging suspended in the air. The fields spread away from the house toward Sugar Creek and its stands of pine and oak. The couple had quickly planted the land in cotton for their main money crop; sugarcane was planted for its sweet properties, and corn for the livestock and for eating. Mitt also planted pecan trees, peanuts, peas, tomatoes, onions, potatoes, collards, watermelon, squash, and beans.

As the farm slowly developed, Gene had what was called a "two-horse farm." It was actually a two-mule farm. Gene occasionally plowed one mule, and his only helper at first, a black named Willy Johnson, plowed the other. It didn't take Talmadge long to realize that a successful farm owner does not spend his time between plow handles; he hires others to do the work for a share in the crop. Gene wanted a diversified operation like his father's, and this took more men and machinery than he owned, and management. Fortunately, he had a good organizational mind and an excellent manager in his wife. Mitt had taken reluctantly to farming, but soon preferred being out in the fields to doing housework. She had quickly determined that more money lay in peanuts than cotton and had soon cut cotton acreage. Gene allowed the operations of the farm to depend on Mitt while he concentrated on acquiring some cattle and pursuing his law practice and his endless games of checkers. As the farm grew through the years before World War I, tenants were hired, and a white sharecropper moved on the land to assist Mitt. The sharecropper bought his own tools and materials and was allowed to live on and work the Talmadge land for a share of what was harvested. The tenants owned nothing and were paid a salary for their efforts. Their relationship with the owner was usually paternalistic.

Gene worked blacks and whites alike, judging the laborer solely on his merits. He would later be accused of everything from refusing to work blacks to beating them and paying starvation wages. To say he would not work them is not true. He worked mostly Negroes, as is testified by photographs and numerous friends. His attitude toward them was no different from that of his neighbors, or the state at large. He paid his workers the standard wage of the area. No Negro would have worked for Talmadge if he could have received better pay down the road. Farm workers, black and white, were traditionally paid badly. And this was a major reason thousands of blacks and whites were leaving the Georgia countryside during and after World War I. A close friend related, "Gene was like a lot of farm bosses back then, he'd knock the hell out of a black if he crossed him. I remember when he was Governor, he hit one of his farm niggers up side the head with a pistol and the pistol went off. The nigger ran up under the house holding his head and Gene got a little scared that he'd killed him. He told me to go look under the house and see if he was alright. By the time I got there the nigger had run home, packed his bags and left." He later admitted flogging a Negro man and appeared ashamed of it, saying, "Good people can be misguided and do bad things." [5] Disregarding this remorseful apology, Talmadge's attitude toward blacks was that they were childlike, basically stupid, barely removed from a savage ancestry, and should be closely controlled. He did not hate the race, but he had very little respect for blacks as human beings. Tragically, this attitude was hardly unique, but Talmadge's hot temper and penchant for overreacting probably made him more fearsome to McRae's blacks than other whites were.

Little was said about it, but Gene had also been in his share of fights with white men, including one McRae judge on the lawn of the Telfair County courthouse. The judge accused him of selling some of his land to the county at an inflated price, and the fiery Talmadge flew into the judge who later became one of his closer friends.[6] Talmadge himself best expressed the foundation of his racial and cultural beliefs: "I am a native Georgian and my ancestors on all sides of my family have been in Georgia for 150 years. I am steeped in southern tradition and background. Neither I nor my people have ever strayed from the pasture of southern tradition. We have not even leaned against the fence." [7]

Attesting to the complexity of the black-white relationship was the fact that Talmadge, an avowed segregationist, invited his black workers to eat lunch at his table in his home most everyday during the farming season. When the dinner bell clanged out over the fields, the male workers came to the back kitchen door, washed the dust from their hands, to take their place at Gene's table. Mitt sat always at Gene's right, and the blacks across from her. The sweat of their collective labor seemed to create a brief and very real comradeship. They were together in the fields under the searing south Georgia sun, together in a common and equal effort. Their lives meshed smoothly out in the fields, and extended through the lunch hour and on through the afternoon work. At that point it stopped, and each race returned to its own carefully delineated position—the black toward his tiny shack, the sharecropper to his house, and Gene to his even larger owner's house.[8]

Gene's invitation to dinner did not brand him an integrationist, though many white farmers wouldn't have dreamed of doing it. The practice did show how every white, to a degree, drew his own line of segregation independently, and it showed how closely whites would let Negroes enter into their lives as long as the white felt the Negro was staying "in his place." This "in his place" criterion was the white's interpretation of the point at which a "nigger was acting like a nigger and not like a white." As long as no overt, obvious move was made by the black which aroused in the white consciousness a feeling of encroachment, or a feeling that his superiority was being threatened, the Negro was allowed latitude bordering on social integration. If one of the blacks at Gene's table had attempted to sit by Mitt, the line would obviously have been crossed, and he would have been run off the Talmadge land.

Gene became known early as one who "kept blacks in their place," because of an incident that happened one August, during World War I, in McRae. Two versions account the story; both involve a northern Jew, his wife, and their black servant. One version published in the *Saturday Evening Post* said the trio's car broke down while traveling through McRae from Florida; the other, told by Henry Spurlin, said they had gotten off a refueling train. However they arrived, the woman and the butler were soon seen strolling through McRae eating apples together. This act inflamed the local merchants who came to the doorways of their stores to curse and threaten the pair. There seemed a near panic about what to do about this violation of McRae culture. The news had no sooner reached the courthouse than lawyer Talmadge exploded out of its door waving an ax handle furiously above his head. He was followed closely by another lawyer with a hammer. The black saw the two men racing toward him screaming hysterically, "I'm gone git you, nigger!" and he bolted away from the white lady and ran off down the street for his life. As Gene galloped past the startled woman, she suddenly started throwing her apples at him and swore loudly in her strange northern tongue. Her husband, in the meantime, returned to his car, where he found an angry crowd of whites who demanded he take his wife and get out of town, which he promptly did, leaving the fleeing black to fend for himself. No one ever did find the poor servant. The incident reflects the complexity and the cruelty of the racial situation. Gene saw nothing wrong in having Negroes eat at his table and cook his food, but he considered it unthinkable to have a Negro man accompany a white woman down the street eating apples together, no matter how innocent their motives.[9] To explain his position toward blacks in the 1920s is to explain that of most Georgians.

Gene was not a satisfied man in 1918, although he had been in the area some years. His farm was increasing modestly in productivity, but his law practice was still little more than pitiful. He was still very much an outsider in the eyes of the city lawyers, and the courthouse gang soundly disliked him. To himself, he was just another struggling dirt farmer and a small-town lawyer. Eager for politics, he saw his chance when the office of solicitor of the city court became vacant. It was a minor post, but it did guarantee some money and a little more respect, or so he thought. Gene wrote his father, telling him of the vacancy, and asking that he speak to Governor Dorsey—who would appoint the solicitor—about giving it to him. Tom Talmadge was a respected man with many friends in Atlanta, and Dorsey was delighted to comply with the request. Gene was elated and the McRae lawyers were infuriated; their hatred for the "nigger who came to town" deepened. Unfortunately, Gene's victory against the gang was somewhat short-lived, for the gang had immediately demanded that its state representative have the legislature vote the office out of existence. The humiliation and embarrassment he suffered were acute, but he maintained the office for two years.[10]

The spring of 1919 gave the irrepressible Talmadge his second chance to crack the courthouse gang and return to an even more powerful office. The reason most often quoted for Gene's becoming interested in politics was that he could not get a road graded so that it was passable out at his farm. Since no elected officials would respond to his requests, he took it upon himself to enter politics. There is probably some truth in this, because the roads around McRae were incredibly bad, as they were all over the state in the 1920s and much later. But to accept this as the sole reason he came to politics would be naive and a gross misreading of the driving ambitions that burned in the man.

He did align himself early with men associated with roads. He met the man who would later become his best friend, John Whitley, during his early years in McRae; and he became friends with Telfair's most knowledgeable road builder, J. C. Thrasher, in 1919. Road construction in 1919 was still in its primitive stages in Georgia, and indeed in the whole South. Machinery was crude, and full-time contractors were practically nonexistent. Georgia roads were rutted, rock-strewn quagmires most of the year; and when they were dry, they were so pitted and eroded by the weather that to travel on them by buggy was to risk a broken axle or wheel. To travel on them in the first autos was almost impossible. The roads were for horses and walkers. Each county provided for its own roads, with work usually done by the chain gang. Roads were an issue in politics in every election year. The sophisticating economy and mechanized means of transportation were requiring better roads.

Whitley was one of the first men to get in the road business with decent machinery; after World War I, he became one of the largest contractors in the state, and one of the best. He met Gene while working on the highway that went by the Talmadge farm. Gene was plowing for cotton. Whitley often talked with farmers as he passed their land and had a better than average appreciation and understanding for them.

Gene "did a little grading" for him around the farm, and the two men struck up a fast friendship that would extend through Talmadge's lifetime.[11]

Gene's friendship with J. C. Thrasher evolved mainly out of Thrasher's aspirations to break into the courthouse gang. The two men met on a common ground in this respect. Thrasher had recently been cut out of his job as warden for the chain gang and county road builder; he was eager to avenge his loss by gaining control of the power office in the county, the county commissioner. Gene thought Thrasher, a huge man who ate food incessantly out of his pockets, could take the post, and signed on as Thrasher's manager. Since Thrasher was by far the most knowledgeable road man in the area, his ability to construct good roads would be the issue. This was, that is, until Gene got wind of what happened to poor "Ole" Bill Harrell, the janitor at the McRae courthouse.

Harrell, a white man, could usually be found asleep in his broom-closet or under a tree in the courthouse yard; he was likable but said not to be worth the powder and lead it would take to shoot him. Notoriously sloppy in his work, he constantly neglected to wash out spittoons, ashtrays, and the bathrooms. But Harrell, in his more active moments, had sired a huge family that lived in a ramshackle house out on the Ocmulgee, and he seemed to be the only member of the family who even pretended to work. Although a lot of people didn't care for his work habits, no one had the heart to fire him. He also had a lot of relatives who voted, and in that day of huge clans, the Harrells, if all came to the polls, could swing a lot of votes.

The incumbent county commissioner, Bill McKechen, however, was not impressed with Ole Bill's family mouths or votes, and while passing through the courthouse one summer day in 1919, he found Ole Bill leaning on his broom half asleep and the place in disrepair. "Goddamn it, Bill," snapped the disgusted McKechen, "why don't you keep this damn courthouse clean! The spittoons are overflowing and filthy, there's paper and dirt and cigars all over the floor." Harrell promised meekly to do better. A few days later McKechen made another inspection and found the old white structure in worse shape than before. When he finally found Harrell, he angrily told him, "Bill, if you can't keep this place any cleaner, we'll find someone who can!" That night Ole Bill went out to the river and told his children and kin that McKechen was going to fire him. This was tantamount to the clan's starvation, and the panic-stricken multitude spread the word that Ole Bill was getting fired and they would have nothing to eat. The news quickly got back to the sensitive ears of Gene Talmadge, and he knew he had his issue. Damn the roads! "That damn sorry McKechen was going to fire poor Ole Bill Harrell, and all them children would starve." [12]

Gene knew Thrasher couldn't beat McKechen if he ran as a Democrat, because the gang, then partially controlled by the commissioner, was the Democratic party. They controlled its machinery and counted the votes. Gene convinced his man that he should run as an Independent. It was highly unorthodox, almost irreverent, but Gene worked the electorate relentlessly, so that McKechen was soundly defeated and the courthouse gang was finally cracked by the "nigger who came to town."

Thrasher had no sooner entered office in January, 1920, than he appointed Gene to the powerful post of attorney for Telfair County. The two men controlled the county's purse strings and immediately went to work on the largest road-building program in the county's history. The dethroned gang drew bitterly together and started a long series of grand jury investigations into every move the pair made in hopes of throwing them out of office. No wrongdoing was ever found, though a lot of people wondered how Gene and Thrasher managed to turn the county's $20,000 surplus into a whopping $89,721.44 deficit in two years. The answer was simple; they did it by building roads and making other improvements, though this explanation was not accepted by a lot of the locals who would rather believe they had stolen half of it.

After having been attorney for the county for only a matter of months, Gene attempted to capitalize on the notoriety of his new position by running for a more substantial office, state representative. This would place him beyond the gang's influence and give much more satisfaction to his demanding ego. His wife let it be known early that she cared nothing for his getting into politics and complained about his abandoning the farm for such a pursuit. But he was an impatient man; and, disregarding her advice, he wrote out his announcement for candidacy and left it in the offices of the Telfair *Enterprise*. The card looked more like one from a man running for dogcatcher than for serious office. Short on words and thinner on programs, Talmadge promised the voters nothing except personal honesty. He did allude to the poor, and intimated that he had firsthand knowledge of that condition, but he offered to do nothing for them. Much of the Talmadge future in politics can be read in this first announcement: know the poor voter, articulate few problems and fewer solutions, and bear down heavily on your own honesty. Do nothing, but do it with honor. The paper ceremoniously and incorrectly called him "Colonel." His card read: "I am different from most of the other boys who want to be politicians; I have no long list of bills to save the country from ruin."

"A good lawmaker," his card continued, "should know from personal experience how the poor make a living." He would "keep an eye singled to the interest of the producer and the consumer." Obviously, he cared little for the Negro vote (few were registered; few voted) when he said, "I want to see every white man, woman, and child before election day." He solemnly promised that if elected he would fulfill "my trust . . . so that I shall not be ashamed to meet you again face to face."[13]

He started with absolutely no organization, no money, and few supporters. He didn't have the support of his wife, though her protest had now turned to just being quiet about the matter. Gene ran alone and showed good instincts. Up before dawn, he would ride the country roads, greeting farmers as they moved out into their fields and waiting at their shops and stores as they arrived. Railyard workers would find him peering out of the morning darkness, ready to mount a rail tie and speak to them over the fires they built to break the night's lingering chill; and every railroad warehouse worker came to know his square face as he walked the high platforms, working his way through the grain and fertilizer and seed sacks. Often a neighbor's boy would ride with Gene in his badly deteriorating Model T as it clattered over the flat, sand roads dusting the dew-dampened leaves and grasses on either side.[14] It would be a lonely, hard run. Perhaps overeager, but knowing that he had to combat years of bad publicity from the gang and many unpopular court fights, Gene had started his campaign with his announcement on May 27. The election was not until September. His opponent, D. W. Phillips, apparently thought Talmadge the most unpopular man in the county for he did not announce until August 5.[15]

For all of his efforts, Gene lost his first race for elective office, 756 votes to Phillips' 1,187. The maturity and control he showed in defeat must have amazed many of his critics, who remembered his fist fighting on the courthouse lawn. The September 9 *Enterprise* printed his concession of defeat. "Good wishes to everyone in Telfair County. My hat is off to the victor." Talmadge was no fool. He knew he had established a position of sorts, had won some minds, and it had taken years to do it. He would not jeopardize the fragile foothold he had established. He would make no enemies in defeat because he was determined to run again. Following the defeat, he sat on the curb outside the courthouse one September night along with one of the boys who had traveled with him. The boy was crying over the loss, and Gene tried to console him by telling him the story of David and Goliath, of how little David overcame overwhelming odds to win. "I kind of think of myself as David," he said, a faraway look in his eyes. "This defeat don't mean nothin'. We'll come back until we beat 'em!" [16]

The city slickers up in Atlanta would have called McRae a backwater town, but it was a microcosm of small-town and rural Georgia during and after World War I. The later assertion that "half a century of political isolation" had ended with the election of Woodrow Wilson in 1913 and the breakdown of sectionalism in the South seems invalidated by the Talmadge mentality and its omnipotence in post-World War I Georgia.[17] More than Wilson, the war would have a long-term effect on the rural South. It would set southerners up for one last economic wipe-out. The war had raised cotton prices, and following the pattern set by his forefathers, the Georgia farmer fell unerringly into the tragic cycle of buying more land, tools, mules, and seed in order to grow more cotton to take advantage of the high prices. Old land, now grown with young pines or honeysuckle thickets, was cleared once again and planted. Huge debts were incurred in order to buy the materials necessary to plant.

The excitement and the profits, however, were short-lived. The boll weevil had been in the state since 1913, having come from the West, and its damage had reached disastrous proportions by 1920. Many who had enjoyed profits because of high war prices found themselves suddenly in debt for the new machinery and land they had bought to take advantage of the high prices. The weevil had literally eaten their profit away. To compound the crop losses, which hurt the tenant farmer and sharecropper terribly, the industrial age was finally creeping into rural Georgia and driving those on the bottom of the labor scale out of work. The tractor and other machinery were tearing up the red earth faster and better than ten struggling men could ever do. A great migration that had started with World War I received new impetus as thousands gave up their lifelong fight with the land and moved into the towns with their mills and increased opportunity. Erosion, worn-out land, dropping prices, and due bills on land and tools combined to wreck the hopes of thousands of the state's farmers.

While much of the nation was enjoying an unprecedented prosperity, Georgia's primarily rural population had once again been flattened by a crushing series of circumstances. The new century had given millions of Americans such wondrous inventions as the telephone, the automobile, and the electric light, but the impact of these marvels had been largely deadened by the isolation and poverty of the great mass of Georgians. In 1920, 98 percent of Georgia farms were still lighted by kerosene or oil lamps and 70 percent had no telephone. Illiteracy was still high among many white adults and a large number of Negroes of all ages. Children were sent to one-room schoolhouses where the grades were mixed and the curriculum limited by the provincialism of the teachers. The young adults started leaving the farm life in great numbers after World War I, for industry and technology were opening up in the cities.[18]

Large numbers of Georgia's Negroes had left during the Great War to work in defense plants for the first real money and security they or their kind had ever known. And many were leaving for another reason—fear. Negroes had once again become the scapegoat in a time of declining rural economy. A new age and century had also given rise to a concomitant philosophy. The mind of the North was liberalizing again as it had done before the Civil War, and was again casting its critical eye to the South. While a new sophistication washed over the North, its journalists made it fashionable to attack the rural South as an intellectual and cultural wasteland. The southern reaction was as it had been seventy years before, defiant and withdrawing. Southerners were aware of the relative opulence in the North and resented its blatant display during the twenties. A people down on their luck, heavily in debt, and apparently not destined to partake of the American dream were in no mood to be ridiculed and derided. In most criticisms of the South, the plight of the black was usually alluded to and whites were scorned for their continuing oppression of the black race. The southerner's reaction to this criticism was a new isolationism and a psychological withdrawal backward into history and old passions. They cried out at the Negro in a violent backlash, accusing him once again of being dull and apelike, the reason for all their troubles. Tom Watson, champion of the impoverished farmer, rode the crest of this reaction back into politics and became one of its most vehement articulators. He was, in his last days, the great warrior, the escape valve, for the redneck who had nothing and knew it, who saw the fabulous riches of a new world dangling just beyond his reach and heard the harsh words of northerners and foreigners, who made him look around at what he had and the way he lived. And he was frustrated and angry and sullen. He had no representation in government, no voices or weapons to attack his critics, nothing to do but to march back onto another man's land and continue working for a share of the cotton. It had always been a sorry existence, but never had so many suddenly realized it. The only man, the only group, the frustrated farmer could turn on to vent his anger was the only man who was having a harder time of it—the black. The wealthy Jew also became an object of Tom Watson's torment. Watson, who had spent his life fighting the crippling feudalistic one-crop system of the South, had turned to a baying demagoguery fed by old age, a life of frustration, and alcohol. He snapped like a cornered old dog at everything foreign to the South, and his anger gave voice and vent to a statewide wailing by a mentally dispossessed people.

Gene Talmadge grew up in these times of sudden fortunes and dashed hopes, of realizations of backwardness and inferiority. And no one boiled quicker about disparaging attacks on the South than he did. The years around World War I had started to crack the stronghold that ruralism had held on Georgia since her birth. The Telfair County farmer had heard these sounds of change and had reacted in a paradoxical way. He was eager to possess the new products of the industrial age, but while wanting its material output, he cared nothing for its disciplines or philosophic dictates. As many of the youth of both races fled to the spawning grounds of industrialism in the cities and thereby accepted many of the new consumer society's demands, the great mass of older Georgians refused to move—either psychologically or physically. It was a generation that fled back to the old times at every opportunity, even as the urge of its children and the age moved unalterably ahead. The twentieth century wore slowly against and into the cultural barriers that had not yielded for a century. The feudalistic cotton economy yielded begrudgingly to advancing technology, but it did begin to yield. The war had exposed many young Georgia men to the outside world for the first time, few having left the state before. They returned with a different outlook. But more than their change of heart and mind (when it did occur), the war had forced an economic change on the state that had a far more profound effect. Thus, if the decade from 1913 to 1923 seemed one of fantastic promise and bitter despair, confusion and uncertainty, it only reflected the great societal changes which were shifting and sometimes crashing into an older America. The movement was audible and sometimes illuminated by explosions. It was a time of yearning and despair and fear, uncertainty and hope for rural Georgia. The times held "large components of frustration, failure and defeat." [19]

After cracking the courthouse gang, Gene Talmadge had become a lot more palatable to a lot more people. Certainly one of the most important friends he made at the time was the old leader of the gang, Lamar Murdaugh. Not having an office or a law library, Gene had been working out of his farm and the courthouse, borrowing other lawyer's books. He was a lawyer without the tools of his trade. As his friendship with Murdaugh developed, Gene frequented the other lawyer's office; and the two finally agreed that Gene would work out of the office, though he would not be a partner. Neither would he pay rent. Rural lawyers often did this to help a poorer friend. "I liked Gene all right," Murdaugh said, "and I didn't mind helping him out. He came and went as he pleased, and used my small library. He couldn't very well practice out of the courthouse hallways, and I guess he couldn't afford his own office. Seems like every time I walked in, he was there reading. He was a studious law reader, but he was not attentive to the law. His interests were split between the courtroom, local politics, and his farm. I remember the one book he read most was the Bible. It wasn't 'cause he was religious; he wasn't, but he felt the Bible was good history and a good teacher, and Gene was a learner." [20]

Gene had tasted the fruit of political victory and in 1922 prepared to try again for elective office. This time for the state senate. His abilities as a campaigner and his popularity had increased substantially, for he won the popular vote in the three-county race. But fortune was not to be his, for McRae was still thick with Talmadge enemies. The old courthouse gang still controlled the Democratic party in the area and ruled that the election was subject to the county-unit system. The local Democrats ruled that although Gene had won the total three-county vote, he had lost the unit votes and the election. Victory was snatched from his hands. He had been out-maneuvered again. Equally disturbing to Gene was the fact that he could not get elected in his own county. The lawyers who disliked him from the first not only counted votes, but their voices were heard in every corner of the county.

So fierce had the battle to defeat Talmadge become that some of the courthouse lawyers had actually brought a case against him before the McRae grand jury, accusing him of having had intercourse with his plowing mule. It created a sensation during his race for the senate, with the standard anti-Talmadge statement being, "You wouldn't vote for no mule-screwing sonofabitch, would you?" Gene would later laugh about the whole incident and how he had been one-upped by the boys, but at the time it was an extreme embarrassment to him and his family. [21]

4

"Papa, We Have
Beat Them
to Death"

By the time he was forty, Talmadge had a pretty spotty track record as a politician. He couldn't get elected to office in his home area. His father's influence had gotten him his first post and he had earned his second on someone else's coattails. He had cracked the local power structure, but they had always managed to turn the tables and wreak their revenge. Because of his determination, his name had been slandered from one end of the county to the other. But he had retained his self-confidence, and his commitment to politics had grown into a blind passion. He had turned into a good farm manager, but farm life was too plodding; his internal tempo was too fast. He cared little more for practicing law, probably because he had never made over $400 a year at it. He was a fair trial lawyer, but not a great one. He came to discuss politics endlessly with his friends, and their dialogue invariably ended in discussion of one office: state agriculture commissioner. In rural Georgia, with its weak central government and strong agricultural economy, this office had emerged as one of the more powerful. Henry Spurlin remembers Talmadge telling him the story of why he ever entered the race for state office. "Gene got to be pretty down. He'd been beaten every time he ran for local office. He couldn't win a case. He didn't like farming. He was always broke. So he just got to playing checkers and messing around with the boys. Mitt got so damn mad at him she threatened to run him off if he didn't go to Atlanta or somewhere and get a job. He took the train up there and went to the Kimball House Hotel. He was hanging around the lobby when this huge man with a big hat walked in surrounded by a bunch that made him appear to be important. Gene asked someone who the man was and they said it was J. J. Brown, the agriculture commissioner. Gene said he had gone up there to take on the biggest dog he could find and that seemed to be the dog. He returned with his mind made up to run against Brown." [1]

32

Through the patronage of his office, J. J. Brown had built up a powerful statewide political machine that controlled the votes of counties and legislators. He maintained his hold (probably second only to the highway department as an intergovernmental center of power) by rewarding supporters with jobs as oil and fertilizer inspectors. He had hundreds of these men over the state, doing little more than collecting paychecks. It was a fat job in hard times, with the kind of pay that made a man real hungry to have such work.

The fertilizer inspectors were supposed to check the chemical and material composition of the fertilizer, but they did so only at the manufacturing plants, and not after bagging. Quality, mass-produced fertilizer had become one of the great boons of the industrial age for the farmer. It had been produced in manufactured form since late in the nineteenth century; but improved production, technology, and better distribution over new rail lines had greatly increased its value to the farmer. It was a particularly critical product to Georgia, because practically all of the arable land had been depleted years ago by one-crop growing. Farmers had lacked both the patience and the money to properly work their land and protect it through crop rotation, letting it stand idle, and fertilizing it. The credit system they lived with was also a factor; they could only get short-term loans, payable when the harvest came in. This did not provide them with surplus capital to invest in anything more than seed for the next crop. Brown's drive for power had made him too close a friend of the fertilizer companies to be of service to the farmer. For a farmer who spent his precious earnings on a bag that was often half-filled with gravel and sand, the loss was profound. Yet Brown fought every attempt to improve inspection and guarantee fertilizer quality.

Brown's department was also responsible for inspecting and taxing oil and gas that came into the state. It arrived in railroad cars, and the state charged the gas companies one cent per gallon. The oil inspector received one-half of that cent. To inspect one tank took only about fifteen minutes, and, obviously, given enough tanks, a man could eat well on peering into oil cars. Each town or county had its own inspector, responsible only for those cars that came into his town to empty their contents. This meant that each inspector could make about $100 a month, and in 1924 that was a lot of money. Brown appointed these inspectors on a patronage basis. They not only had to promise him their unqualified support, they also had to actively campaign for him during elections. Being an inspector was a highly desirable job in an area where clod-busting was the normal occupation; and the man whose county went against Brown in the elections immediately found himself out of a job, with a more enthusiastic supporter in his place. The Brown machine and its stranglehold had reached scandalous proportions.[2]

Gene Talmadge knew all of this, and he figured Brown and his office to be one of the most vulnerable in the state. Gene's problem during the period under consideration (1924 and early 1925) was that he was uncertain just how to get into the race. He was absolutely unknown, had no organization, no money, few backers, and an embarrassing local reputation that said he couldn't get elected by his own people. He and Murdaugh traveled to Atlanta a number of times to talk with the one influential friend they both had, Clark Howell, editor of the powerful Atlanta *Constitution*. Howell was interested, as were a lot of people, in seeing Brown defeated, and he gave Gene "a lot of encouragement" in his desire to run. He never told Gene that the paper or he himself would unequivocally support his candidacy; but his continued encouragement indicated he would give every ethical advantage in reporting Gene's candidacy, and that was considered an enormous advantage.[3] This solidified Gene's thoughts on which office to seek and gave him a tremendous emotional boost. The two lawyers returned to McRae to discuss further entry plans. Gene still needed an "in" into the arena. Coverage by the paper would not, in itself, be sufficient. However, without their knowledge, a series of events were happening in Atlanta that would open this long-sought-after door.[4]

All through 1925 a young legislator from nearby Hazlehurst, Tom Linder, had been trying to muster support for a bill that would put more teeth into the fertilizer inspection laws. He wanted bags checked after they had been filled and the contents written on the outside of the bag. Brown had told the agriculture committee in the house that he didn't want Linder's proposals let out of committee, and such was his influence that they never reached the floor of the house. Shortly after this, Brown was reported to have said, "I've got them legislators wrapped up in my vest pocket."[5] This so infuriated the growing number of anti-Brown politicians that they drew together, determined to run him out of office. Their motivation was increased by tremendous pressure from their farmer constituency, which was enraged over Brown's refusal to help them. The solons held several secret meetings in vain attempts to settle on a candidate they might run, and in desperation they appointed Linder to find someone to oppose Brown. They didn't care who the man was; they would give him their support. Linder, ironically, was a fertilizer salesman. He returned to his south Georgia home to think on the responsibility and to sell fertilizer.

Hazlehurst is just northeast of McRae, and in the early spring of 1926, Linder drove over to work that area. The roads were notoriously bad around Telfair County, and he parked his car to walk and see his customers, who, being farmers, usually were found in their fields. Heavy rains had swollen the creeks in the area, and he was forced to take a different path than he normally took in the Scotland community. He encountered a farmer in his field and failed to make a sale. The man told him there was a farmer Talmadge over the ridge who was plowing his fields that day and might buy some fertilizer. Linder walked that way, and as he approached the Talmadge land, he saw a thin man sitting on the wooden handles of a plow pouring dirt out of his boots. A mule stood silently in front of him. A number of chickens and pigs, wandering through the field around the man, were feeding on the worms and roots the plow had turned up. The freshly plowed clods lay heavy and thick and dark with the moisture of the recent rains, and the dirt clung tenaciously to Linder's shoes as he walked out across the field. The farmer introduced himself as Gene Talmadge, and upon hearing what Linder was selling said he did not need any fertilizer. Gene had heard of Linder and the two struck up a general conversation about the times, the inadequate fertilizer laws, and Brown's hold over the agriculture department. Linder said he had been appointed by one hundred legislators to find a man willing to run against Brown and had had few takers. He found himself running late, and left Talmadge to resume his plowing.[6] Gene wasted no time in getting to Murdaugh's office and telling him of the conversation. It was a godsend. Any man who started the campaign with one hundred legislators behind him would have a tremendous advantage, even if he were a small-town political failure who couldn't win a case or an election.

A few nights later, early in the evening, Linder answered a knock at his door. There stood the thin McRae farmer, dressed in a suit, and another man, Lamar Murdaugh. The two were obviously excited and immediately launched into the purpose of their visit. Gene Talmadge wanted to run for agriculture commissioner, and he wanted Linder to call the one hundred legislators and tell them he had found his man. Gene's credentials were paper thin, but his willingness to take on the awesome Brown impressed Linder, who was frank to admit that he could not find an alternative. If this intense farmer-lawyer wanted to take the chance, it was all right with him. He also liked the idea that Talmadge was an unknown, a man without interests or powerful enemies. Linder agreed to contact the legislators and tell them that he had found one Eugene Talmadge, a farm boy and a lawyer from McRae who wanted to run against Brown and that he was suggesting they support the man. Gene and Murdaugh disappeared quickly into the night, elated over the sudden favorable turn of events.[7]

Mitt claimed she was one of the last to hear of his plans. Gene knew her feelings about his interest in politics. She wanted him on the farm and had told him so, but his spirit had never been there, other than to raise cattle. It had brightened only when he was waging his battles in McRae. She would find out while shopping in town that he was a candidate for the office of agriculture commissioner and would raise the roof, to no avail, that night.[8] Once she saw his commitment, she offered to help out as best she could. Gene said she could start by lending him enough money to pay his qualifying fee. Mitt sold butter, eggs, and milk so that Gene could have the money to ride the train to Atlanta and become an official candidate for state office.

When Talmadge qualified he had only three official supporters: Murdaugh and two McRae businessmen, Zack Cravey and Morris Cameron. One of Cameron's greatest contributions was his shirts. Gene was so poor he only owned one dress shirt, and the tiny staff agreed that he would have to be better dressed to run for state office. Cameron, being more successful, had a closet full.[9]

The first task was to travel the state quietly, visiting the one hundred legislators who had agreed to back Linder's choice. Georgia's road system in 1926 was an appalling collection of mud paths, potted asphalt and rain-gouged dirt roads that had kept the state isolated for so long. Gene's beat-up car reportedly could barely stand the trip into McRae from the farm, so they took Murdaugh's and the Talmadge organization hit the road in one car. The visits with the legislators were quietly and effectively conducted, though they constituted a very long and arduous trip. Gene later said he slept four nights out of the week in the back of the car.

Once the long trip to meet the legislators was over, Lamar had the unenviable task of telling the local courthouse gang that Gene was going to be a candidate for the agriculture office. It was considered critical to Gene's chances that he have the support of his own people; and if he were to do that, he had to have the backing of the county's politicians. Calling "the boys" together, Murdaugh boldly announced that Gene

Talmadge was a candidate for agriculture commissioner, "and by God, you're going to support him!" A chorus of indignation shouted back, "What the hell are you going to do that for!" But he was not going to be drawn into any arguments about the matter, saying only that Gene had the *Constitution* and one hundred legislators behind him and that he was going to win. A silence settled over the group; and even if they did not like the new candidate, they appeared resigned to the fact that he was going to run and they would not openly fight him. Some, obviously, did go straight to J. J. Brown and offer to provide him with "the goods" on Talmadge, for Brown would soon prove that he had a sensitive ear in McRae.[10] Most of Gene's enemies were delighted to see him take on Brown. If he lost, and they knew that he would, he would be such a laughingstock he wouldn't dare leave Sugar Creek again. And if by some miracle he won, finally he would get out of McRae and out of their hair. It was a strange final peace Talmadge made with his old enemies.

Gene headquartered out of Murdaugh's law office. A few girls were hired to answer the phone and type letters and generally run the office, and a very small group of McRae men drew together to form a loose-knit advisory committee, though they knew from previous association with Gene that little of their advice would be accepted. Talmadge had long ago decided on the thrust of the campaign and its issues. The power-hungry, patronage-ridden, insensitive Brown machine and its gross negligence of the people was the only and obvious issue. It was agreed Brown had overextended himself and was ripe for a fall.

The first step in entering rural Georgia politics was to get out and make contact with the county power holders and communication sources. Murdaugh was designated as Gene's contact man, and he quickly set out to let the state's machinery know that a Eugene Talmadge existed and was running for office. The routes he took were common sense and standard for the times, and they set a path that Gene would follow all the days of his political life. Murdaugh described it: "I'd drive into a town and go to the newspaper first where I'd try to find out who was what in town; then I'd go to the courthouse gang where I'd do my best to know them and collaborate with them. Thirdly, I'd go to the ministry who were the most difficult to handle, but they knew a lot of folks. Good word-spreaders. I guess the old newspaper editor knew the most, certainly about the gang—everything about them. In the 1926 race we couldn't offer any deals, because that was what we were fighting Brown about. We stayed clean."

It is doubtful that J. J. Brown had ever heard of Eugene Talmadge before 1926. But as that year progressed and word got around privately that Talmadge was the man the legislators were backing, Brown at least came to know Talmadge as their man. This fact alone elevated Gene to the rank of contender and sent the Brown forces and the other candidates to probing the background of the new man. Brown was confident he could win reelection, but the fact that for the first time a strong effort was being made to oust him had him marshaling his far-flung forces. The word went by phone, letter, and mouth that any oil or fertilizer inspector who wanted to be back on the payroll after election day better make sure Brown carried the inspector's county. In face-to-face encounters, Brown would unequivocally tell the frightened inspectors, "If I don't win your county, you're out!" [11] He told them his election depended on their passing out Brown literature and talking him up in their areas. They were his mouthpieces in an era and a state where there were few means of mass communication. Hardly anyone who lived in the country had a telephone. Radio was nonexistent, and most of the newspapers were poorly read weeklies.

A consideration of the times and the temper of the times in which Talmadge made his first state race is important. To say they were hard times is to say nothing, for the Georgia farmer's history was a long and bitter scenario of hard times. New elements had entered into his life that made the problem of making a living a relatively acceptable crisis. More unsettling were the monumental changes that were daily creeping over the land.

One of the most disturbing things to the rural populace was the cornucopia of goods and services that were pouring from the mass production lines of the industrial age. Few of the country folk could afford these new luxuries, though they instantly realized that a status was being attached to their possession. The city people had brought shiny cars to their land, and the rattling machines that dusted the roadsides were making the boys hungry. This was an urge to possess that was stronger than any their fathers had known. Inventions had come and gone before, but none had ever elicited the cravings for ownership that the automobile, the radio, appliances, and the myriad other new "necessities" elicited. Whereas luxuries once included new shoes, a city-bought dress, a coat of some fashion, store-bought tools, store-bought liquor and cigarettes, and even coffee and salt, the rural Georgian suddenly, in the early twentieth century, was confronted with a new dimension in purchasable goods and services and a subsequent disturbing new dimension in desire for ownership of those goods. A new set of social rankings evolved with the goods, and the farmer who had always equated success with the size of his fields, house, and crops now found that this did not necessarily have meaning if he rode into town on a horse, or owned no telephone, gramophone, auto, tractor, or similar status symbol. If nothing else, the 1920s offered the Georgia farmer the chance of becoming a lot more dissatisfied than he had ever been before.

Gene Talmadge knew these dissatisfactions, particularly the old ones. He had been there—briefly, but he had been there: defending unpopular cases in tiny, opinionated villages; rarely getting paid cash; alone on a farm, breaking his back behind a mule trying to eke a living out of the land and realizing small reward for his labors. He knew about it better than J. J. Brown, and he could tell about it better than the host of other candidates. He had developed an uncanny intuition about the emotional motivation of the farmer. He knew the country people called wool-hat boys. He knew they were gut-motivated, responsive to emotional appeals and extremes, and had a strong propensity for irrationality. They possessed great pride, a fantastic sense of their past and appreciation for it; and they were suspicious of things strange and alien. He also knew they were leaderless and looking. It was a comfortable and natural standard for him to pick up, and it had Tom Watson written all over it. As the campaign schedule approached, he was anxious, impatient, exuding enthusiasm, ready. To the professional, he seemed ill-prepared for the challenge, but to the man Talmadge, he could not have been more ready. He had tasted the fruits of politics and had become delirious with it. He had endured a long and often embarrassing struggle to make his mark in the local arena, and he had discovered that neither farming nor practicing law were the goals of his life. They did not fulfill him. But politics did. His days in June, 1926, became a fury of activity.

One of the major problems the Talmadge campaign confronted was money. Without a large organization, ties with wealthy special interests, or the backing of the Democratic purse holders, Gene had to look to family, friends, and supporters in his area. They found early that money could be obtained, but it was usually in the form of coins. The people of the area simply had very little money. It would be said later that Gene had run for office on money derived from cotton his wife had grown. It was also said that he spent his father broke, nearly bankrupting the big Talmadge farm at Forsyth. Unquestionably Gene did spend money derived from his family. But the charge that he ruthlessly took all the earnings of a helpless wife and generous father was not valid. The highly independent Mitt initially hated politics and her husband's constant figurings in them. She did not like his taking the farm money to run for office, but knowing the determination of her husband, she knew it was pointless to fight him on the matter. She also knew he had too good a business mind to spend the farm broke, and she was right.

Gene knew that he would have no problem getting help from his father, though Tom Talmadge was adamantly against his son's running. When he found out that one of Gene's old buddies from Forsyth had been working hard to bolster Gene's desire to make the race, he angrily rebuked the man, saying, "You're trying to make a damn fool out of my son!" [12] Tom Talmadge had been around the powerful inner circle of state politics, and he respected the workings of strong organizations like Brown's. He could not conceive of his son defeating such expertise. When Gene and his small entourage proudly traveled to Atlanta in early June to qualify, he avoided running into his father, because he had heard of his feelings and he feared the elder Talmadge would try once again to talk him out of running.

Gene was struck by the many strangers who came up to him and gave him small change. He could tell by their dress, their mode of travel, the lean look of their faces, and the tired look of their eyes that they placed great value on what they had contributed. They were banking on him with a desperation that was almost unnerving to witness. Surprising to both Gene and Murdaugh was a Jewish boy from McRae, Billy Brant, who turned out to be their most prolific contribution-gatherer. "We never could figure out where he was getting all that money," remembers Murdaugh, "but he kept coming back to us with pockets full." Few records were kept of the money because of the manner in which most of it was collected and spent. Gene would receive it while walking down the street, then spend it a few hours later on gas or food while on the road. Money did come to the headquarters, and that was kept by the girls working there until Gene or Lamar came through needing some more. Records were kept of this money and who sent it; much of it was saved for the hard summer campaigning. At the outset, there wasn't enough money to buy paper for pamphlets and letters, so Murdaugh got the LaGrange newspaper to give them the paper. And so it went.

When Brown announced his candidacy on June 11, he saw no reason why his reelection could not be accomplished. And by June 24 he felt even more certain, as a host of candidates had entered the race. The vote would be badly split, with people traditionally voting on a geographic basis; the local boy would get the local vote. Besides Brown and Gene, the candidates included Charles E. Stewart, James H. Mills, J. S. Shettlesworth, and John R. Irwin.

The latter four were compounding their lack of fame by exhibiting an obvious fear of Brown. Their trepidation gave an added appeal to Gene's infectious enthusiasm and confidence. A more important contrast between Gene and the others was the excellent coverage Clark Howell and his Atlanta *Constitution* were giving Talmadge's candidacy from the outset. The Howells would later vehemently deny supporting Gene, but the proof was on the paper's pages throughout the campaign.[13] This coverage was giving the Talmadge name and campaign a certain credence and status. He became at the outset more than a small-town politician, and this elevation from backwater brawler to noteworthy contender was valuable in spreading his name to the public at large and in improving his trading position with the courthouse gangs throughout the state, men whose only desire was to back a winner. The *Constitution* gave Talmadge that smell. It would be an ironical association, but it was momentarily one that prevented Gene Talmadge from entering the race as a laughingstock. At the same time it seemed almost incredible that a big-city newspaper and one hundred legislators would be backing a man who was unknown, untried, inexperienced, and without organization or popularity in his own town. But it happened, and in the space of a few months in 1926, a diverse group of political centers had merged into a movement that was alive. The Atlanta press and the Georgia legislature had provided flesh and blood to a skeleton conceived and bound together by the tremendous energies and aspirations of Eugene Talmadge. He was, in essence, the organization—its brains, manager, decision-maker, most tireless worker, and dedicated booster. He set a precedent of total involvement and management from the start, which figured nicely into the character and self-perception of the man; and he would learn that this total commitment had high appeal for the farmer mentality. Gene Talmadge presented himself as the lonely fighter, a highly independent, self-sufficient man, alone against all comers. There was heroism in solitary battle. It would not be the Democrats and Gene, or special interests and Gene, or slick politicians and Gene. It was just Gene.

One thing neither Talmadge nor anyone else had to worry about was a platform. The issue was clear-cut, the battle lines drawn by the incumbent. The unresponsive, self-serving, and ever-expanding Brown machine was the great bulwark against which all challengers would do battle. As the campaigns opened in June, all of the warriors issued forth with loud, fuming attacks against Brown's arrogance in power, his horde of oil inspectors, his refusal to allow reform legislation to pass on fertilizer inspection, and his patronage base of power. The fact that all contenders were running on more or less the same platform became an immediately recognizable weakness that tended to lump them together into one indistinguishable voice. It became obvious that his parrot-like stance would result in a badly split vote along local lines and an easy Brown victory. But simultaneously it became obvious that one candidate was extricating himself from the pack. It was not so much what he was saying, but the way Gene Talmadge was saying it. A showman had come to Georgia politics, a prancing, dancing, arm-waving holy-roller, circus barker, medicine man. His language was as fresh and topical and relevant as the new cotton shoots that sprouted in the fields around him. He was speaking the language of the cotton and corn, the tongue of the dirt farmer, a tongue that was provokingly reminiscent of Tom Watson. There was such a hunger for a second Watson that the yearning helped ease Gene Talmadge into that hallowed mold, a mold that Talmadge wanted and felt he needed if he were to win. He was his own man, to be sure, but there was an undeniable Watson-consciousness and appreciation about Talmadge that he could not contain. The analogies were quickly drawn and the word spread with the speed and fervor that would be attendant to a Second Coming.

The strategy of erecting faceless enemies and conspiracies warring against the "little man," the haves against the have-nots, had been used definitively by Watson, and the disciple had learned well from the master. In fact, a lot of Watson devotees were angered at what they felt was rank copying by an imposter, a pretender to the Watson throne. The accusations had begun as soon as Gene had started his speeches by saying "My fellow countrymen," an echo of Watson's "My countrymen." The influence of the mentor had been strong, as it had been strong on many Georgians, particularly the deprived dirt farmer. Talmadge would think twice before he would launch into an approach different from Watson's. He played off Watson's fame and appeals, but it was not an entirely dishonest effort. The words he spoke were more often his own. Certainly, his feelings were his own. He was committed to helping the farmer; and having made that commitment, he styled his manners and presentation around that commitment. He was fiery, indignant, angry, corny, and iconoclastic. His language could be earthy, profane, grammatically atrocious, and very provincial. In isolated rural areas it was tailored to be understood by the most ignorant farmhand. It was a simple, uncluttered, blunt discourse, punctuated with Bible passages and rural humor.

His language was also very adaptable. He was a highly educated man, a man capable of polish and refinement and of sophisticated dialogue. But this appeal did not fit his place or its people as did the imagery of a swashbuckling rebel, the shrewd country boy battling the big-city crowd. The farmer needed a champion and Talmadge knew it. Farmers also made up the largest mass of voters in the state, and he knew that. There was a power vacuum left by the passing of Tom Watson, and Talmadge rushed to it. If he took advantage of a rare political offering and exploited it to the hilt, the wool-hat boys would not sit in judgment, for they needed help, and if Gene could give it, he was their man.

By the end of June, it had become obvious that there were too many candidates opposing Brown; consequently, no one stood a chance against him. Murdaugh set up a publicized meeting with candidates Irwin and Shettlesworth to see if they couldn't unite against Brown—or, in Gene's words, to see if the "outsiders" couldn't present a solid front to the "insiders." Murdaugh would first try to reason; then, as a last resort, he would offer to pay them "to get the hell out of the race."

The meeting with Irwin and Shettlesworth quickly turned into money talk. Murdaugh offered Irwin his campaign expenses to date if he would quit and come out for Gene. Irwin had been wanting out, thought Gene a good man, and agreed to take the "reimbursement," as it was called. This type of offer was standard practice in backroom deal making and was not considered wrong by the participants, since all that was paid was the candidate's sworn expenses. Shettlesworth, upon hearing of the Irwin offer, later demanded twice that amount. He was told he could have half of his own expenses, and he took it and got out. The men had emerged from the July meeting to say to the public that nothing had been accomplished in the way of unity and that each would continue his own race. Irwin waited a few days for appearance's sake, then dropped out. Shettlesworth waited a little longer. Their endorsement of Gene created a little boost and was well worth the money.[14]

The most devastating phrase of the campaign became Gene's euphemism for the oil inspectors. He called them the "oily boys." It struck with a sting, and was typical of his unusual talent for coming up with simple, easy-to-remember, funny phrases. They were demeaning in a good-natured way, and the laughter they inspired slowly destroyed the other candidates.

Talmadge modified his speeches in the second month, carefully positioning his image. He broached the new theme early in July, when he continually referred to himself as "a real dirt farmer." He was trying to build further identification with his audience and attempting to offset the accusations by Brown that Talmadge was no farmer and not much out. Shettlesworth waited a little longer. Their endorsement of Gene politicked and lawyered in town, and Brown had had his men scour the county digging up mud about Gene. Gene was incensed by these accusations and knew that if they stuck he would be ruined. He pushed the dirt farmer theme hard. A redneck with mud on his shoes, dust in his nostrils, and calluses on his hands, he was one of the boys.

Brown's staff felt that a series of debates could finish Talmadge and embarrass the solons who had backed him. Brown would teach them all a lesson. They let the word leak out that they were going to challenge Talmadge to three debates, and the first would be in McRae. The news was met with great trepidation by the Talmadge staff. The thought of actually debating the man they had painted as one of the ogres of Georgia's history was unsettling. For all of its slow progress, the campaign had at least been moving, and everyone knew what would happen if Brown whipped Gene in his own hometown. It could decisively end the campaign.

But Lamar Murdaugh was not so frightened. He knew what kind of speaker his man was, and before making up his mind he traveled to several of Brown's speeches to size him up. He returned convinced that Gene could easily "get the grin" on Brown; he had not been as impressed as he had expected to be. Gene was game for anything; he feared no man and told Lamar to get the word out. They would meet in McRae and then in Brown's hometown, Elberton, and finish up at neutral Dawson. Apparently, Brown's spies in McRae had told their man that Gene was one of the most unpopular men in town and could easily be defeated. Brown did not think it such a bold move on his part, for he never questioned that he could take Gene. But he was making an obvious mistake. He was basing his decision on the words of critics. Also, he had not personally heard Gene speak. Finally, he was drawing tremendous attention to Gene's candidacy, and if the speech was no better than a tie, Gene would have gained notoriety and credence as a candidate. What Brown had underestimated was Gene's ability on the stump, and the tendency for small-town people to draw together in the face of an outside threat. Brown was not reading his own constituency well.[15]

It was a natural card for the main event of the campaign. The hometown boy, a novice dirt farmer who had never won anything but hard knocks, was taking on the big-city politician, the slickest manipulator, the biggest boss in state government, and all middle Georgia was talking about it. A few had heard Gene speak and knew he was good, but many more had heard Brown, and all who had seen him knew they were seeing a speaker from the old school. A man of enormous proportions, his massive head was mantled with thick flowing hair that swept back like a mane, and his face was accentuated by a large mustache. His booming voice carried easily to the back rows of his crowds and he spoke in long, well-reasoned passages. All were quaking at the thought of poor old Gene Talmadge taking on the mighty Brown. All but Gene and his small cadre. They had their man where they wanted him, and they were counting on the pride of the local people to draw them to the local boy.

In the few days they had preceding the speech on August 3, the Talmadge organization had completed its hurried but thorough orchestration of the county's leading people. Every man who had ever won anything, plus a lot of plain dirt farmers, was asked to prepare a little speech for Gene. They would be asked to come on the stage and tell how they knew Gene to be a good man and a dirt farmer. This led to a community-wide involvement and created a flood of excitement. Men who had piddled for years in backwater politics would get their chance in the spotlight. The night before, Gene's little group of advisers huddled in Murdaugh's office and completed their plans for the next day. Mitt was out at Sugar Creek, scared that her ambitious husband was going to be embarrassed by Brown. Everybody in town thought they were going to be embarrassed also. They all thought Gene would lose.[16]

The platform had been nailed up in the town park the day before the speech. Its fresh pine floor was sticky with sap and smelled of the liquid where the wood had been pierced by a nail or saw. It was a small platform, made just high enough to look over the heads of the crowd. The August sun found Gene already up as it cleared the hardwoods at Sugar Creek. Talmadge was very calm, and his movements were precise. There would be a final meeting that morning in town; it was important that the townspeople be prepared to mount the stage. But if anything was underestimated that day, it was the people of McRae. Unquestionably this was viewed as one of the biggest political events in the town's history and few people wanted to miss it, particularly since it was that Gene Talmadge fellow going at it again. Storekeepers expected a brisk trade, and enterprising farmers could be seen setting food stands out on the roads. Apple cider, peanuts, and other light fare spilled from the stands, beckoning to those riding the long, flat, sandy roads to McRae. Good clothes were pulled out by the local ladies, and white shirts were ironed for the men. The children would wear their shoes and bathe before going. In the long August days, the debate offered high entertainment. And the people filed out from their far-flung homes to fill the roads before the morning sun had made itself felt. A few came in cars and trucks, but most plodded along by oxen or mule or horse. And some walked. Indications of family income could often be seen in the manner of travel, and the roads to McRae that day told a story of hard times.

Stick candy and soft drinks moved well in the stores as the crowd slowly assembled; and out at the park, watermelons were disappearing from large wagons parked nearby. Since the speaking would last only a few hours, most people didn't bring food other than some cold chicken and biscuits and jars of iced tea wrapped tightly in newspaper. The crowd was in a jovial, festive mood, and their din was punctuated by laughter as they nervously discussed and joked about the debate. Cigar boxes and paper sacks were carried through the crowd by Talmadge supporters looking for contributions.

Brown mounted the platform amid polite applause and hushed, apprehensive conversation. His appearance was almost majestic. Gene Talmadge took his place with good applause and cheering. His dark skin and wiry frame contrasted obviously with Brown's appearance. Gene looked almost indistinguishable from the farmer crowd through which he had just walked.

Brown, smiling and confident, started first. His speech was prepared and rather long. He touched briefly on his record, claiming he was doing a commendable job for the farmer; then he tore into his opponent with a long list of accusations. He said Talmadge was an unpopular lawyer who claimed he was a farmer in order to justify his running for the commissioner's post. He and his crony Thrasher had nearly spent Telfair County into bankruptcy, and their tenure in office was characterized by constant grand jury investigations. Brown also said that Talmadge was a man who would cheat his own people, as evidenced by the fact that he had tried to sell some of his own land worth $10 an acre for $30 an acre to the county. He also said Gene was not much of a lawyer, as anyone who read the courthouse records could see. The old politician had done his homework well. Somebody in McRae had talked plenty to his people. Having been provided such a wealth of negative information, it was hardly surprising that he had confidently challenged Gene to a debate in his own hometown. But of all the attacks on the Talmadge record and character, probably none was more important to disprove than the assertion that Gene Talmadge was just a lawyer and not also a dirt farmer. No farmer in Georgia was about to vote a man who had never farmed into the agriculture office.

Talmadge took the podium as though he had been in on the Brown strategy sessions. Without uttering a word, he allowed what appeared to be every citizen of the community to march up on the stage and say a few words for McRae's boy. It must have been one of the longest introductions a candidate ever had. When the long procession finally ended, Gene stepped forward—lean, cocky, intense, his enormous round-frame glasses enveloping his dark eyes like goggles. And he immediately drew the crowd into the fray by shouting "Now how many of you people want to see me quit?" A chorus of "No"s and "We want you to run, Gene"s echoed through the afternoon heat. Talmadge then slowly went about picking apart every Brown accusation, often with a bit of fancy verbal footwork; but the crowd was pleased, and he moved with all the comprehensiveness of a lawyer to refute the allegation that he was not a dirt farmer. He asked his farm foreman to come forward, and Gene asked the man if he had ever seen Gene Talmadge plow, and the man reacting like someone had just asked him if he'd ever chewed tobacco, answered with great certainty, "Sure, Gene, I seen you plow plenty of times. I plowed with you." And then the speaker asked the creased faces before him how many of them had ever seen Gene Talmadge plow, and arms shot up above the sea of white shirts and another chorus of approval rocked the park. The speaker then rocked back on his heels and said smugly, "I guess that about proves I done some dirt farmin'." The disgruntled Brown was heard to sneer from his chair, "lawyer!" but the point had been made, and the day won. Next Talmadge blasted the Brown record, and served his coup de grace by asking for a show of hands of those who would vote for the local boy. Not a hand was left dangling, and Gene Talmadge, "the nigger who came to town," stepped from the platform as Telfair County's new fair-haired boy and the state's leading contender to end the rule of J. J. Brown. He had met the fearsome patronage king and had sent him off, according to a local lady who passed his entourage as it left McRae, "looking like a man going to a funeral." [17] The news of the debate flew from the town on a thousand voices; Gene Talmadge from Telfair County had whipped Brown on the stump. It was the type of delicious news from which heroes were made, news that struck terror in the hearts of the "oily boys" and the fertilizer inspectors, and the hundreds of other members of the great Brown machine who had escaped the poverty of the farm through the patronage of government. But then Talmadge had been on his own ground, and country people love their own. The tale would be told at Elberton when J. J. would be in his own hometown for the second debate. That was north Georgia, and that was another story.

Some of the boys were sent up early to start working the Elberton area. Their weapons were their mouths, that very developed and much-used means of communication that an isolated, partially illiterate populace necessarily erects as its major means of communication. Gossip, rumor, and all manner of embellished tales were spread from the small shops where people gather and listen to the stranger in town who has seen a revelation in a distant place, who has seen and heard a great new leader—a man who speaks the heart of the farmer, a dynamic and courageous man who talks a whole lot like old Tom Watson. And that man was coming to Elberton.

The second debate was on August 12, and it was a stunning defeat for Brown. His attacks on Talmadge were prosaic and nebulous, with the strongest objection to the Talmadge candidacy being the allegation that Gene was a "stalking horse" created by the Atlanta newspapers. By contrast the Talmadge speech was strong and colorful. He deflated the pompous Brown machine with his earthy humor: "The oil inspectors and fertilizer inspectors are sucking a teat under Brown"; the commissioner was "leading two hundred jackasses around the state with high patronage positions." [18] The second debate had its winner before the day began. The people were ready for Talmadge and he delivered, in a style that would mark him as the new star on the Georgia political horizon. He had come quickly to the essence of rural political appeal—emotionalism in all of its facets. He was making politics fun; he was making people laugh. He was a touring carnival, a dopey cousin, a profane, rambunctious, devil-may-care, good old boy who "didn't give a damn." He was "just one of us."

Word spread quickly from Elberton. Brown had been run off the stump in his own hometown; the judgment would ring like a death knell across the state. Even Tom Talmadge was now convinced that his son could win, and he started campaigning actively around Forsyth, stopping in hardware and seed stores, saying to the customers, "Boys, I've got a son, Gene Talmadge, who's running for agriculture commissioner. I want you to vote for him." [19]

Gene returned to McRae for the September 8 election returns. He would hear them by radio. As the votes rolled in, he was ecstatic. "Look at them votes roll in," he shouted, "Ain't I a runn'n fool!" [20] Indeed, he was. The final vote gave him 123,115 popular votes to Brown's

66,569. Gene won the majority of the votes in 139 counties out of the state's 169, or 362 unit votes to Brown's 52. [21] So complete was the victory that it generally defied an analysis by geography or demography. Gene did lose 2 of the large 6-vote counties, but this was mainly because of a strong Brown organization in those areas. He was so elated after the win that he called his father and exclaimed, "Papa, we have beat them to death!" The relieved father pontificated: "Son, be humble. Never gloat in victory."[22]

It was officially reported that the Talmadge campaign had cost $4,985.68, and that Brown had spent $13,305.70.[23] The figures were low and in the case of Talmadge did not account for the hundreds of dollars handed to him and Murdaugh as they moved through the state, monies they stuffed in their pockets and spent as the need arose. Nor did the official reports take into account the two candidates who quit the race because the Talmadge organization had paid their expenses to that point. Murdaugh had attempted to pay a third candidate, Stewart, to quit, but he had refused the money, saying he was quitting to support Gene out of conviction only. Murdaugh estimated that the total expenses came to between $7,000 and $8,000.[24]

The victory had been rather unorthodox. Disregarding state party machinery, having little money or patronage to promise the courthouse gangs, and with little experience, finances, or organization, Gene had defeated one of the most entrenched powers in the state. Some said that Brown was ripe for a fall and most any candidate could have effected it, but this assessment seems blind to the masterful psychology and execution exhibited by the Talmadge organization, and particularly by Gene himself. He knew the southern rural mind—its fears, loves, hates, and needs. He tested his delivery on the crowds until he could turn their emotions at his will. Beyond this analytical ability there was something dynamic and passionate and magnetic about the man. Many thought it was in his eyes, others in the rapid-fire way he talked, and others in his total delivery. He was many different things to many different people. Very dissimilar men could identify with this strutting, irreverent, bespeckled figure. His speech and its contents had a memorable quality, but it was primarily his iconoclastic qualities that stood out. To a populace who took their religion fundamental style, his hand-wringing, cadenced, preacherlike style created a revival atmosphere. He could bay like a hound, cry like a baby, sing, dance, howl with laughter; right there on the stump, whatever they wanted, he could deliver it. He had brought laughter to politics, and those who had heard him grinned long into the Georgia fall of 1926 about the victory of Gene Talmadge.

5

"Yeah, It's True.
I Stole, but
I Stole for You."

He had been elected as a reform candidate, a man of the people in the old Populist tradition. He ran under the auspices of the Democratic party, but no one thought of him as a party man. To prove his lack of ties to the old machine, he had vowed during the campaign to fire the legion of agriculture department inspectors, and to fire every man he found in the offices of the department. "He said he was going to clean house, and when we went over to his new offices for his first day on the job, he found out that a lot of people had taken him seriously. There wasn't a soul to be found in the whole agriculture department. He seemed a little disappointed and surprised. It was kind of a lonely experience, a letdown. He felt that somebody should have been there to greet him." Gene had taken one of his most trusted campaign workers, a young lawyer named Hugh Howell, over to his new offices, so that someone could share in the excitement of that first day in office, but as Howell remembered, the fury and the accolades of the campaign had been ringing too loudly in Talmadge's ear. He had expected an office of eager workers to be waiting on him; but he had scared the hell out of Brown's staff, and they had left with their leader.[1] Even the janitor had gone.

Gene showed quickly that he was going to be a man who flexed his muscles. He asked Governor William Hardman to reduce the oil inspectors from two hundred to ten, to put the state veterinary under his control and make its employees "subject to his dismissal without cause." He made public appeals to the farmers to pressure their representatives into accepting the Talmadge reforms, but lobbying was hardly needed. Such had been the desire to get Brown out of office, and such was the weight of Talmadge's win, that the normally quiescent lawmakers were in a cooperative mood. Usually reformism of any degree rarely nudged the stagnant state party, but it could surge, on occasion, with a vengeance against individuals who had overextended themselves and gotten caught at it.

In his first term as commissioner Talmadge got his office bonded, cleared out the last vestiges of the Brown machine, reduced the number of fertilizer inspectors, and expanded his department into food and drugs and marketing. And most important to his own designs, he gained a firm control over his department and its employees. He did not, however, get a new fertilizer law.[2] His impact through the first term, as it came through the state's presses, was resounding. His movements, judgments, and words were locomotivelike. The man seemed unable to do anything quietly, and the farmers who had voted for him loved it. The only valid criticism of his initial efforts was against his practice of hiring so many members of his family, including his stepson John. Gene defended himself by saying that his relatives were the best people he could find for the job. The truth probably lay closer to a paranoia about the Brown forces' ability to infiltrate his department.

The *Market Bulletin*, a department newspaper founded by Brown, found great favor with Gene. Only a handful of Georgia's rural homes had a radio in 1927, and fewer had telephones. Newspapers were the primary mass medium, but most local weeklies covered only church and social news. It was very difficult to communicate on a continuing and current basis with the whole farmer class which accounted for about half the state's population at that time. The *Bulletin* offered a means, and supposedly a nonpolitical reason, for communicating with the far-flung farmers. The columns soon fatted, however, with Talmadge economics and philosophy. But this practice was not always self-serving, for Gene's sincerity in helping the farmer was evidenced in the new agricultural information and advice he presented. He soundly preached diversification and the need for a processing industry. But, paradoxically, he advised the farmers to remain on the farm and gut it out, even though many were destitute and unable to diversify or start a processing industry for want of the capital or the skills. Gene's great solution was for farmers to keep their products off the market, thereby forcing prices up. To the man near bankruptcy that rang with the sound of insanity. But people were getting used to Gene's barrage of advice; and oddly enough it came to them more as entertainment than as rhetoric, so that its importance was not in the substance, but in the presentation. In the simple fact that the man obviously cared, appeared to be a reformer of sorts, they found solace and the ability to forgive his mistakes. That forgiveness even covered his penchant for touring out of state with carloads of friends to "observe agriculture in other states." Old Gene was having a ball, but what the hell, maybe he would find something out.

All this activity, this propensity for charging headlong into opponents and programs, guaranteed the commissioner opposition in 1928. And not so oddly, his ability to "make people mad" became the campaign issue. G. C. Adams of Newton County, Gene's only opponent, said that Talmadge had caused strife and chaos in the department, all due "entirely to the incompetency, the bull-headed obstinacy, the rule or ruin policy and the one man domination of the commissioner, Eugene Talmadge." [3] Claiming he had little money with which to campaign, Gene answered his opponent with a few sweeping brush-offs, saying he was a Brown puppet backed by the tobacco crowd. These simplistic generalizations kept Adams at bay, while Gene ran a campaign based on his supposed martyrdom. He humbly admitted he had made mistakes but beseeched the voters not to "break the vase to kill the fly," and he said his errors had been of the "head and not of the heart." [4]

While most of the state's presses were favorable to Gene's reelection, the Cobb County *Times* scoffed at his self-proclaimed accomplishments. "If any official made a complete fizzle of office, Mr. Talmadge did." [5] But Gene felt confident of victory, knowing his opponent was a prosaic front for the fertilizer people. Therefore, he ran a short campaign based solely on his record and the promises he kept, and he defeated Adams 129,868 to 98,631. Gene received 289 county unit votes to Adams' 125. [6]

The Talmadge victory, while never in doubt, was much smaller than it had been over Brown. This probably substantiates the assertion that people voted against Brown more than they voted for Talmadge in 1926. Gene's abrasive, brusque way of doing things had offended the sensibilities of a lot of people, and the remnants of the Brown machine had made sure that every Talmadge junket and court fight had been thoroughly dragged through the mud. Gene had lost Atlanta and other highly populated areas. His strictly redneck mannerisms and language had become a little too much for the city people, who were usually trying hard to forget the miseries of the farm life most had just left. Adams compounded his own problems by issuing spurious and meaningless campaign attacks. He had failed to fathom the real weakness of Talmadge's tenure and instead had attacked the man personally. Ironically, he attacked that part of the Talmadge personality that was his strength, his adamant independence. The fact that Talmadge was making big-city bureaucrats mad delighted the dirt farmer. Tragically, one of the few satisfactions the farmer enjoyed from his state government was the fact that it had been stirred and angered and cussed at by Gene Talmadge.

Attacks on bigness and big government in particular had crept into the Talmadge campaign speeches and his *Bulletin* columns, and it was difficult to separate his own independent convictions from the profound Populist influence of Tom Watson. His column over the next few years became a lengthy invective against the haves and their supposedly ruthless domination over the have-nots. His voice sounded populistic, but it was Populism tempered with very narrow provincialism; it carefully paid tribute to the culture, mores, and attitudes of middle Georgia, which was in essence a direct philosophic extension of the Old South mythology. He made a poor imitation of Watson in October of 1930, when he described the rich capitalist as being like a mastodon whose legs would be eaten off by the poor like mice. "The pitiful part of it all is that the people who raise the raw materials out of which all the wealth is produced are being trod down by these monsters." [7]

If his overzealousness and frustration at fighting things, seemingly beyond his own control, made him sound melodramatic, his thesis was coming close to target. Northern capital had been used more to hold the agricultural South in dependence than to make it an equitable partner. The old inferiority and oppression fears that had found voice in a civil war were the soundest of realities to Talmadge in the late 1920s. They infuriated him to the point that his hatred and distrust drove him beyond Old South conservatism to the point of know-nothingism, and a semi-rejection of all things geographically and idealistically removed from the South. Naively, he could not understand why southern bankers did not come to the aid of the South and its farmers. They, for some reason inexplicable to him, appeared to be leaving southern interests to the mercy of Wall Street and its uncaring financiers. These political appraisals would usually be followed by a paternalistic admonition in the column. Talmadge warned "his people" to watch out for railroad crossings, work hard, save money, go to church, and believe in the life on the farm. His grasp of economic realities was embarrassingly meager for a man in a position of economic leadership.

While the first Talmadge term was spent in solving immediate local needs, such as improved fertilizer laws, and in gaining control of the power inherent in his department, the second term was much broader in its vision and goals. He attempted to bring relief to the farmer through protective tariffs, higher prices for crops, cooperatives to help the farmer control markets and prices, and more "sympathetic money" from lenders. His goals were grandiose in scope and highly commendable in principle, but practically speaking, they were quixotic in their potential for fulfillment. His limited knowledge of economics hurt his ability to bring changes and damaged his credibility with those in power. He constantly and erroneously placed the sole blame for the South's woes on Wall Street and its bankers, ignoring the fact that cotton prices and markets for southern goods were controlled by a number of interrelated variables from around the world. Reflecting this naivete, he wrote in the *Bulletin* on April 3, 1930, "The bankers of the South should fix the price of cotton." He had expanded the enemies of the farmer from the confines of his state to include the American corporate structure and American financial institutions. He had found in his first year that he could effect changes against enemies from within the state, but he found out in his second term how small his office and his powers were when he attempted to expand his influence outside the state. Big institutions cared little for his populistic concerns, especially when they saw that the concern did not extend into traditional areas of populistic reform and progressivism. Gene wanted reforms against national institutions carried out within the tight perimeter dictated by Old South conservatism. These limits allowed for absolutely no controls or obligations from any outside institution, such as those incurred by government lending. Talmadgism was more a cultural isolationist doctrine that oddly enough avoided direct, detailed confrontations with the most critically deprived groups of his impoverished constituency, the sharecroppers and the Negroes.

The stubborn loyalty that poor whites attached to Talmadge during his commissioner tenure often defied rationality. Although Gene's appeals were aimed at the emotional and educational level of the sharecropper, his programs more often favored the farmer who owned his own farm. The destitute and ignorant tenants were participants in a grinding economic cycle, fueled by opportunism, greed, inherited debts, and plain stupidity. Their situation was of such magnitude that no amount of Talmadge philosophizing, dragon-chasing, or paternalistic advice would ever substantially improve their lot, particularly since he was telling them to remain where they were and keep doing what they were doing. They needed help, the kind that comes with government intervention and sweeping societal changes. The Georgia conservatism of the 1920s had been unwilling to have much truck with movement. Gene's answers lay in his traditional conservatism, in the sacred value of hard manual labor, rugged individualism, honesty, and frugality. If he was short on economic pragmatism, thousands of farmers seemed as though they could not have cared less. They found his defiance, his concern, and his folksy mannerisms sufficient cause to rally to his side.

The depression came hard to the Georgia farmer, though many share-croppers and tenants would have sworn that its next-of-kin had been an historical resident of their fields and pastures. The measure of success that had followed World War I had all but vanished ten years later. Following the decline in the economy, there had been a profound decline in the farming population; by 1930 (and actually a little before), for the first time in Georgia's history, less than one-half her population was living on a farm. The drama of this move is found in the fact that 10 percent of the state's people left the countryside in the decade of the 1920s. The mass exodus resulted from a combination of hard times, no lending capital, technological forces, bitter discrimination against Negroes, compelling desires for the new materials and services of the emerging consumer society, new levels of consciousness and perception, the growth of urban areas because of industrialization, education, and alternative lifestyles.

The Georgia countryside, apparently impregnable even into the twentieth century, appeared to be crumbling overnight. The rural exodus had been going on for years, but never had its rate been so pronounced or the rise in levels of consciousness so obvious. There was a new world moving beyond the pine trees and many a wool-hat boy packed his trunk. Perhaps if cotton and hogs and produce had kept their price and the depression had not sledgehammered them, the farmers would have stayed. Perhaps they would not have been so enthralled by the new age and its society and products. Perhaps if some of those newfangled things like the telephone, radio, and automobile had not brought the reality of the world so unmistakably to them, they would still be there today—isolated, independent, poor, suspicious, changeless. But, listening to the siren call of the late 1920s, the farmers annointed that time the gestation period for the dramatic cultural upheavals of the 1930s.

Statistics of the era attest to the economic devastation that was occurring. Cotton acreage fell by a million acres in ten years. Farmland worth $37 an acre in 1925 fell to $18 by 1933. The cotton crop worth $96 million in 1930 fell to $46 million one year later. Manufacturing establishments numbering 3,175 in 1927 fell to 2,812 in 1931. One of the few increases, one which ironically reflected the unfolding tragedy as much as the decreases, was the statistic that farms operated by tenants rose from 63.8 percent in 1925 to 68.2 percent in 1930.[8] More farmers were selling their farms, or turning them over to creditors, and working their old land for another. Gene Talmadge, with departmental state responsibility for this rural class, saw in the monumental exodus more than escape from economic deprivation; he saw escape from a culture which had been the backbone of his society. He knew that culture would not survive in the cities, and thus he made his seemingly irrational plea for the farmer to remain on his land.

Talmadge ran for a third term in 1930. His old opponent, J. J. Brown, unable to find someone to run against Gene, entered the race himself. Running on his record, the incumbent trounced Brown 148,150 votes to 57,219, and 406 county-unit votes to 8. It was an unparalleled victory, and it established Talmadge as a man of great political potential.[9] But there was also great irony growing with the emerging career of Gene Talmadge. He was winning big; he had garnered a large, solid core of supporters, and yet his advice to this core on how they should solve their problems and the reality of how they were solving their problems were growing further and further apart. He was saying stay on the land. They were leaving in droves. He was saying, "We do not want to become dependent on our government," [10] and they were desperately looking for relief. He said hold your cotton off the market, and they beat a steady path to the cotton factors. Whatever he advised, they ignored, and yet they were voting for him in overwhelming numbers. Gene was so blinded by his dogmatic philosophy that he could not fathom the enormous attitudinal releases, cultural readjustments, alternative awarenesses, and self-identity changes that were occurring. The crushing economics of the day had destroyed the sense of infallibility, the frontiersman identity, and the concept of self-sufficiency. The Georgia farmer had lost the will to care for himself because he had lost the ability. This forced him to think beyond himself, to expand his consciousness and realize that his was now a world of alternatives, whereas in its two hundred years of history there had been no viable alternative to staying on the land. And yet these new directions in which the farmer was moving were apparently creating a problem of conscience; and by supporting the voice of the past, Gene Talmadge, they were absolving these guilt feelings about leaving the past. Gene was left shaking his head, warning, "borrowing from the government is leading us into bad habits."

In fact, bad habits were becoming a subject of discussion about the Talmadge tenure. There was the habit he had of forever driving with carloads of friends to places like Charleston's Botanical Gardens on the way to "study agriculture." And he had still a bad tendency to hire members of his family and let the state pay for the cars he and they wrecked on their own time. And he was quite derelict in not reporting to the state treasury the agriculture department tax money he collected, but placing it instead in a friend's bank. These things, plus his blunt, roughshod approach to everything he did, had been festering in the legislature until it exploded in a storm of criticism when Gene bought eighty-two carloads of hogs from Georgia farmers and shipped them to Chicago for sale—on state money, all unauthorized, about $14,000 worth of hogs.

The Talmadge decision to have the Bureau of Markets buy and sell the hogs was, oddly enough, one of the best political decisions he ever made. It had come after much agonizing in his office over a period of time in January, 1930. Hogs were a major Georgia product, but their profit had been eroded badly because of high, unfair shipping rates and low prices from the big Chicago packing plants. It was like everything connected with agriculture at that time: nothing seemed to work. Gene was beseeched by farmers to at least do something—even if it were illegal—to salvage the hog market. Meetings and deliberations ensued in the Talmadge office, resulting in the idea that he have the Bureau of Markets actually buy and then sell the hogs. It was unprecedented, and he knew it would never be approved by the governor, Richard B. Russell. His friend, Lamar Murdaugh, was in his office at the time: "Gene was reluctant to buy the hogs, though he was convinced it was the only course left. There were a number of us in the room, and he asked us what we thought he ought to do, knowing the state would raise hell when they heard about it. We said 'buy the Goddamn hawgs!' and his voice snapped the way it did when he came to a decision, 'I'm gone do it!' It was one of the most deliberate decisions I ever saw him make, because I think we talked about it for days." [11]

At this point Gene was supposed to make a request to the governor for the money and receive a warrant for it. Instead he ordered the hogs bought just under Chicago prices and shipped North in eighty-two carloads. Gene later claimed he forced a slight increase in what the hogs sold for, but official investigations of the affair reported that the state lost $12,176.28.[12] This amount has also been given as $10,521.83, and $14,000. The legislature, being out of session in 1930, was unable to react until the following year. In the meantime, Gene began appealing to Washington for protective tariffs. He was attempting to organize the southern agriculture commissioners into a sort of marketing bureau that could determine prices through coordinated actions. Neither of these well-intentioned moves worked. He was particularly disturbed over the Federal Farm Bureau's lending money to cooperatives which were trying to bring some control to prices. Talmadge was not anti-cooperative per se, but he saw the bureau emerging as just another bureaucracy that was betting the farmer's money on futures. He also opposed the bureau's proposal that farmers plow under every third row to bring down supply, going so far as to say, "It is un-American for any man to advocate a policy of reduction of acreage of any staple crop."

Richard Russell had been elected governor in 1930. A young man emblematic of the beginnings of new political thinking in the South, Russell instigated vast governmental reorganization, none of which included the agriculture department. That department was given, however, commissioner control over who would be paid and when.

By the end of July, 1931, a senate investigating committee headed by an angry and determined W. H. Duckworth was directing its attention toward Talmadge's conduct. It started the investigation by ordering Gene to give the committee a list of the names of his relatives who were working for him.[13] On July 30, the committee disclosed that Gene had paid $40,000 in salaries to himself and members of his family over a three-year period. This also included their expenses, such as a yearly trip to the Kentucky Derby, where the agriculture commissioners met, and damages to state cars that both Gene and his stepson had wrecked while using them for personal reasons. Gene was also accused of taking $500 from his department to help fight for a tariff, his personal fight. The committee was particularly angered over the $200 his stepson, John Peterson, was receiving for services as fertilizer inspector. It irked them that the boy's mother, Mitt Talmadge, was getting half of the twenty-five year-old's salary, "to teach the boy to save money." Gene, in typical fashion, was defiant before the committee's charges. He brushed the investigation off, saying he only employed the boy and a third cousin because they were as good as anyone else for their jobs. Why not hire someone friendly to him, if he was competent? He innocently justified his trips to the Derby because of the annual commissioners' meeting there, and he said he thought he was right in buying the hogs. But Duckworth was not impressed; he demanded that Gene appear the first week in August to answer further, more serious charges of misappropriation of fertilizer money.

When Gene refused to reappear, claiming that the committee had no power to demand his appearance, the committee asked for contempt proceedings and hinted at impeachment. These actions and threats were based on Gene's alleged use of collected fertilizer funds that he had failed to send directly to the state treasury as required by law.[14] Instead, as his department had collected them, Talmadge had placed the monies in the out-of-town banks of friends.[15] His defiance of the committee and the rude indignation he displayed in refusing to answer their summons, shocked many legislators who had otherwise chosen to stay out of the matter. Practically all of the lawmakers represented rural constituents who had made known their strong attachment to Gene Talmadge, but the strength of the accusations and the defiance had caused many of the normally reticent lawmakers to join the anti-Talmadge forces. The fact that Gene had no real organization to back him, no special interest groups or money men behind him, made it all the easier to ignore the fact that he was a winner at the polls.

The uproar became so strong, Gene was forced to meet with the senate investigating committee. Meeting them head on, he glared proudly, "If I stole, it was for farmers like yourselves!" [16] It was an electrifying statement that reflected the sheer desperation of the times as much as it did the dishonesty of an official. It moved a number of powerful legislators who had long been impressed by Gene's determination to help the farmers, to get him off the hook. House member Roy Harris was one of them. "Gene was a good boy, and we knew it. He hadn't meant any harm, and it was about to get out of hand. We discussed the matter with the right people, and got a minority resolution to impeach him defeated 114 to 22." [17] An angry senate demanded that Russell take Gene to court.[18] The governor dodged the issue by asking his attorney general, John A. Napier, to "make a thorough investigation and take such action as you deem necessary to conserve the interest of the state." Napier researched the matter and wrote Russell that he felt some real errors in judgment had been made. He recommended that Talmadge pay back to the state the $14,136 he had spent on the hogs, plus $1,600 "paid out illegally to John A. Peterson as clerk in his office." Napier said he felt Gene's purchase of the hogs was within the powers of his office, citing Section 3, Paragraph 8, of the Market Bureau Acts, which gave the commissioner the power "to take such steps as may be deemed advisable to benefit the producers," if he ever determined that "any agricultural products" would "depreciate in value for lack of ready market." [19] Napier felt hogs could be considered "agricultural products." He did think Gene was wrong in not getting a requisition to spend the money, and he was particularly angered over Talmadge's bonding company's refusal to answer any inquiries. Napier closed his letter to Russell by asking the governor what he wanted to do now. Russell wanted to do nothing. In preparation to run for the United States Senate in a few months, he wanted no part of angering the farmers who supported Gene. He tried to pass the buck back to Napier, saying it was his job to prosecute, but Napier was having none of that, and the investigation fizzled out.[20] Senator Duckworth moaned to the press, "God pity this great state"—having an attorney general "who can see no legal wrong committed." [21] The house in voting down impeachment had voted to sue Gene for $14,136, but Gene refused to pay it and Napier refused to sue.

Talmadge emerged a Robin Hood, taking from an unresponsive state to help the poor farmer. The fact that the farmers saw nothing wrong in a public official more or less stealing money from their state said something about both their economic plight and their historic attitude toward state government.

The investigations concluded that Gene had erred in paying his stepson the sum of $200; in guaranteeing watermelon freight bonds; in buying hogs and poultry for the state; and in putting $9,850.65 in fertilizer tag funds into an Ailey bank owned by his wife's cousin instead of turning it over to the state treasury.[22]

Representative J. H. McGehee, chairman of the house committee investigating Talmadge, concluded: "Two laws were broken. One when money was collected and not turned into the Treasury and the other when it was disbursed without an executive warrant." [23]

Only his sale of the hogs caught the public ear, and he played it to the hilt. During all of his late summer speeches he received thunderous applause for shouting, "Yeah, it's true. I stole, but I stole for you, the dirt farmer!" This was a spine-tingling commitment—and surely a unique admission in Georgia's political history.

During the investigations Russell had sent Gene to New Orleans to hear Huey Long present his cotton holiday plan for raising the price of cotton. Gene became totally enthralled with the idea, and returned to Georgia to stump the state in late summer seeking popular support for a holiday. He then rushed off to Texas to speak before that legislature, trying to convince the legislators that they should pass cotton holiday laws. They refused, and Gene returned to Georgia once again to call a mass meeting of farmers at the state capitol on September 16. He would try to force Russell to call the legislature back. It was a grandstand play that drew a respectable crowd. Gene worked them into a lather with fiery speeches; then they all marched on Russell's office. The governor thought the idea wrong, but Talmadge had created such a spectacle, the governor did not want to appear too much against it. He passed the buck. If Texas would pass the law, he would call a special session if the lawmakers would serve free. With this the crowd dispersed, and for all purposes the cotton holiday movement in Georgia peaked out. The legislators refused to serve free, and Texas voted a holiday on only 30 percent of its land. Gene called the legislators by phone, asking them to return for a session, but no Georgia politician had ever told a farmer not to grow cotton, and they weren't going to be the first.

Gene had spotlighted himself so severely in 1931 that even his writings in the *Market Bulletin* came under fire. The general assembly ordered him in December to stop writing for the paper.[24] They accused him of propagandizing. With characteristic martyrdom he promised, "I will try to find some other way to keep in touch with the farmers. I believe this to be my duty." He would continue writing in the *Southern Cultivator* for a brief time.[25] Gene had greatly extended his voice through the *Bulletin* and, in the farmer's eyes, had extended their own voice. Gene wrote as they thought and spoke, blasting their enemies, praising their God, laughing with them, and most of all showing them that someone cared.

Many thought otherwise. Attorney General Napier said, "Mr. Talmadge acts and talks as if the general assembly and the courts of Georgia were mere sideshows when compared with his power and authority."[26] One L. L. Lowe accurately wrote, "I know he is a good honest man, but he doesn't seem to have the necessary farming and business experience to cope with the changes that are now taking place."[27]

The year 1931 had created a solidified constituency for Talmadge, but more than that the Talmadge phenomenon had reflected the posture of *government* in Georgia: a figurehead affair; a cultural perpetuator, an oratorical platform from which the ghosts of the past were revered; a curator turned relic; a museum-keeper turned as stonelike as the objects it guarded. The gist of it was, if Gene Talmadge had stolen from this inanimate object—so what? Desperation stalked the statistics of the day, and only one state politician had laid his reputation on the line to do anything about it. The fact that he didn't seem to know what he was doing half the time was irrelevant.

The Wild Man
from
Sugar Creek

It was 1932, election year, a time for traditional speculation in Georgia about who would run for what. The Atlanta *Constitution* added fuel to the rumor mill by asserting that Talmadge "holds center stage" in the governor's race.[1] The Macon *Telegraph* was not so quick to give laudatory headlines to anything Talmadge had done or might do. It reported in late February that he was "pondering" his next move, afraid that he could not defeat Governor Russell for his office, or Senator Walter F. George for his. Neither had the liabilities of a J. J. Brown. Regardless of what he did, the *Telegraph* considered his tenure in state office a farce. It termed the $14,000 loss on hogs a "foolish, futile, impotent gesture" and said that as far as farmers were concerned, Talmadge had "given them no tangible help." A closing swipe said, "We don't think the department is being even intelligently run." [2]

Whatever the speculation, Gene had eliminated the possibility of running against George and his massive state organization. He didn't want to run against Governor Russell either, but considered his chances much better against him if he were forced to choose between the two. Russell wanted very badly to run for the senate seat of William J. Harris, but didn't want to run against Harris. Harris was a sick man, and through the winter of 1931–1932 it became increasingly doubtful that he would stand for reelection. Confusion marked the camps of both Russell and Talmadge through February and March; then, as if on cue, Harris died on April 18. The way was thus open for Russell to seek the vacant senatorial seat and Talmadge the governor's chair. Aspirants seemed to jump from behind every pine tree, but none moved faster than Talmadge's man Lamar Murdaugh, who had been watching developments from McRae. He knew Gene wanted the governorship, and with Harris' death he quickly raised money to cover Gene's qualifying fee. Singlehandedly, Murdaugh gathered up the money and a loud group of McRae citizens and struck out for Atlanta without Talmadge's knowledge. Barging into the agriculture department, they found a surprised Talmadge working at his desk. As the raucous group jammed into the small office, Murdaugh announced with great determination, "Gene, we gonna run you for governor! We have raised the qualifying fee, and we're about to march across the street and qualify you. You can come if you want to, but it don't matter if you don't. Like it or not, you're gonna run." Talmadge laughed, jumped to his feet, grabbed his ever-present hat, and said, "Let's go!" [3] The band marched across the street to the capitol, and with much fanfare signed up their beaming candidate.

Talmadge had known nothing of the plans, but he liked the way it looked—the hometown folks making the long trek to Atlanta, like a pilgrimage, to beg the hometown boy to take up the torch, to say "yes" to a plea from the people. It was in keeping with the master strategy he used; stay a part of McRae. Go to her people for readings. Return to her frequently and let her share completely in the rising career. The maintenance of these ties had given him a concrete political base and an ally in the most desperate of times. He never forgot the humiliation he had given Brown in his own hometown of Elberton. The strategy was not totally self-serving, however. McRae people were his kind. He knew and understood them. He hunted and joked with them, sat in the courthouse and shops, chewing, smoking, cussing, and laughing with them. They talked about cows and cotton, money, politics, people, and hard times. Six years in Atlanta had not changed him. His talk about the "big city" was as derisive as the suspicions of his people demanded. He called city dwellers and the politicians that served them "that sonofabitchin' crowd."

That kind of talk was mainly politics. He thrived on the vibrancy of Atlanta, particularly its social life. Gene was a partygoer. The bigger and noisier the affair, the better. His wife hated the city. She was a loner, even more independent and blunt than he; and she had refused to move to Atlanta when he was commissioner. When friends would kid her about Gene "high-steppin' " it in Atlanta, she would snap, "I don't give a damn, as long as he stays away from here!" [4] Publicly the two seemed to compliment each other. Privately they seemed to be always at odds, pulling in opposite directions. Their relationship was more businesslike and companionable, and its strength lay in a strong mutual respect for the type each was. They knew neither would ever change, and neither tried.

Two days after Gene qualified, Murdaugh organized a rally through the McRae American Legion in support of Gene's candidacy. He was again trying to create the image of a grassroots candidate, a man running for office because the people had spontaneously asked him to, not because a machine had. He knew that if the Legion put it on, the taint of politics would be minimized. The rally would serve as a kickoff for the candidacy; and to give real honesty to the whole affair, Gene was not invited. To insure a crowd, the rally was advertised as a free fish fry. And word was spread by mouth that there'd be plenty of corn liquor—to be sipped discreetly, of course. The efforts were successful; a good-sized crowd came out to the Ocmulgee, twenty miles from McRae. There were a decent number of local politicians determined to speak up for Gene; and following their rhetoric, Murdaugh was asked to speak, though he had been sitting low in his seat hoping he wouldn't have to get up. As he stepped to the platform he saw his cousin, Oscar, weaving drunkenly in front of the stand, eating catfish chowder out of a paper lard container. Oscar liked his corn liquor and had an empty bottle in his pocket to prove it. Murdaugh said a few words about Gene and was interrupted by the high-pitched drawl of Oscar. "Lee-mar, Lee-mar." The long, thick-tongued intonation drew the attention of the crowd to the cousin. "Lee-mar, didn't you say last year that Gene Talmadge was a sonofabitch?" The crowd became dead quiet, and stood with broad smiles to see just how "Lee-mar" would extricate himself. Murdaugh shot back, "Maybe I did, Oscar, but that's all in the book [in the past]. I do know that if he is a sonofabitch, he's *our* sonofabitch!" The crowd roared its approval, and the day was saved. Word spread from the banks of the sluggish Ocmulgee that McRae had turned out to rally for Gene, and the Talmadge campaign was underway.

The Ocmulgee rally was indicative of the lack of sophistication and complexity of the Talmadge organization. It was primitive by almost anyone's standards, and almost totally dependent on a grassroots upwelling of enthusiasm and a bandwagon psychology. The country-unit system forced politicians to deal with the courthouse gangs, and herein centered the state political machinery and patronage. Gene had been able to sidestep to a degree this normal channel of power-giving by building a strong bond between himself and the people. An organization, apparently nonexistent in off-election years, would suddenly spring forth at election time, based as much as anything on a genuine feeling of fondness and loyalty to Talmadge. He had by 1932 made a substantial number of county contacts, all quite willing to join his campaign, and the old group from 1926 had again gathered about him to form the nucleus of his advisory and management group in 1932.

Gene had entered the race naming the issues as "high taxes" and "high government spending." The other candidates joined him in unison. The entire slate were by-the-book, old-line conservatives who, to a man, saw the answers to the day's problems in yesterday's solutions. By early June, Gene had been joined in the race by J. I. Kelly, Arlie Tucker, and H. B. "Hellbent" Edwards, a man of renowned volume and radically conservative convictions. After a tenure that overshadowed those of most officeholders, Gene was clearly recognized as the man to beat; and true to Georgia political form, the other candidates quickly moved to make this a campaign of personalities rather than issues. Even the depression did not alter this pattern. Personality clashes had always been a tradition in an area where issues were at a minimum. Local heroes were forged from the battles on the stump, and their erection and maintenance had come to be what Georgia politics was all about.

The Talmadge campaign staff at headquarters included Hugh Howell, Tom Linder, Charles D. Redwine, Lindley Camp, and James Peters, lawyers and bankers, all trusted, conservative, intelligent men who had been with Gene for some years. Their method of operation was informal: several relaxed general meetings to discuss strategy and organization had been held through the spring. Gene did not dominate the discussion; the give-and-take was free and open. The depression was an obvious base issue, and Gene's response to it occupied much of the conversation. Another important topic was the determination of the status of Georgia's counties in regard to Gene. County attitudes toward Gene were listed and rated in what came to be called "the Black Book," though it was not a book as such, but a number of lists. Talmadge's key advisers had a wide range of acquaintances, and by county they would list local leaders whom they knew and felt they could call upon to give support. The probable candidates had been taken into consideration along with their past records as vote-getters in their own areas. After the names were compiled, the strength and character of the various courthouse gangs were analyzed to determine how much control they exercised, what demands they asked for their support, and what their past records were as power-brokers. The Black Book list would form the core of the campaign.

Phone calls and letters would be sent out for support, and invitations sought for Gene to speak. With money and time limited, Gene mainly wanted to speak in counties where all agreed he was weak, but stood a chance. These "swing counties" were top priority. Only if he had nothing else to do and was in the area would he speak briefly in a "Talmadge county." The dates were lined up as far in advance as possible, because of the enormous size of the state and the difficulty in getting about on its atrocious roads. Before the big summer speeches began, most of the key staff members spent their time on the road in private conferences with courthouse crowds or local supporters talking Gene up. He was tied to his office, spending hours on the phone trying to put together a state organization. He could rarely be found at his hotel headquarters, but dropped in briefly to leave ideas he had written on scraps of paper. Some of the messages were instructions to secretaries for letters or speeches. He had instructed the staff to be very conservative in their patronage promises. There would be no money in the state coffers with which to do anything. Road contracts could be alluded to and a few offices promised, but only to critical counties where the bargaining got tough. Talmadge was promising as little as any candidate ever had to the power-brokers; and if he could get away with it, he would emerge a man of substantial power with few strings attached to pull him down.

The organization had little money and would depend heavily on small contributions until Gene could appear to be winning, and the big-money people would then come through. Speech organizers were instructed to have a number of people pass through the crowds with cigar boxes and paper sacks to ask for contributions. Organizers were also told to be sure to have a local band in attendance, to have local leaders prepared to speak, to build a platform or find a large field or fairground, and if at all possible to have food available. Nothing would draw a rural crowd faster than a free barbecue or fish fry.[5]

Gene and his staff agreed early on a platform and issues. Economy in government was considered the cornerstone of the platform. This reflected a twofold thinking. First, Gene's conservative philosophy was that a government should take a bare minimum of tax money from its citizens, because it had no need or right to be so involved in their lives that it needed much money to operate. And second, he felt he knew what a big government with money could do to the minds of the people. He had been appalled when he heard presidential candidate Franklin Roosevelt tell some Georgia Democrats that a larger, more involved federal government was needed. Gene knew that if the starving farmer were given food and money as a handout, there would necessarily be controls, and a dependency on government as thinker and doer would emerge. The southern farmer would, therefore, remain in subjugation, only this time to the government instead of to the local bank or the Wall

Street boys. It would be a psychological indebtedness far worse than the region's traditional financial indebtedness.

Other planks included reorganizing the ponderous highway department, getting freight and utility rates lowered, and abolishing the ad valorem tax. Payments to teachers and Confederate veterans, a favorite of every candidate, were other planks. The veterans issue was a particularly emotional one for a people not far removed from the most momentous event in their history. The ties with the aged men prompted every candidate to include them at every chance, but in Gene's case the desire to do was more out of personal sincerity than political motivation. For his philosophy had been theirs, and their culture, almost vanished, represented the way of life he was earnestly supporting. As the industrial age belatedly crunched over rural Georgia, nothing in Talmadge's regressive politics would become more futile than his role as standard-bearer for these men from the past.

Concomitant with his economy cornerstone was a promise to pay the state debt. He literally could not stand deficit spending, partly because of his acute awareness of debt as a southern burden and heritage. His obsession with debt as an evil was an example of his inability to distinguish the symptom from the disease. His 1932 platform was flawed by this failing, and he thus attacked peripheral issues that ironically served to maintain the very problems he was trying to cure.

Throughout the spring of 1932 the topic of every cracker-barrel and shady-tree conversation was the depression. No one loved to gab more at these gatherings than Gene Talmadge, and probably no one else absorbed more of the comments and stories. It was not surprising that out of one of the whittling, checker-playing sessions emerged the most memorable issue of the 1932 race—the three-dollar tag. Shug Fussell of Ben Hill County had driven into McRae with a load of firewood he had cut off his land. Pulling up to one of these gatherings, Gene had asked, "Shug, how you gettin' along?" Shug answered, "Gene, I gotta git a three-dollar tag for this truck that cost me five dollars. I borrowed my neighbor's tag to bring the wood in. If they would lower the cost of tags we could buy more gas to offset the loss [in revenue]." [6]

Gene seized on the idea like a man possessed. In his scheme of simplistic solutions to the depression, the three-dollar tag fit perfectly. He reasoned that thousands of dollars could be saved by the poor, many who couldn't afford to drive their cars, because they couldn't afford the tag. Besides it had the ring of memorability about it, like his famous "oily boys" phrase of 1926. In an economic situation of staggering complexity, everyman could understand the three-dollar tag, and it would benefit the poorest of voters. It was common-denominator stuff.

Preparation for the stump opening of the Talmadge campaign had begun weeks in advance. Never before in Telfair County history had such excitement and activity been generated. It appeared they had all learned to love Gene. Miss Laura Brown was appointed chairman of the serving committee and was responsible for feeding the throngs. She enlisted one hundred women to help, then designated Trix Wilcox to be in charge of all food except barbecue. Trix found fifty men to be pickle-dishers, bread-carriers, barbecue-cutters, and tea-pourers. They would also clean up after the event. Norman Graham, known locally as the "Barbecue King," was asked to oversee cooking. Miss Brown saw to it that letters were sent to the area farmers asking for donations of pigs, goats, cows, and chickens. Asking for money to buy these foods was never considered. It was not the custom of the place or the ability of the times.

On Thursday, July 1, the farmers began arriving with their livestock and poultry. They were taken out to City Park, in the middle of town, and turned over to Graham, who immediately saw to their slaughter and cleaning. This took all day Thursday and Friday. Miss Brown had the carpentry committee build rows of high tables—you stood while you ate—"in the pretty pine grove behind the high school," where the people could eat in the shade. She also saw to it that hundreds of watermelons and cantaloupes and gallons of tea were being made ready. Her music committee engaged a brass band in Atlanta to come and provide music, and she had the sheriff call Macon to arrange for "forty of Macon's finest policemen" to be there to handle the anticipated jam of cars and wagons. The platform committee brought colored paper in from Macon and made red, white, and blue bunting. They also acquired dozens of American flags from the Legion.

The Barbecue King was up early on Saturday, July 3. He planned on cooking ten thousand pounds of barbecue and one thousand gallons of stew. The King admitted that even he was awed by his task. For that amount of meat and stew, twenty-four to thirty-six hours of continuous cooking was required, and he started at dawn on Saturday in the shallow pits and the big kettles. There would be no flames for the pits, only simmering coals; but wood would be needed for the kettles.[7] All through the day and far into Saturday night the searing wood and coal burned beneath the one hundred kettles simmering the thick stew, and the pits hissed with the drippings from the meat racked above them. Townspeople came out to stand and to hunger over the vast array; and as they looked into the succulent red-brown juices they would grin and mumble with a shake of the head, "Boy, ain't that gonna be somethin'." Then they would move off, content that they had seen the largest barbecue-ing of their lives. Some were so enthralled by the enormity of the scene that they stayed long into the night, close by the dull glow of the coals to stare into the fires the Barbecue King had built and to be able to say "I was there." Insects swirled and buzzed crazily out of the night, whiz-zing around and crashing into the string of naked light bulbs that wound over the pits giving a hard brightness to the cooking area. So many bugs flew into the kettle of stew—drawn there by its sweet aroma that no pepper had to be added for flavor. "Bugs was good spice."[8] By morning the stew was bubbling heavily in its juices and the meat over the pits had turned a succulent tan; the dark red-brown barbecue sauce had hardened to a crust where it had been tirelessly basted over the animals' skins.

Morning dawned over City Park, mixing its slow light with the pale smoke from the fires. The smell of the meat drifted far beyond the area and greeted many an early riser with its richness. Miss Brown, who had been busy the day before with the trimmings, began calling her forces early to make sure the pickles and tea and watermelon and bread and paper plates and cups were ready to be moved out to the park. Trucks and wagons had come in at dawn with their melon loads, packed in straw and ready for the pocketknives' puncture of their thick green skins.

The trip to McRae would be long for many people, and the day and night before had kept the wives of those coming busy washing and press-ing shirts, seeing that shoes seldom worn were polished and ready. And not a few of the men drew up a good medicine bottle full of their favorite drink, to be concealed in coat pockets and used to help ease the heat of the day and make it more pleasurable. Others, more enterprising, filled up extra bottles to be placed in the car boot for those who were so in-clined to purchase some good corn sold at the edge of the crowd. It would be a festive day. It would be an old-time Georgia political spec-tacle. A day to forget the mortgage, the hungry kids, the empty pocket-books, and to soar with an uninhibited release on the heroic words of Old Gene.

Ten thousand people showed up. They clogged the streets of the small town with their cars and mule-drawn wagons. Arriving on the grounds early, they chatted and laughed and traded stories about the times. But mostly people talked about Gene; how he used to live over in Ailey, then Mount Vernon, and how he farmed and lived right here, in McRae, and now he was running for governor. Who'd ever have thought. . . ?

Gene had been out at the Sugar Creek farm doing minor work on the speech, conferring, checking on the preparation (how'd the crowd look, what counties were coming in, and was the barbecue ready?), and greeting the endless line of well-wishers who had come out to the house and wanted to be in the motorcade into town. Word came that a giant crowd had the town bursting at the seams, and it was time to go; with great excitement the house and yards emptied as the Talmadge party moved off for City Park. The sounds of the Tech High Band, which had "added pep and pleasure to the event," had scarcely quieted and its young members cased their instruments, when the motorcade pulled up into the throng. Horns were pressed down tight, bells were rung, and the crowd roared its approval. Talmadge strode quickly to the platform, stepping with a bound onto its fresh-cut pine planking. He was preceded by a long line of local politicians, all suddenly eager to come out for Gene. Surely some among them saw the irony of the most disliked man in town drawing the courthouse gang that had fought him and the townspeople that were reluctant to elect him, drawing them all before him in worshipful attendance. Many of the gang still detested him, but that hat in the ring for governor was enough to bring his worst detractors out to to be a part of a run for greatness that they would never make. It would be the first speech Gene had made before the public in McRae since his memorable debate with Brown six years earlier. This speech would not and could not have the profound effect of that early one; it would not be as raw, and the audience would not be as small or uncertain. He had now earned his place with these people, and the hot July air that lay around them would not crackle with the delicious suspense or expectation of 1926, but it would swell and soar with adulation.

The planks he dwelled on in the speech were simple, designed for the rural mind: (1) making an honest living; (2) educating the children; (3) securing good roads. The crowd cheered wildly at every pause and carried him triumphantly from the field on their shoulders. Perhaps the most significant thing about the speech was the complete coverage the Atlanta *Constitution* gave it. With ten candidates speaking throughout the state that day, only Gene rated in-depth front page coverage, plus a large photo. Although publisher Clark Howell would later hotly deny any favoritism, his paper obviously gave Talmadge better coverage by far throughout the campaign.[9]

After the speech the huge crowd moved quickly to the long tables of barbecued meat and stew, bread, pickles, watermelon, coleslaw, cakes, and tea. With heaping paper plates that bent in a V under the weight of food, they crowded into the "pretty pine grove" where they ate. There was much talking and laughing and speculating about how Old Gene was "gone whip Hell out of 'em." After the thousands of pounds of food were consumed and the area strewn with plates and cups, watermelon rinds and seeds, the men walked out to the baseball field where a game had been organized. Many went home after the "eatin' " to sleep and rest up for the big dance that night to be held at the Harris House. Some of the men who had been seen at the field's edge during the "speakin'," taking long swallows from their jars and forming their own suspicious little groups around car trunks, had to be driven home because of the combination of corn and sun and standing all day; these things had reddened their faces and numbed their brains into sleep. It had been a good day for McRae and for Gene Talmadge.

Gene left McRae for a grueling two-month campaign tour of the state with a message that would never substantially change. He had given it all on July 4, and state reporters were left writing different slants on the same script. He was labeled as the man who "represented the heartbeat of the masses" by his introductory speakers. He said on July 14, in Statesboro, that he was being called the "wild candidate," "cussing Talmadge," and "the wild man from Sugar Creek." He repeated these names with pride, saying "Sure I'm wild, and I'm going to stay wild!" [10] The iconoclasms, the vulgar, earthy language, the haughty rebelliousness seemed to remove him from the depressing, unconquerable realities of the day; and those who attached their dreams to his words could in small part escape those realities by believing in Gene Talmadge, "the wild man," and in what he was saying.

An old friend moved into the Talmadge inner circle during the July campaigning. John Whitley, the state's largest road builder, remembered Gene Talmadge as the dirt-poor lawyer-farmer who had lent out his mule and scraper to help grade roads around McRae. Now, Gene was the "ring-necked dog" [11] who was the leading candidate for governor and the man promising to bring the giant highway department to its knees. Whitley knew that if Talmadge won and carried through with his promise, he would have more control over that powerful and lucrative department than any recent official. It was to Whitley's advantage that he provide Gene with information on irregularities between the department and the strong gubernatorial candidate, John Holder. This, though not critical to the outcome of events, strongly endeared Whitley to Talmadge, and he moved as close as any man ever came to Gene Talmadge.

Roads had for some years been a great political football, patronage source, power lever, and an issue that was safe and sure. Georgia had never had good roads. The state was a huge area of land with a widely scattered people who were farmers and who used roads only to transport their goods to a market town or to go to town for purchases. The economy, that all-pervasive influencer, had historically helped determine that a vast and good road network was not a top priority. This feeling had changed with the advent of railroads and industry in the 1890s. As markets and means of transportation became more sophisticated in the early 1900s, the need for better roads had not only become critical, it had become a reflection of the backwardness of the state. Politicians seized upon road construction with a religious fervor, as though it would be the salvation of their people. By 1932 the highway department had become a monstrous, uncontrollable appendage of state government, and Gene Talmadge was afforded another populistic enemy to battle.

The Talmadge campaign assumed a steamroller, bandwagon effect by August. Gene was pushing the three-dollar tag hard, for it had caught on better than anyone had dreamed. He was also getting good mileage out of calling the opposition the "baseball nine." [12] It was effective rhetoric in that it put all the opposition in the same bag and individualized Gene's candidacy. He had accused them of joining forces to split up the county-unit vote, thereby causing a run-off. It was the type of grand conspiracy that added spice to the battle, and its picture of a sinister movement afoot had high appeal for the entertainment-starved farmers who knew enemies had to be on the land, but could never identify them. The times required enemies, and Gene had a bag full of them.

The Talmadge record, and not his platform, became the point of attack by his opponents. They continually hammered at his near impeachment and his handling of the agriculture department, particularly his selling of the hogs. His retort had already become one of the most famous phrases in Georgia politics and was a part of nearly every speech that summer. From the crowd one of his plants would shout, "Tell us 'bout them pigs you stole, Gene!" And on cue Gene would lean low over the podium like a man about to stare down a charging bull. He would give an awful grimace and slash the crowd with his piercing glare. His arm would fire out toward them like a spear, and with a fist clinched white he would point a finger so menacing that the crowd rocked back as though they were about to be impaled. With his head cocked slightly to one side, hair flopping disdainfully over his forehead, he would say with an icy disgust that chilled every man who heard it, "They say I stole!" The "stole" would roll off his lips like it was dipped in persimmon juice. There would be a long pause as the audience hung quietly waiting on this man who was admitting publicly that he had been accused of thievery, and he held them there until they were uncomfortable in their quietness, almost sorry anybody had mentioned it, waiting until they were ready to shout, "Hell no you didn't steal"; and at that precise moment Talmadge would jerk upright, and he would yell from his stomach so that it rocked the back rows, "Yeah, I stole!" Another very slight pause. "But I stole for you. You men in overalls. You dirt farmers!" The roar of the crowd after the admission was deafening, and absolute in its endorsement of the theft and the man who made it. The opposition scoffed at this Robin Hood rationale, but their attempts to attach guilt to it failed.

Talmadge had brought a fiery campaign to the trail, but for all of its apparent spontaneity, it had become by August a well-organized, smooth-running affair. The campaign's purpose became more than selling the Talmadge platform per se; its goal was to make each speech an unforgettable event in the lives of the people who attended it, and through the excitement and emotion of the moment, loyalties would be won. The Talmadge organization was proving to be an extremely successful structure composed of inherently political people, organizing and politicking on a local level in a manner that was traditional to the region. There were no great secrets about what appealed to the mass of Georgia voters, for they were all of similar backgrounds; it seemed hard to believe that only Talmadge was really hitting at those basic appeals.

Certain organizational methods had emerged that came to prove successful at almost every stop. Counties were first of all carefully selected on the basis of how weak they were for Gene. If they were lost to him, or all for him, their priority for an appearance was reduced. But if they could swing either way, a speech was set up. A local site was then worried over, one easy to reach and well known. It had to be a field or a building that would present an overflow situation. If outside, platforms had to be built, flags bought, and if at all possible food offered as assurance of a draw.

Supporters had to be obtained who would serve as plants in the crowd to assure applause and laughter. A handful of plants who knew their job could turn a crowd for Gene. They would arrive early and start working the crowd before the speaker ever arrived. Since people were naturally talkative and friendly at these events, there was no problem in gathering a group if one talked loud enough. Once Gene started speaking, they would move like shadows as they led applause and response. Their constant movement gave the appearance that Talmadge support was scattered throughout the crowd. Gene had used this technique since the first frustrating races in McRae, and he knew its value. The plant had another equally important purpose—cueing Talmadge about things he wanted to speak on. Because he rarely used a written text, he needed someone to cover him in case he forgot a subject. The plants did this at first, and then the crowds would do it on their own. The plant also served the purpose of creating a running dialogue between Gene and his audience. His speeches were characterized by this speaker-audience relationship. People had no qualms about yelling out questions as he spoke; and if they were proving timid, he would direct questions to them or get them to hold up their hands in support of him or an issue.

Probably his most famous plants, though not a part of the Talmadge organization, were some brothers named Haggard from Danielsville. They became fascinated by the growing Talmadge mystique and began to follow him throughout the summer campaign. For some reason they loved to sit in trees around the platform, and they became known as the Tree-Climbing Haggards. They were informally taken into the entourage but were never told what to cue Talmadge about. They appeared to have memorized his set speech, and after hearing other plants, they quickly learned what the cue lines should be. The cue always started out with "tell us about," as in "tell us about the three-dollar tag, Gene," or "tell us about the baseball nine, Gene"; and Talmadge's response would always be "I'm a-comin' to that." This type of give-and-take gave the Talmadge speeches a unique intimacy, a sharing, a revivalist atmosphere that made the audience become involved. There was great ego satisfaction in standing in a crowd of ten thousand and hearing yourself talking with a platform speaker.

Not all of the plants were carefully selected. At one speech, on a particularly hot day, an old gentleman asked if he could help cue Gene. Requests for plants were never turned down, and it was agreed the old man could sit at the base of the platform directly under the speaker's dais. Unfortunately, the introductory speakers were too long-winded and the heat too oppressive; the old man was lulled into sleep beneath an enormous straw hat. Gene came to the podium and moved quickly into his speech. He knew the old man was to cue him on a subject, and as he came to it, he asked his customary lead-in to a cue, "What do you think of that, brother?" Looking down from the dais, Gene could not see that the old man was asleep under the hat, so he reached down, tapped him on the head, and yelled, "What do you think of that, brother?" The man sputtered out of his sleep in surprise and accidentally spit out his false teeth as he did. They fell into the dirt at his feet and he went scrambling for them, forgetting about his cue. Responding to the embarrassment of the moment, an elderly lady near the old man suddenly sang out in a crackling voice, "Talmadge Red, Talmadge Blue, I wish my name were Talmadge too."[13] The old man by that time had his teeth back in and yelled out his cue to the delight of the crowd. Talmadge was one of the few men in the race who could turn this type of situation to his advantage. His mind was very quick, and it enabled him to carry on constant chatter with the crowd with little worry of being caught without an answer. Although they were never instructed from Gene to disrupt opponents' speeches, the Talmadge plants could wreak havoc on the other candidates. Their tactics did not include booing, but they did go in for causing suspicious accidents like setting a car on fire during an opponent's speech. The resulting smoke and sirens would invariably send the crowd racing toward the fire, leaving the hapless speaker without an audience.

Another campaign trick Talmadge adopted early, and with great success, was arriving late at speeches. He would have his driver park outside of town and wait until ten or fifteen minutes after he was supposed to have arrived, and then his motorcade would come racing up with blaring horns and a cloud of dust. His tardiness would create a tension, an anxious wondering that diverted attention from other speakers. The tumultuous arrival would totally disrupt the speech that was being made at that time. Another tactic included exploiting the size of the crowd. Statewide communications were so poor in 1932 that a candidate had difficulty informing the state at large how his campaign was going; often, small-town newspapers did not cover politics beyond their own city limits. Gene attempted to create the impression that he was the leading candidate by seeing that his speeches were held in a field or courthouse that was too small to hold the expected crowd. Overflow crowds at every speech soon became the talk of the campaign. The size of the crowd a speaker could draw had traditionally been considered a barometer of success, and to the newspaper readers Talmadge was apparently way out in front. He became obsessed with crowd numbers and made sure that every reporter got an estimate. Courthouse appearances, therefore, became more desirable than field speaking, because Talmadge could jam any courthouse. Crowd estimates also served the crucial bandwagon strategy. Normally if the speech was held in town there would be no barbecue. Barbecues were enormous affairs that greatly taxed the staff, and particularly Gene, because these events required his spending the entire day in one town, and this cut heavily into his schedule.

The Talmadge entourage, which by August was taking on the appearance of a traveling circus and medicine show, brought on another attraction. Atlanta singer and composer Fiddlin' John Carson was a country singer who had seen better days, but he could set a foot to stomping with little effort. He and his daughter, Moonshine Kate, came on with the organization, and it was their function to entertain the crowd before Gene arrived. They also set the tone for the speech, appearing as corny, redneck characters, a little down and out, but happy.

Motorcades became, through accident, another device. Like crowd sizes, they were touted as barometers of the Talmadge bandwagon. Motoring had been a popular sport for some years, with numbers of families loading up their cars and going for long rides and picnics. There was an exhilaration with the new freedom of movement that had been denied a people dependent upon the horse. Talmadge supporters in counties surrounding the city where Gene was to speak would organize motorcades; contests were set up to see which county could bring in the most cars. Huge signs were drawn up with the county name, and as the long lines moved down the highways, it seemed as if whole areas were making a pilgrimage to see Gene. The scene was a stimulus for those along the road to join the movement.

The roll call of counties also became a part of every Talmadge speech. With people from a county sitting together, Gene would ask whether a certain county were there and, like cheerleaders, the section would let out a roar designed to sound louder than the preceding county's. The result would be an ego involvement for the participants, a feeling that they were part of a crusade; and another blast of publicity would resound over the state that Gene Talmadge had pulled in people from thirty-five counties.

After the roll call of counties, Gene would call on the sheriff: "Sheriff, would you come up and estimate how many people have come here today"? With great officiousness, the sheriff would come forward to cast

University of Georgia Sigma Nu fraternity picture, with Gene standing at far right. Photo courtesy Atlanta *Journal/Constitution*.

Train depot in Ailey, Georgia, where Mitt worked when she met Gene.

Ailey boardinghouse Gene lived in when he began courting Mitt.

Mitt and Gene's first home in Mt. Vernon, Georgia.

Old law office in which Gene worked in Mt. Vernon.

Fields surrounding old Talmadge farm at McRae.

Sugar Creek, behind the Talmadge farm.

Talmadge family at McRae farm. From left to right: Mildred Talmadge, Mitt, Gene, John Paterson, Herman Talmadge, Margaret Talmadge. Photo courtesy Atlanta *Journal/Constitution.*

Mitt and Gene in McRae, in the 1920s. Photo courtesy Atlanta *Journal/Constitution*.

an intensely critical eye at the throng, and all could see the mathematical calculations running through his head. A hush would fall over the area as everyone stood a little taller, certain he was being individually counted when that cold eye of justice passed over. After such scrutiny the sheriff would look very serious, as though a great official judgment were forthcoming; then he would give his figure, which was usually "about 15,000." A chill of excitement would sweep the crowd. The number rocked the mind; 15,000 was usually more than the county held. Gene would say cautiously, "Would you say that was a record crowd for this here town, sheriff?" And again the official would bring the boys to the edge of their seats with another long and even more determined deliberation, because this was one for the books, a record. Now caught up in the theatrics, the sheriff would say with great certainty, "15,000 has got to be the record!" The tension would be released in a great sigh of relief. The farmer for the first time in his life had been adjudged part of a record. Gene would then go into a humble recitation of thank you's, saying, "I find it hard to believe, and it makes me deeply thankful, that this many working people would take time to leave their plow to come all the way to here just to hear Old Gene speak. I never expected this many would come. But I'm proud that you did." [14]

In trying to analyze the Talmadge phenomenon, and it had become that, Gene's hometown newspaper sent a reporter to Quitman to cover the August 10 speech. The writer arrived late to find the courthouse jammed with a mass of sweltering farmers who took up every seat and sat on every inch of floor space. Gaunt, stoop-shouldered men in overalls, pressed tightly around the walls of the courtroom, effectively blocking the windows and a small cooling breeze that was trying to move in from the big shade trees outside. The throng spilled out onto the steps and into the street, where they sat fanning with their straw hats, trying to hear the man inside; but his voice had been muffled by the heavy air and the packed bodies until it emerged as a distant indistinguishable droning. Those in the yard stood silently, straining to hear, and pressing desperately forward as a roar would blast from the inside. Old Gene was "laying it on 'em." Inside, Talmadge stood small in the jam of humanity—dressed in white, coat off, shirt clinging to his body with moisture, suspenders blazing with an incredible red, a red bandana clutched tightly in one hand, the other hand tearing furiously at the air, a long shock of black hair dancing across his forehead. There was a decided religious fervor about the whole scene. It was in the eyes of the people, in the very real intensity of the speaker, and in his high-pitched voice that came close to frantic, but was still controlled. It was a cadence one had heard at revivals; it held a rhythm that beat ceaselessly against the mind of the listener until it tore him loose from his constricting self-consciousness and had his heart pounding and his eyes popping. Gene called it "a weavin' and a wavin'."

Gene drove to Irwinton the same day, to address another sweltering mass in a similar courthouse: "You farmers haven't had anybody fight for you since Tom Watson." The Telfair *Enterprise* reporter noted, "The statement struck fire from the crowd," and one man yelled, "We've got you NOW, Gene!" The reporter concluded, "He spoke the language of the cotton and the corn field; he swept his audience along with him." [15] So moving, in fact, were the speeches, that an old Negro was overheard saying, "There's a man what really is worthwhile."

By late August, he had made over fifty speeches and talked before 75,000 Georgians, in what was emerging as one of the most remarkable and effective political campaigns in the state's history. Fiddlin' John Carson had even provided the campaign with a song. Probably the corniest piece of music ever to grace a political race, "The Three-Dollar Tag Song" was played at every speech by the strumming Carson and his daughter. It went:

> I gotta Eugene Dog, I gotta Eugene Cat,
> I'm a Talmadge man from my shoes to my hat.
>
> Farmer in the corn field hollerin' whoa, gee, haw,
> Kain't put no thirty-dollar tag on a three-dollar car.[16]

Despairing of hard times, Talmadge said, "When a man gets some money in his pocket the first thing he spends it for is food, and then he pays the rent and last year's doctor bills. Then he buys Mary a dress and himself some overalls. If there is any left he is sure to buy an auto or some new tires and maybe some fresh curtains for the living room and a chair or two. Then he looks around and about the time that that hole in the roof gets big enough to throw a chicken through he will buy a roll of rubberroid and patch it." [17]

The Democratic white primary vote for governor was held on September 13. Talmadge was at his Ansley Hotel headquarters with a large, boisterous group of supporters to hear the results. Farmers seemed to be on every inch of Atlanta sidewalk. Everyone expected a run-off, until the votes began pouring in through the night and the following day. It became obvious that Gene had achieved a phenomenal victory, that he had in fact received 264 county-unit votes against 146 for all the others combined. He had won 114 counties with over 42 percent of the popular vote, that being 116,381 votes of a total of 240,242. His nearest competitor, Abit Nix, had received 78,588 votes.[18] The county-unit vote enabled him to become the Democratic candidate for governor, which was tantamount to victory.

Gene's allegiance did not lie in Atlanta or any other urban area; therefore, his victory celebration was held in McRae. He would make a pilgrimage to pay homage to the strength behind his power, to his power source, the rural electorate. The victory motorcade was welcomed into McRae by a huge, gaudy neon sign saying "Welcome Governor." A local "orchestra" was asked to "furnish jubilee music, and a grand and glorious time was had." Appropriately, Gene was introduced on a hastily built platform by one Enoch Buttram, a farmer, who held the great distinction of having trudged twenty-two miles on a rainy day to vote for Gene. In a short speech Gene attributed all of his success to the common man. He said, "It was the people upon whom I was depending and the common people didn't let me down." [19]

Gene and every man that voted for him believed that statement, but it desperately needed qualification. In 1932 Georgia there were few people who could economically qualify as anything but "common people." Certainly the poorer of the poor voted heavily for Gene, but in a state where a devastating depression had brought a vast leveling of incomes, to use the word *common* to define a particular segment begs an explanation because of its vagueness. It was, in fact, an intentionally spurious statement, for Talmadge was attempting to create a personal image and resurrect a culture, both of which demanded an emphasis on Georgia's very large farmer class. If the depression had not given so much publicity and general recognition to a condition that had always existed during these people's lives, it is questionable whether the "Rise of the Common Man" theme would have worked. The truth was that although the little man in Georgia had been the traditional power base, he had never chosen to use his power and never demanded it from the planter class or, in the 1890s, from the new industrialists who took it from the planters after Reconstruction. Gene had convinced them that a "Champion of the People" type politician was needed, and hard times made convincing them a substantially easier task.

The Hapeville *Statesman*, a newspaper controlled by Talmadge, wrote in September that "Eugene Talmadge is NOT wild." In fact, he was heralded as a reformer. Someone on the paper's staff had taken a long look at the tremendous Roosevelt victory, for it was said Talmadge "will bring about a new political deal in Georgia." In the same issue, on September 15, the *Statesman* said the Talmadge victory was a "remarkable demonstration of the strength of the farm vote." This, like the "common man" rhetoric, needed qualification. In that period of rural to urban and agriculture to industry transition, definitions were difficult. Certainly those thousands moving to the cities still retained their rural philosophies and for the most part their lifestyles and customs. Practically every Georgian had parents who had either lived on a farm or lived in a town so small that some of the family land was used for farming. The farm, in 1932, was either physically or psychologically still the traditional homesite for Georgians. To speak of the "farm vote," therefore, was to speak in the most sweeping of general terms. It could not be accurately defined in either geographic or vocational terms. Perhaps a more incisive reflection of the *Statesman*'s analytical ability was given at the start of the campaign when it editorialized, "We believe the present so-called depression is simply a God-given lash of discipline," aimed at redistributing the wealth.[20]

Many would later be astonished that Gene was being termed a "reform candidate" by the Atlanta press, particularly since he was against the Roosevelt proposals.[21] But in the context of Georgia politics there was a certain validity. His promise to lower freight rates, clean up the highway department, and adjust taxes had a certain reformist ring, as did his interest in farm cooperatives and crop diversification. But his emphasis was on items like the three-dollar tag, hard work, poor government; and these were not curative, progressive, or even populistic issues.

The times were extraordinary; something had to be done. And in that time of insecurity, fear, and uncertainty, Talmadge stood out as the rugged, tough, fearless individual—a man for hard times. If his tools for fighting were forged in another era, it bothered few Georgians. The solutions were simple, easy to understand, and the fact that they had never worked appeared to bother no one.

The year 1932 had provided one of the more colorful spectacles in Georgia politics. Gene had brought more than a political campaign to his state: he had created something akin to a religious experience. He had brought hope and laughter where there was none. He had become a spectacle unto himself—a circus come to town, with bands and fiddlers and banners and flags, oxcarts and moonshine. Gene pranced and danced, sang and hollered over the sap-wet planking, cajoling, scolding, preaching. He was the showman, the rainmaker, the medicine man, the ranting, magnetic evangelist. He spoke a simple language. He cussed, brayed, drawled through his words as though he'd never had a day's schooling. It wasn't what he said, but the way he said it. His strength as an orator was in his presentation. He had become a master of the rural mind. So completely had he sold his image as one of the boys, that in one small town the big limousine in which he was riding was turned back, because they thought he would resent so much wealth being displayed at a Talmadge speech. Hugh Howell, whom no one there knew, was driving the car. Gene was not recognized in the back seat. Howell turned the car around and drove outside town where a farmer driving an oxcart was hailed down. Gene climbed on board, and in more acceptable transportation was enthusiastically welcomed at the gate from which he had just been turned away.[22]

7

"I Love
a Fight"

Mitt had no recourse now but to pack up their two girls and two boys and move to Atlanta. "I didn't want to go up there," she recalls; "I didn't like big towns. I just wanted to be left alone to run my farm." The Talmadge clan rolled into the capital city like a band of unwanted country cousins. The governor's mansion was located in Atlanta's highly fashionable and established Ansley Park. Its society matrons were hardly prepared for the rambunctious Talmadges who arrived with their farm animals and cotton seeds, apparently intent on turning the mansion into a farm. Mitt remembers with a twinkle in her eye, "It was all politics. Gene had been promising if he was elected governor he'd plant cotton at the mansion and bring some farm sense to the place. We hadn't hardly moved in when he told me he wanted me to build a chicken coop in the back; he wanted some chickens. I built it myself and got the chickens, and we put an old cow on the lawn, but it was all just politicking." The local cocktail parties, however, reverberated with shock over the whole menagerie, especially the cow that kept running off down the street to eat grass and tear up the well-manicured greens at the posh Ansley Golf Club.

"I'll tell you something else about that mansion," Mitt said; "Dick Russell had left the place in a mess! He was a bachelor you know, and didn't have nobody to clean up after him or worry about the house. The whole place was so run down when we moved in. Wild onions had taken over the grounds. I cleaned up the place myself and replanted the lawns." [1]

The daughters, Margaret and Mildred, and the younger son, Herman, were in school; and Mitt's son, John, was working. The mansion, therefore, was maintained more as a place of business than of family. Mitt had been forced into the role of politician's wife, and by the time of the move to Atlanta, she had come to relish much of that role and was one of her husband's most trusted advisers.

On January 10, 1933, Richard Russell made his last state of the state address. It was little more than a rundown of the ravages of the depression on Georgia. But significant were the accountings of his reforms and reorganization.[2] An interesting contrast to Russell's progressivism was the Talmadge inaugural speech. First on Gene's priority list came the famous three-dollar tag. "I do not know of anything that would help the people of Georgia more and help business more." Equally nebulous was his advice to the general assembly to "watch the common schools and protect them," with no more substantive solution than that. He promised economy through a very weak government, though he did remind the lawmakers that there was a desperate need for some action. "You are fresh from the country. You have left good men, women and children, especially white women and children raggedy and barefooted, some of them ashamed to go to church and . . . school." [3]

A split that would long haunt Talmadge began forming with the Russell speech. The governor had submitted a list of last-minute appointments which was a customary payoff to supporters, and it never failed to irk the new governor, who had his own people to reward. If the senate approved the appointments, the incoming man would have few vacancies to fill. Gene asked the senate to return Russell's nominations. It refused. Russell's popularity was immense, and from Washington he could be far more powerful than Talmadge. Gene saw the refusal and the nominations as a deliberate move to block him, and he vigorously pressed the senators. House speaker E. D. Rivers later said the Talmadge obstinance created a strong anti-Talmadge core in the senate that wrecked his programs. The senate voted 42 to 1 against Gene's request.[4]

Gene sent a written and very detailed version of his program to the legislature on January 13. Along with the rest of his platform it included advice against a sales tax. His reasoning: "Any sales tax . . . taxes the bare necessities of life—the coffin, the plow point, the widow's bonnet, and the corn meal of hungry children." His text also asked that he be given extraordinary powers over the various state agencies. He wanted "a law giving the governor authority to put a stop to extravagance and waste . . . in any and all departments." [5] It was a request that sent a shudder through those who remembered the power grasps of his previous office.

He quickly found that the senate rebuke was only the start of his troubles. His program soon ran head on into the traditional apathy of the Georgia legislature. Wallowing in an historic ineptitude and obsessed with local interests, the body was refusing to budge. Gene had said throughout the campaign that he wanted small government but was unprepared for the degree to which the lawmakers were taking him at his word. The Atlanta press started blaming everyone in sight, including Gene, for poor leadership and the legislature for high absenteeism.[6] The legislature's failure to act on Gene's program could in part be attributed to the one-party system in Georgia. It had become such a myth and status-quo server, rather than a political tool or lever, that it appeared to have lost its usefulness as a governmental machine. It was a custodian of custom and culture. Thus a candidate in reality ran on his own name. This meant loyalties were not attached to party candidates, for everyone was a party candidate. Loyalties were attached to men. Talmadge's platform wasn't perceived as a Democratic platform in 1933; it was a Eugene Talmadge platform. The *Constitution* quoted one legislator as saying, "Talmadge was elected on a three-dollar tag platform and we were not."[7]

Southern political scientist V. O. Key wrote soon after this time, "The Democratic party in most states in the South is merely a holding company for a congeries of transient squabbling factions most of which fail by far to meet the standards of permanence, cohesiveness, and responsibility that characterize the political party."[8] The upshot of this was that strong personalities and special-interest groups dominated elections and government.

With his three-dollar tag floundering in late February, Gene made a strange appeal to party loyalty out of desperation. On March 1, he asked that the house compromise bill be accepted by the senate, because the tag was a part of the "Democratic platform."[9] The compromise provided for a fifty-cent additional charge on vehicles over three thousand pounds.

Gene had taken a large festive group to the Roosevelt inauguration and used the occasion as a belated excuse to speak before the assembly on March 7. His platform was splintering all about him, and he needed to build public pressure. In the speech he chided Roosevelt for his banking legislation and welfare: "There has been enough charity in this country, and sometimes I think too much." Intrigued by the governors' meeting that had been held in Washington and the movement by some to unify and raise cotton prices, Gene had picked up Huey Long's cotton holiday idea and attempted to push it onto his platform. With typical shortsightedness he told the assembly, "The prosperity of the South depends upon cotton," but its surplus was, he said, "hanging over our heads like the sword of Damocles."[10] His speech concluded: "We must pass laws and put our boys and girls back on the old washed-away, fallen-down farms." [11] (It was a statement of precisely why the boys and girls would not go back.)

The March speech had little result, and Gene's planks fell one by one. The house refused to pass his reduced ad valorem and utility rates.[12] His holiday for cotton was defeated.[13] And his badly needed highway reorganization bill died in the senate.[14] The cherished three-dollar tag did not survive the senate either. The planks that did pass included one promising back pay to teachers and Confederate veterans, a recommendation that school book contracts be gradually dissolved, state expenditures be reduced, and county officials responsible for local money be bonded. The assembly also failed to provide for adequate income, appropriating four million dollars more than state revenue accounted for.[15] Of the two hundred bills the legislature passed, Gene vetoed forty. A complete breakdown had occurred between the executive and legislative branches of government, a breakdown that extended into the Talmadge camp. Three of his strongest supporters, Roy Harris, E. D. Rivers, and Wesley Culpepper, had fought him on the sales tax, which he vetoed.[16]

Gene blamed the broad governmental failure on the strong lobbies that camped at the capitol,[17] which was about as valid a theory as the half-dozen others flying around town. There were other factors, of course: Richard Russell's lingering influence and the anti-Talmadge forces it had fostered; the traditional staunch conservatism of the legislative body—an inherent trait that rebuked action as surely as a man draws away from fire. The domineering bull-headedness of Gene Talmadge had its negative effects, as did the clear lack of qualification of many of the lawmakers. They were either farmers representing farmers or courthouse gang members representing that special-interest group. Certainly their hearts and souls were committed to the rural life, particularly the history that gave it spiritual sustenance and the economy that formed its foundation. Neither the courthouse scrapper or the farmer-lawmaker knew anything else. This background was making their initial acceptance of the alien demands created by the depression and the industrial age very difficult. It was easier to live with mythology, reaching from it to grasp at the more delectable fruits of the new age—the auto, the telephone, the tractor, electricity—while being careful to avoid the new cultural demands that extracted obedience and compromise in return for a full sharing in the cornucopia of goods. The legislators had been born close to the Civil War. Their fathers had fought in it. In a strange sense they were war babies, for they were children raised during a profound societal reversal. They were reared in the rush of the desperate psychic yearning for identity that created a postwar culture based upon the half truths of a prewar culture. The men who sat in the 1933 legislature had been carefully tutored in the legends, the battles, and the warriors of the war and before. Their fathers and grandfathers were living substantiators of all that was told. There was no one to deny, no one to refute. Everyone drew up his own figure for blame, but few could see fault in the shadowing hand of the past.

Certainly it was more delectable to blame it all, as the Macon *Telegraph* did, on the nights of liquored revelry, the "fish frys and bird suppers." [18] Scenes of drunken legislators reeling about the streets of Atlanta accompanied by slick lobbyists flew about the state, and Georgia politics became a charlatan affair. Perhaps no story brought more laughter or winces than the fact that Roy Harris of Richmond County had threatened to have the members of the house arrested and brought back to the capitol in order to make them remain in their seats and perform their legislative duties. [19]

Gene suspected that he had been set up for a colossal fall by the Russell forces who were working through the senate. Without hesitation he moved. As soon as the legislature had adjourned (not to meet again for two years), he suspended all state taxes until the next session, using authority granted in an 1821 law. [20] This enabled him to order that all taxes on motor vehicles be dropped down to three dollars. His cherished tag plank was instant law, and overnight a whirlwind of elation swept the state. It was a coup that made the lawmakers look even worse and in the public's eye propelled Gene out of the whole mess. The motor vehicle commissioner didn't like the idea and refused to sell tags for three dollars. Gene immediately told the man that he was off the state payroll, and almost as quickly the commissioner notified the governor that tags would be sold for three dollars after all. [21]

Pressure was exerted during April for Gene to call a special legislative session to legalize beer. He had been sidestepping the issue all spring and attempted to laugh off the whole matter as inconsequential in view of the day's problems. "Beer? Why this is hard liquor country. Beer's a fad," he scoffed. [22]

With the defeat of his reorganization of the highway department, Gene was forced to change tactics in his attempts to bring about fiscal control. He felt that the only way he was going to bring about change with the road department was either to take personal control of it or to have himself recognized by the highway board as their superior. This attempt at taking over a department or agency of the state would mark a prophetic step in the Talmadge career. Continually blocked or baffled by inept legislatures, he would seek to rule through the state's agencies. Any means would come to justify this end. It would prove the only sure way he could have his programs and philosophies realized. In order to humble the highway department he would attempt to fire some of their engineers for the farcical reason that they were abusing their free passes on the railroads for personal trips, something many state employees did often and everyone knew about. If that firing was accepted by the board, the Talmadge authority over the board would be established, and he would then move to fire employees and lower expenses. The number of highway employees seemed to him unnecessarily high; those seen along the roads holding surveyor sticks or standing in gangs around an early morning fire seemed forever idle.

He knew going against that department would be tough. Its lobby was the unquestioned heavyweight in the legislature, as evidenced by the 53 percent it was taking out of the state budget. Those millions enabled it to become a giant patronage center used particularly by the governor. It was the political lever, the tool of manipulation by which counties were kept under some semblance of control. It supplanted the Democratic party as an energy source for political action. Through its intricate patronage network, Atlanta was interconnected through obligations with the state's courthouse gangs. Enterprising county officials either owned or had ties with local road construction companies. For promises of support, the county politicians or the legislators would be given a certain amount of the road fund. The construction of roads employed local men and made the county men who took all the credit look good. The isolated farmer was happy because he was being connected with a market, and he would naturally vote for the man who gave it to him. The system made people happy from the governor's office all the way down the lines of power to the power base, which was the farmer or small-town people.

The Russell Reorganization Act of 1931 required state department heads to submit quarterly budgets to the governor for his approval. No appropriations could be drawn until he approved the requests. When the department routinely sent its second quarter requests in, Gene refused to issue warrants for payment until the request was cut and five of its engineers fired for "waste and extravagances." The highway board accepted the cuts, but was shocked by the attempted firings and refused to fire the men. Intense pressure was again brought on Gene to call a special session to legalize beer and bring Georgia out of prohibition. A majority of the legislators signed a petition saying they would vote beer in if called back. But Gene saw much more behind the movement than a vote on beer. His attack on the patronage-heavy road people had hit a very sensitive nerve, and the system had reacted up and down the line, to the tune of "get Talmadge." He suspected that the senate would use the session to kill the three-dollar tag and strip him of his ability to hurt the highway crowd. Thus Gene told the petitioners that if they could get "the religious people of Georgia, the church and Sunday school people," who had started the bone-dry movement, "to say they made a mistake" and now wanted the state wet, he would call the session. Obviously, no God-fearing Baptist was going to admit he had been wrong about booze. The beer issue was a detour that angered Gene, for he thought it a waste and a trap.[23]

On May 5 Highway Board Chairman Barnett released a letter from the Federal Bureau of Roads hinting that federal money might be withdrawn if Gene didn't let up. On May 26 it was learned that Gene had refused to compromise with the board who agreed not to pay the engineers, but reserved the right to refuse to fire them. Their salaries seemed inconsequential when it was reported that the state of Georgia had only $13,000 in its treasury.[24] Exasperated at Gene's refusal to compromise, Barnett angrily said that he "would not and could not" fire the men.

While the road problem simmered just below the boiling point, Gene abruptly joined battle with the Public Service Commission. A major Talmadge plank had been to lower utility rates. This plank had failed to pass the legislature. Rates had not been lowered in deference to a crippled economy. In June, Gene ordered the five commissioners to show cause why they shouldn't be removed. He charged a conspiracy within the utilities to build monopolies and "charge exorbitant rates." He claimed power to take his actions under Section 2118 of the Georgia Code. This empowered the governor to "remove state officials who are derelict in their duties." He also referred to Section 2620, which "gave him the right to appoint their successors." [25]

Talmadge left his battles long enough to go to New York on June 13 for Flag Day exercises. Strong rumors followed him, suggesting that he had already set in motion a military occupation of the state capitol and treasury. National guardsmen were seen quietly moving about the capitol grounds armed with machine guns. Simultaneously, it was leaked that two million dollars had been taken from state depository banks and

placed in the treasury vault because the highway department was going
to sue in federal court. If the court granted in their favor, their money
could not be touched if on state property. It was noted that Gene's New
York entourage included four smartly dressed national guardsmen.
When asked by reporters about the sight of armed men on state grounds
and the movement of the money, Gene would only smile and say, "Military matters must necessarily be secret." [26]

Many were shocked by the sinister sound of the answer, by the constant presence of a military guard around the governor, and his apparent
fondness for militarism and its trappings. It was obviously disturbing to
Georgia politicians that Gene might resort to strong-arm tactics in order
to control a part of state government. Whatever he was up to, he was
taking his actions without consulting anyone outside his very small inner
circle of advisers and friends. These advisers disturbed many observers,
for some of their backgrounds were questionable, and the weight of
their influence on the governor was not discernible.

Barnett was not impressed; he spoofed Gene's militarism by saying
he was calling out a troop of boy scouts to guard the highway department stamp fund of $1.50. In the meantime Gene was doing his own
maneuvering on a more unprecedented scale. He was determined to end
the highway department confrontation quickly and decisively. On June
19, he stunned Barnett and everyone else by proclaiming a state of martial law at the capitol. He was taking personal control of the highway
department. In his executive proclamation Talmadge wrote a long di-
rective citing the duties of the road department leadership and their obligations under law. He then cited his lawful powers over that department,
particularly its monies. This was followed by a detailed list of grievances
he had gathered against them: they had run up huge debts; their employees were angry over the board's decision to cut their salaries; the
convict labor that did so much of the highway work would have to be
turned back over to the counties and the state because of the cutoff in
funds, and once placed in prison where they had nothing to do, their
idleness would result in "disease, escapes, mutiny, and rebellion." Gene
also made the accusation that "certain of the highway commissioners
have been profiteering"; he said that the board, led by Barnett, had
failed to file a budget for the quarter: therefore the department could
get no operating money. After carefully citing these wrongs, he said
that his real justification for taking control of the department was that
board members Barnett and William C. Vereen had abandoned their
offices and were "aiding and abetting" in "practices circulated to incite"

insurrection. He said the board, led by these two men, had also squandered and wasted millions of dollars.[27] The charges made for a long list, and most of them were highly debatable.

In defiance of a recent court order, the governor issued a warrant to the state treasurer for $1,313,000 to run the highway department, saying he felt the matter was none of the court's business and that they should not "interfere with the issue." [28] On the same Tuesday Talmadge fired the board members and appointed Jud P. Wilhoit in "supreme command" of the highway department. It seemed an appropriate title in view of the militaristic manner the post had taken. Barnett said he would set up his own offices, that he was still the rightful head of the department.

That afternoon, Deputy Sheriff Sidney Wooten served Gene with a copy of a superior court order "enjoining the state treasurer and comptroller general from diverting highway funds in the state treasury to other than highway purposes." Gene became furious with the deputy. He ordered Adjutant General Lindley Camp to arrest the deputy on the spot, then told Camp to place a military guard around the persons and offices of himself, the treasurer, and the comptroller. The guards were to follow the men even to their barbers. The order to the guards was that "any insistent process servers be arrested." Camp was later ordered to physically remove Barnett and his engineers from their offices, which they did, and which prompted the defeated Barnett to call Talmadge a tyrant and a man with "a deranged mind." [29] The following day Barnett filed an injunction against Gene in federal court.

Talmadge's arrogance had fed the fires of his critics who said he was dictatorial, ruthless, a totally self-centered man bound by no law or convention. In an era of weak political leadership, Gene had exploded on the scene like a thunderbolt. He was able to do this because he had circumvented the traditional power centers in his own rise to power. He had only the people to answer to, and their checks could only be exercised at election time. He had also proven the Democratic party to be a mythical restrainer of individual action when it had also been circumvented in the power ascension. His occasional appeals to party loyalty were shams. He ran under the party label to use its machinery. But with the national Democratic policies reversing the old Democratic dogmas countrywide, he felt even less constrained to follow the dictates of a party. He appeared to be placing himself beyond every governmental check; and suddenly, in the summer of 1933, there seemed to be no way to stop him.

The call to arms created some electorate polarization, with Talmadge defectors moving from the moderate middle-roaders to the anti-Talmadge, more liberal side. The swing vote was slightly reduced, and the staunch Talmadge supporters were forced into a defensive position, moving further to the right. Rather permanent voter lines were being drawn that summer over Talmadge, and their effect would be to temporarily erase traditional localized voting patterns in Georgia. To the dirt farmer the summer battle had been just fine. He felt that Gene was a warrior battling for him, and he could not have been happier that the battleground was in Atlanta, where he was convinced that all manner of evil lurked. No one loved a scrape better than the wiry, sun-baked man out in the piney woods, whose existence was a battle that appeared to have no victory. He vicariously enjoyed Gene Talmadge's calling out the militia: he was entertained by it, it broke the boredom and the insignificance of his life. It was all made easier to enjoy by the fact that the dirt farmer felt very little identity with the political establishment in Atlanta. It had done little for him. He owed it no allegiance other than his loyalty to the Democratic party. The traditionally weak government system was paying the price for having been weak. It could not muster the support of the people to check a strong governor. Gene had slain the highway department dragon, and in the process emerged a much stronger leader than he was at the close of his election victory. He had also slain the weak and divided legislature by circumventing it, but the completeness of that victory could not be known until the next election.

He had pushed himself out to a point where detractors felt he was on the verge of political ruin if he continued to defy a federal court order. He spent the morning of June 22 conferring with his legal advisers, Judge Eschol Gresham, Hugh Howell, and William Mann, on how best to fight Barnett and Vereen. They advised him to accept the service of the suit. The news from Washington further supported their advice against fighting the federal establishment. Secretary Henry Wallace notified Georgia that ten million dollars in road funds would be held back until the state solved its road dispute. Wallace cared little for Gene, but he was chiefly concerned about what Gene might do with the road money. Gene wanted to use the money for roads plus other state needs, and he was very much disturbed about the cutoff.

On June 23 Talmadge was scheduled to have lunch and make a brief speech at the Atlanta post of the American Legion. Held at the Ansley Hotel, it was a routine appearance for the governor—a nice manageable group, all loyal supporters—the kind of undemanding occasion a politician doesn't mind. It was also the kind of relaxed occasion that can have a lulling effect on the mind, allowing the tongue to become a little too loose. The luncheon started out badly. As Gene ate, two deputy sheriffs suddenly burst into the banquet room; Deputies Charles Poole and W. G. Smith strode directly to the long table at which Gene was seated with a huge cigar in his hand. As he looked in amazement, they handed him a $25,000 damage suit ordered by Deputy Sheriff Wooten, whom Gene had arrested on Tuesday for trying to serve him a court injunction. Wooten was charging "humiliation and illegal arrest." Gene reacted the same way he had with Wooten: he blew up. So furious that he could only sputter, he repeatedly barked, "What is this! What is this!" He then tore the process papers up and threw them at the startled men. Turning to his right he ordered Adjutant General Camp to throw the men out of the room. As the surprised deputies were escorted out, the Legion commander got up and stumbled through an embarrassed apology which was met with enthusiastic applause.

After lunch Gene delivered an informal talk, simply standing behind his chair. It was casual, filled with idioms of the day and spiced with his own frank expressions. Perhaps he was still angry from the confrontation, for suddenly he made one of the most damaging comments of his career. He was denouncing the United States for its forest conservation camps and cotton acreage reduction policies. "They're sending those fellows out into the woods," he said, "to cut down bushes in the summer and plant trees in the winter, and they're paying the United States soldiers in charge of the camps just half of what they're paying these bums and loafers." They had cut the pay of disabled veterans, yet the government was paying to "let a lot of young fellows run around in the woods." He then lit into the government plan to plow under cotton already planted as being "against nature," and "an act of desolation." [30] His solution was a cotton holiday. The American Legion story was duly noted in the next morning's papers—front-page stuff, but no major headlines. The routine coverage, however, created a storm of protest and indignation. To the thousands of jobless Georgians, the government work programs were a godsend. The reforestation plan was one of them, and a good, honest way to make a small living. The fact that it was work created just to keep people employed and had been initiated by the government irked Gene. He had very definite opinions about what was work, or honest labor. To him government work programs were a subtle evil that fooled a man into thinking he was personally being bettered, while he was actually being made dependent upon the government. It was welfare in disguise. It was a sham that destroyed the individual.

To those families who were eating off that money, and to those men who could look others in the eye and say they worked, it was no sham. It was not welfare. The South had always honored the man who worked and looked down on those who didn't. And now, those who had stood in breadlines with their heads bowed could again feel they had become a part of acceptable society, because they were again sweating for their money.

As if the day had not brought enough problems, a federal judge ordered Talmadge, Camp, and Wilhoit to appear on June 30, to answer Barnett's charges of illegal martial-law government. Gene rather quietly said he would accept service of the papers and would answer the charges. It had been a very bad day.

The weekend, the last in June, was filled with meetings and conferences on how to handle the court fight, and what the strategy should be for Monday morning when the public service hearings would open. He had promised the people he would lower rates but had received no help from the legislature or the utilities. He would not act to force the commission out of office. He was severely criticized by some for being the sole judge and jury over the hearings. They were called a sham. Since it was widely known that he was not pleased with the commission, everyone figured the outcome was foregone, that he had already made his decision and was merely trying to garner support for that decision. The hearings were not necessary, because he had the legal authority to fire the commission in a much quieter fashion.

The hearings opened early Monday morning to a jammed chamber in the capitol. The afternoon papers noted the happenings, but they also reported two other interesting stories: Gene had come out in favor of a minimum wage for textile workers, a real bit of liberality for him; and the United States had asked farmers to cut cotton acreage in 1933 and promised that they would be compensated. Ironically Gene's staunchest supporters were the main beneficiaries of this type of federal recovery program, while he was dead against it. He was offering the cotton holiday as a solution to lower prices, but he did not promise compensation for abstinence. The United States did.[31]

On Friday, June 30, at the federal court hearing, Gene was called an "outlaw" and accused of being "like a South American dictator" by highway board lawyer Ruben Arnold. The governor was over at the commission hearings and was represented in court by lawyer Gene

Smith, but his mind was on the court proceeding. He knew he would win the fight with the commission; he was toying with them, and he thought he had the highway thing tied up, but now the unpredictable eye of the federal judiciary was looking around and it could spell disaster. He had gone too far to lose gracefully.

Suddenly, it was discovered that Gene alone held the winning card. Under a recent reorganization bill, the state attorney general had been given the sole right to represent the highway board in court. Therefore, on July 1, the chief counsel for the defense asked to be made the chief counsel for the plaintiff. In the same breath Attorney General M. J. Yeomans asked the court to dismiss the case. The highway board reeled in disbelief at the apparently impregnable Talmadge. They asked for a week's delay to see if there were any pieces left to pick up. The long struggle was over on July 10 when Talmadge-man Yeomans was ruled the board's attorney.

On July 4 Gene traveled to Albany to make an Independence Day speech. An enormous crowd turned out for a full day of activities; there were stunt planes, fireworks, boxing, baseball, and dancing. Gene was in town to do some explaining to "his people." [32] And he started off by flatly denying that he had ever called their sons and husbands who were working in the restoration camps "loafers and bums." What he said he meant was that the government programs were going to make loafers out of honest men, and that was bad. He also defended his martial-law order, saying it was necessary to "force economy."

The public service hearings continued into July, with dozens of witnesses filing through the house chambers. On July 21, eleven days after the hearings had started, Gene announced the firing of the five-man public service commission—effective until the legislature met in 1935. The hearings that had run from June 26 to July 10 produced no surprises. Anti-Talmadge forces called the whole affair a kangaroo court staged for the benefit of Talmadge's career. Cries of "Dictator" were heard again, but not out in the piney woods, where Old Gene had slain another dragon and the Little People had supposedly benefited. Gene took the summer crisis all in stride. "As for me . . . I love a fight," [33] he said.

Gene completed his reorganization of the two most powerful departments of the state government by appointing relatives and friends to their boards. He then moved to have released the ten million dollars in federal funds that were being held. Friend and foe alike were objecting to this holdup in road money, and Gene took the train to Washington to find out what the government, and specifically Secretary Wallace, were going to demand he do in order that the money be refunded. Wallace told him the militia would have to go, and Gene would have to assure him that federal road money would not be spent in other areas of state government. Gene gave assurances the road department was in better shape than ever, and on the day of his return the state militia was sent home.[34] The occupation had lasted from June 19 to July 29.

Gene then hit the stump, going after the state senate. "I do not want those people back again. I want you to give me a senate that will back my principles."[35] It was late summer; and on the long hot days, Gene was good entertainment at county fairs and church gatherings. He beseeched the rural audiences: "We have got to get back to fundamental principles . . . go back to your Bible . . . get back out in the country; do not let the old schoolhouse and church rot." Gene was conscience, but his words rang with a tragic narrow-mindedness. He asked the victims of the cotton economy to return to their historic treadmill of speculation and debt. His answer to the continuing depression: hard work and virtuous living. It was too simple; yet the people flocked to him like a quixotic army clinging desperately to the fast-fading world of their fathers.

In trying to bolster his continuing charisma-building efforts, his propaganda sheet, the *Statesman*, called him a "He-man," though it admitted he "cussed a lot." And stretching its defenses to the limit, the paper said that public opinion, not the courts, was the final law; therefore it was all right for Gene to utter "Damn the law!" as he had done during the highway fight.[36]

Though his messages to the people of Georgia seemed to dwell on internal affairs, Gene was basically fighting a battle against the new expansionism of the federal government. This fact would not fully emerge until 1935, but Gene had sought through 1933 to strike some kind of cooperative stance with Huey Long against Roosevelt. This was an affair doomed from the start. Long broke with FDR in the fall of the year over patronage and degrees of liberality. Long "emerged as the leader of the American left," which was diametrically opposed to the direction in which Gene was traveling. Huey wanted to share the wealth and dispense welfare; Huey was a reformer. Gene wanted earned wealth, little welfare; Gene traveled under the guise of reformer, but he reformed very little. Perhaps as important as their philosophic differences was the fact that neither wanted to be second fiddle to the other. Neither could give, or submit.

Symbolic of the Talmadge stance was an almost pathetic plea he made in December of 1933. "This land has got to come back. If it doesn't come back everything else is gone. The value of this land and a day's work in the sun has got to come back." As out of tune as this was sounding, it was the kind of talk that had brought profound change to Georgia's voting pattern. Talmadge had wrecked the power structure of the state and its old voting lines through the immense force of his own personality. Georgians had traditionally been localized in their voting patterns—a reflection of their highly provincial perspectives. The pervasion of the one-party system had furthered this localization by voiding the chance for issues or alternative platforms which would have projected voter interest beyond an egotistical desire to get the local boy elected. The Democratic party had become an integral part of the culture. To believe in it was a duty of citizenship.

Political scientist V. O. Key observed that what happened in Georgia in 1934 was a normal southern reaction to a strong leader like Talmadge. "Factional division of the electorate around a powerful personality is characteristic of southern politics," Key wrote.[37] By polarizing the electorate, Gene stabilized it, creating "a fairly consistent bi-factionalism." The situation had some of the characteristics of a two-party situation, although in reality it wasn't. For Gene was not a truly valid and viable substitute for a political party. Regardless of whether he had achieved "party status" he had garnered tremendous powers in a short explosive period. In a time of economic and psychological depression he had emerged a strong man of worrisome unpredictableness. For the uncertainty of his courses, however, there existed an overwhelming certainty about Talmadge; he represented a constant in a world where anchors had been loosened. The people knew that he would do something, and for a time what that action was was not so important as knowing that Old Gene was stirring something or somebody up. In a less desperate time, what that something was would become more important than the fact that it was done.

The Talmadge impact was such that by late 1934 he would begin precipitating a state Democratic identity crisis. Particularly troubled were Georgia businessmen who were all for Gene's small-tax and little-government philosophies. Many of them had worked hard to get Roosevelt elected, and simultaneously, they backed Gene with money.

But now he was saying that the Georgia Democratic party and the national party were going separate ways, that loyalty to the one meant disloyalty to the other; he was forcing the issue by articulating what they all felt in their hearts to be true. The business community had become one of the two core support groups behind Talmadge—the other being the farmer. They felt that if no one mentioned it, a two-party loyalty could be maintained. But the businessman would find it more difficult than the farmer to maintain a schizophrenic stance over state and federal democratic principles.

8

"Country Folks Don't Believe in Germs"

For a man of enormous simplicity, Gene Talmadge had a paradoxically contradictory effect on many who met him. Close friends could differ as much in their interpretation of the man as the voters he polarized. Crude, ill-tempered, profane, out of control to some, he was a God-fearing, kind, and compassionate man to others. And both of these responses could come from people who knew him quite well.

J. C. Corley, a man who knew Talmadge from childhood, attests: "I never knew Gene to take a drink or to swear, except on a few occasions when he was real mad. And I never knew him to chase after women like everybody said, or to do anything to hurt anybody." [1]

Hugh Howell, Talmadge's confidant and adviser, remembers differently. "Gene was only out for himself. He was mean as hell, and would run over his best friends to get what he wanted. He didn't do a damn thing for the state of Georgia." [2]

Another would say, "I would watch him come into a room full of people, and the effect he would immediately have on that room was something I have seen few other men be able to do. I think it was more than the fact that he was governor; it was more than his office and who he was. He had a very real charisma. He had a magnetism about him. It was almost frightening to watch. And I don't say this because I was his friend, but because it was something that I saw happen many times and I have talked with others who had the same response." [3]

"No matter what you say about the man," recalls Henry Spurlin, a long-time Talmadge friend, "I knew him to be extremely compassionate. He used to give money to some of the prostitutes that hung around the Henry Grady, and I asked him one day why he did this, and he almost looked pained when he said, 'I feel so sorry for those women that they have to do that to make a living.' He would take handicapped children down to the farm. He refused to fire a lame man at the capitol when everybody else tried to run him off. And I remember so often when I was driving him around the state, he would never let me pass up a hitchhiker. He would say, 'Those people are unfortunate and poor, but they own this governor's car as much as I do.' We would pull into a town with hitchhikers hanging out the windows, and Gene packed down in one corner. Everytime I left the mansion with the big truck he would come out and say, 'I want you to fill the back of that up with hitchhikers.' I also remember us coming up on a patrolman checking for licenses, and Gene leaned out the window and cussed the man out for doing it. Soon after that he spoke before the highway patrol and told them their job was not to be stopping the poor people of Georgia, but to help them out. I saw him jump on a game and fish warden down at McRae one day for fining people for not having a fishing license to fish. He told the man, 'These are poor farmers. They ain't got no money for licenses. This is the only fun they can have. Now you keep your ass away from them!'"[4]

Perhaps nothing was so notorious about Talmadge as the stories about his drinking and his women. He was reported to have jumped in and out of every bedroom in Atlanta. Most of the rumors were either exaggerations or pure fabrication, but Gene could thank himself for propagating and nurturing much of what was said. His humor was so often self-deprecating, and he was known to stretch a story to hold one's interest. But he was also a little brazen in exposing his affairs. One of his old drivers remembers, "Gene had a number of girl friends; he had nothing to do with prostitutes like so many of the politicians that hung around the Henry Grady. Whores worked that place like you wouldn't believe. Gene was fairly discreet, except that on his trips, he would often take one of them with him and even introduce her around to the farmers we'd meet. Mitt knew all about it, but what could she do?"[5]

One Talmadge confidant explained, "Gene had a real magnetism around women. He usually had about four girl friends. I remember one day he was going to visit one and was worried that he might be seen. He asked me to get him a wig and a mustache which I did and which he wore that night. But let me say this; Gene Talmadge was no better and no worse than any of us, and he was a damned sight more moral than half the politicians in Atlanta at that time."[6]

These aspects of the Talmadge lifestyle and character had no effect on his service in office, but they undoubtedly cost him as many votes as they got him. To Gene, it was all a part of his almost radically masculine appeal.

The Talmadge office staff in 1934 included seven women and one man, the lone male being executive secretary Carlton Mobley. Although Gene arrived as early as 5:00 or 6:00 A.M., the office opened at 8:00 A.M., and went at an unrelenting pace until 5:00 P.M. Because Gene had based his career upon a close rapport with the people, the influx of visitors and mail into his office was enormous, far heavier than was normal for a governor. There was a decided informality about the office which was created by the personality of the boss. Appointments were made only by people used to making them. If Gene saw a farmer friend standing in the lobby he would holler for him to come on in, much to the displeasure of the appointment-getters. Crowds of farmers seemed forever about the place. They had heard of the easy access to the governor, and he asked them in every speech to come see him, so they came in droves. Families seeking pardons for loved ones in prison were also in constant attendance, pleading for releases. Laughter and loud talk added to the lobby confusion, and a jovial, earthy air characterized the place. It smelled of tobacco and men, and critics were always saying they smelled cheap whiskey; but, if this was true, the drinker had taken his fill before entering the capitol. Gene did not drink on the job, and he allowed no one else to. The receptionist tried to maintain a certain decorum, but the "boys" seemed forever infused with the fun and revelry that characterized a Talmadge speech.[7]

The governor was a demanding boss, but fair to his staff. The inner circle of advisers from 1926 was not entirely intact, though this was not critical to Talmadge's decision-making ability, since he only surrounded himself with men who were totally loyal to him and his principles. Equally interesting is the unanimous observation by the men of that time that, certainly into the early 1930s, there existed a societal unanimity of thought in Georgia on a broad range of subjects. This was just prior to the profound effect of the New Deal, which offered alternative attitudes and levels of consciousness. Prior to the public acceptance of this new philosophy, Talmadge did not have to look far to find men loyal to his beliefs; in fact his task would have been more difficult had he sought opposing viewpoints.

Perhaps the real distinction between the thought processes of Talmadge and those around him was the tight constriction and dogmatic stance with which he held his beliefs. He never vacillated. He was the totally predictable politician. He later told Lamar Murdaugh, "You would never make a governor, because you admit you are wrong too much. I'll never admit I'm wrong, even if I am, and I'll never apologize. If I've made a mistake, I'll ignore it and in time it'll work itself out." [8]

The Talmadge method of operation, once a decision had been made, was to move with suddenness and by the shortest route—decorum and convention be damned. This often gave him the appearance of being brutal, self-serving, unfeeling, beyond control. Talmadge had difficulty delegating authority; his involvement was omnipotent. Remove the man from the environment of political decision, however, and he was all play. Gregarious, affable, though not necessarily warm, Gene constantly joked and laughed, regardless of how well he knew a man. His wife remembers, "I never met anyone who had a memory for names and faces like Gene. We met so many people through the years, and Gene could remember farmers he met at a speech years before. This always made a big impression on people." [9]

Religion was a crucial part of the Talmadge political repertoire. Rural 1930 Georgia was hard-core God-fearing in profession, though not necessarily in practice; and any man who would run for office in that place most assuredly aligned himself with the Lord. Talmadge, almost completely mastering the rural mind as he did, paid homage to the country man's God, a recurrent theme throughout his speeches and his strategy. In the rural make-up, religion served often as an emotional escape valve. More than a hope for eternal salvation (which it was), it was also entertainment and a simple black and white wisdom and code of behavior. Living up to its laws was not as important as professing belief in them. Gene knew the Bible cover to cover. His memorization of passages was stunning, particularly to preachers. Almost every Sunday, the governor could be found in a country church serving as guest preacher. His old friend John Whitley would often travel to hear him. "Gene was the best preacher I ever heard. He knew the Bible so well and he could preach so good I have seen whole congregations crying and yelling before him." [10] Henry Spurlin often drove him to the churches. "Gene used to embarrass the preachers. They would get up and challenge some of his quotations, and he'd nail 'em every time in front of their own congregations. I never saw a man know the Bible so well." [11] The irony of Talmadge's use of religion was, as he told a friend, "I wish I was religious, but I just ain't." [12]

For all of his public bombast, Talmadge was a good and attentive father and family man. His wife had become one of his closest and most dependable political confidants and advisers. Whether he took her advice or not, it was sought on many major decisions. Her opinion and her perceptions were respected not only by her husband, but by so many of the men around him. Gene's favorite child was his son Herman, whom he called "Hummon." During Gene's first term, Herman was busy establishing himself as one of the University of Georgia's most raucous new students. Mrs. John Monaghan, wife of the governor's old college roommate, remembers, "Mr. Talmadge kept my husband busy running over to Athens and getting Herman out of some trouble he'd gotten into. Herman cut a wide swath."[13]

As a conversationalist, Gene was unpredictable. In a group he dominated, but in the company of a friend or a small group of friends, he could sink into "quiet spells" where he refused to say more than a sullen "yeah" or "naw." Often when in one of these moods, he would commandeer one of the boys (that small transitory group of men who were forever hanging around the mansion, always ready to run errands, do valet work, drive, advise, help Mitt, lobby, or just be around for laughs—all on a salary of sorts which showed up on no ledger, but came out of Gene's pocket) to "git the car." Gene would sink low into the backseat of his Buick while the driver sped for the open roads south of Atlanta. For hours they would ride at breakneck speed with Gene either asleep or hidden under the broad rim of his hat. "I remember driving Gene when he was in one of them moods," a friend relates, "and the only words he would ever say were 'go faster, go faster.' And I'd say, 'Goddamnit, Gene, it won't go any faster!' Then he'd say, 'Are you going ninety,' because he knew it would go ninety, and I'd say 'it's on ninety;' then he'd sink back into his spell."[14]

His penchant for being chatty around some and dead silent around others was a characteristic of the rural male who could paradoxically appear overly sociable to the point of being silly and subsequently close-mouthed to the point of rudeness. As a result of the farmer's simplistic lexicon, his language's only adornment was humor.

The use of language was central to Talmadge politics, and this was partly because of recent attention to "the way" people talked. The rural-urban population shift was bringing slight alterations in dialect; whereas everyone had "talked alike," the more pronounced drawl of the rural folk was now becoming a reason for derision by the more educated. Gene was a master of the rural intonations, ruinous use of grammar, slang descriptions, anecdotes, and use of Bible passages. At the same time he did not sound stupid or patronizing. Before Atlanta bankers he spoke with the correctness of the Phi Beta Kappa he was. While many criticized him for his changing dialect, most agreed that regardless of the way he said it, he always told one group what he told the other. Examination of his words doesn't always reveal this to have been true. He was known to have told small-town bankers and preachers, "Come see me and Mitt at the mansion and we'll spit tobacco over the porch rail." But to the boys in the fields he would promise, "Come see me at the mansion. We'll sit on the front porch and piss over the rail on those city bastards." To the ladies club, he would brag, "I'm stubborn as a mule"; and to his men friends, particularly those he drank with, he was forever saying, "I'm just as mean as cat shit." [15]

To Gene it was all theater. The play was basically the same, only the degree of emotion was changed for the different audiences. He felt those who criticized him for playing the role of a redneck in order to beguile the country people misunderstood his politics and his constituency. They wanted a show, and a wound-up Gene Talmadge was the best show in town. Through his entertainment he gained their loyalty and trust, for the essence of his performances was their honesty.

He appeared to be constantly "on stage" around rural people, even when he was riding from one town to the next. His trips took forever because he would constantly pull off to use a farmer's outhouse, walk with him behind his mule, appraise his cattle and horses and crops; and at every stop the people would come "touch him or laugh with him like he was their best friend."

Gene was almost fifty as he entered his second year in office. His face retained a smooth boyishness, and he stayed lean and wiry looking. His eyes remained his striking feature because of the intensity they projected. The squareness of his head and the thin lips that cut tightly across his face evoked a wooden, puppetlike appearance and was cause for derisive comment when nothing else was handy. The skin tone of his face stayed a dark yellow-brown, because of his childhood jaundice and the fact that he was constantly out in the sun. Henry Spurlin remembers the two of them stopping at a remote south Georgia drugstore for a soft drink. It was mid-summer and the men were sweating. Walking up to the counter they asked for fountain cokes, and the old proprietor told Spurlin he could have one, but they weren't serving "niggers" that day, as he glared toward an unbelieving Talmadge. The old man finally threw Gene out of his store swearing he was black. "We laughed our ass off at that one," said Spurlin, "but Gene's skin could get real dark."

He eagerly drank from the moonshine jugs of the boys when he thought it would draw a laugh, but he was wary of moonshine except that which came from one of his neighbors. After the long haul from Atlanta to McRae, he would slip over to a friend's house with his driver for a drink. One night they stayed too long, and the driver let a staggering governor out in front of his farm. Arriving at his own home, the driver got an irate call from Mitt wanting to know, "why the hell did you take Gene drinking?" The driver sheepishly asked what made her think they had been drinking? "Because," she snapped, "when I drove in the governor was manuring in our driveway."[16]

Probably no incident better characterized Talmadge the politician in 1933 than when the State Health Board asked him for support in getting x-ray clinics built in rural areas. They were desperately needed and Gene knew it; but after much discussion, he said in his characteristic way of refusing someone, "Nope, I ain't a gonna do it." The doctors were incredulous that he would deny his supporters this aid and asked didn't he think they needed it. He startled them by saying, "Yep, but I don't believe a x-ray would show germs. Won't show nothing but air." The doctors left his office swearing he was the dumbest educated man they had ever met. When they had gone, he turned to a friend and said succinctly, "Country folks don't believe in germs. If I sent those machines down there, they wouldn't go near them, and they'd swear I was wasting their money."[17] To a certain percentage of the rural people, he was right. But later, noting the rising educational level of these people, he had the facilities built.

9

Roosevelt
and
Talmadge

In 1934 Gene was privately becoming critical of the Roosevelt administration and its policies. Publicly, he was promising FDR's administration Georgia's "undivided and unstinting faith." [1] The increasing social activism and growing federal involvement of the New Deal was positioning itself at the opposite pole of Gene's governmental and social philosophies. He wrote in the January 15 issue of the *Statesman*, "If you have a rich government, you have a poor people, and a depressed people. If you have a poor government, you will have a rich and happy people."

Since the legislature did not meet in 1934 (it met every two years), all interest in state politics turned to who would dare test the power of Talmadge in the summer governor's race. By March only one trial balloon had been lofted, that of youthful Superior Court Judge Claude Pittman from Cartersville. [2] No one responded.

A group of prominent Atlantans opposed to Talmadge met shortly after that to agree on an opponent. Pittman heard of the meeting and figured he would be brushed aside unless he were there. Attending, he sat quietly while the group worried without success over who would be willing to chance ruining his career in a battle with Talmadge. Pittman startled the gathering by announcing that he would do so, then promptly walked out to tell the world he had emerged the candidate of the caucus. There was little the group could do but back the young man. [3]

Old Talmadge friend and worker Tom Linder figured that with Gene's help he could win the agriculture commissioner's office in the elections; he told Gene of his intentions and said he would be leaving the staff to run. Gene snapped, "You ain't a gone do no such thing!"

Dejectedly, Linder walked across the capitol hallway to treasurer George Hamilton's office, where he told his story. Linder said he had helped Gene to the post in 1926, and he was hurt because Gene refused to do the same for him. Hamilton sympathized with Linder and was annoyed with Gene to the point of stalking across to the governor's office where he dressed Gene down. Gene said he needed Linder, that he was too valuable to let go; but Hamilton was adamant and finally persuaded Gene by pointing out that it had been Linder who had agreed to back the unknown Talmadge for the same office eight years earlier. It was one of the few times Talmadge ever changed his mind.[4]

The campaign planning was halted by Gene's annual trip to the Kentucky Derby. This had become a traditional outing, with the governor loading up carloads of cronies for a weekend. A small number went in 1934, since road contractor John Whitley was footing the bill. Because Gene liked to "doll up his friends and staff and make them feel important," he issued everyone a full-dress military uniform. The colorful group from Georgia "made all the parties and had our usual good time," but Gene became restless and wanted to return to Atlanta by train so that he could sleep during the overnight trip. He, Whitley, and highway board chairman W. E. Wilburn left the rest of the group to board a train. When they discovered that the dining car had closed for the night, Gene told Whitley, "John, get off and go find us some coffee and sandwiches. We'll hold the train." Whitley grabbed a porter as he got off to insure his not being left. The station diner had no cups they could take out, so Whitley pulled out a roll of bills and bought one of their huge coffee urns and gave it to the porter who staggered out toward the train. But it was too late. With a sudden lurch the train began to pull out, and the two men so encumbered could only struggle against the weight of their coffee and sandwiches as the train sped away.

Whitley hailed a taxi, stuffed the porter and the urn into it, and ordered the driver to follow the train until they could intercept it. There followed a wild, hair-raising ride through the night. Meanwhile, on the train, Gene was giving the conductor hell for leaving his friends and the conductor was trying to run the Talmadge party off the train because Whitley had their tickets. The taxi, careening through one small Tennessee town, was sirened to a halt by the sheriff. Peering into the cab, the sheriff saw a man in military dress, a black porter holding a coffee urn, and a terrified driver. The sheriff figured it was John Dillinger in disguise with his gang. A long and loud argument finally convinced the sheriff of their identity, and he waved them on into the night. The next morning a very dusty Kentucky taxi was seen pulling up at the Georgia capitol; a man in rumpled military dress waved goodbye to his driver and the porter who still had his arm around the urn. From that day on Whitley was known as "Taxi John," and another improbable story had been added to the burgeoning Talmadge folklore.[5]

As usual Gene succeeded in keeping his name before the press while he was preparing for reelection, this time by defying the state and federal courts which were trying to prevent his lowering utility rates. He shocked the state's lawyers by proclaiming, "I do not recognize the jurisdiction of any court to compel the governor to attend its court." If they held him in contempt, he wouldn't appear. Talmadge's defiant attitude angered many judges. This was a situation he could have controlled by appointing young men to the bench, but he would not; he preferred instead to leave the judiciary pretty much alone. This resulted in the state retaining an unusual number of old judges who owed Talmadge nothing. His court stance received the blessings of "the boys," because the courts were not overly respected by much of the Talmadge constituency—the hard-times crowd who saw their kin put on the chain gang by the court and saw their property taken through the courts because they couldn't meet the mortgage. On the other hand, this above-the-law stance ran thousands of voters off. Gene just plain scared them, and he made no apologies.

His opening speech for the 1934 race was at the cotton trading center of Bainbridge in southwest Georgia. Even hardened veterans of the political circuit were incredulous at the masses jamming the roads into town. Macon reporter W. T. Anderson stopped at a restaurant in Americus and heard the owner exclaim, "My God, what's the matter with the people about this Talmadge fellow? When they talk about Talmadge they act like they want to fight about it if anybody disagrees with them. I waited on them and made change and kept my mouth shut." [6]

The last thirty-eight miles of the road into Bainbridge was a squishy rain-soaked mess. The air was dank and hot, and clouds boiled over the area; but it did not rain. Gene sat in the wet air on the broad veranda of the Bon Air Hotel in a wilting white suit, watching the high school band "make music like city slickers" before moving out to a big field where the speakers' stand had been nailed up, the barbecue cooked, and an enormous throng had gathered.

The platform Talmadge presented that day grew out of an unapproachable confidence that reflected the ignorance of the Talmadge constituency. In the face of staggering needs, Gene offered a simple three-plank platform: (1) creation of the office of lieutenant governor; (2) a four-year term for governor; and (3) payment of the state debt without raising taxes. It was a refutation of the realities of the day—a bold, egotistical statement to the Georgia people that all that was needed to solve their problems was Old Gene. Old Gene and Roosevelt. So enthusiastically did he embrace FDR that the Atlanta press was moved to say he "seemed to glory in the fact" that Washington had acceded to his every request.[7] It was a paradoxical embrace, in view of Gene's ultraconservative platform. But few noticed.

What they did suddenly notice, to the extent that they became the legendary symbol of Gene Talmadge politics, were the brilliant red suspenders he wore. Friend and foe claim the suspenders were always a part of Gene, but his son Herman said they never became such a center of interest until the 1934 race. Speaking in Bainbridge at a working man's club called the Tammany Club, Gene was presented a pair of red suspenders. He began to wear them constantly as a symbol of the working man, and Pittman ridiculed them so much that they became an issue and forever more a symbol of Gene Talmadge.[8] He had indeed always worn suspenders, with a belt, but never consistently red ones. The Macon *Telegraph* wrote in September, "The crowd, or many of them, had evidently been reading the newspaper stories for they cheered the red suspenders." [9]

And the Atlanta *Constitution* reported: "Talmadge gave the crowd everything it wanted and more too. Stripping off his coat the governor revealed a pair of red suspenders which, of course, drew a round of cheers. Pretty soon he began mopping his streaming brow with a red bandanna handkerchief and this brought more cheers. And when he rolled up his sleeves and started speaking with his arms as well as his lips, the crowd went wild." [10]

For all of his pro-Roosevelt talk during the campaign, Talmadge had been firmly, but rather quietly jousting FDR and his department heads for a year. Since the rush of the first New Deal programs Gene had sent a steady stream of telegrams to Washington, complaining and advising about the AAA cotton-reduction program, processing taxes on corn, tobacco prices, and disbursement of road money. Ironically Gene also had beseeched the president to offer some immediate help. In August of 1933, he had written, "The very foundation of this section is the farmer. The farmer must receive some help." To discuss the programs, particularly the huge federal road grants scheduled to come to Georgia, the governor had met FDR at the White House that September. Gene had become so concerned by that time with Roosevelt's impact that he had sent Atlanta's Fulton National Bank president, Ryburn Clay, to Washington, asking for a letter from FDR saying that he was not against Gene Talmadge in the 1934 gubernatorial races—a veiled attempt at getting a presidential endorsement. The request was refused. Talmadge's position through the 1934 campaign, then, appeared to be one of respect for the president, growing concern, if not hostility, toward his programs, but a keen interest in Washington doing something to help the states. Talmadge was insisting, however, that the states have control over the federal money and its disbursement, and that they have the right to ignore any programs of which they disapproved. A split was emerging along states-rights' lines.

The September white primary was a runaway. Winning all but three of Georgia's 159 counties, Gene won 178,409 votes to Pittman's 87,049 and Ed Gilliam's 5,073.[11] In his victory speech Gene noted with little humility, "At times I have felt there was a great force behind me that was holding me up." As reporters moved in for photographs, witnesses said Gene ducked out of the room to change his "sporty" shirt for a rumpled campaign suit. It was also noticed that his neatly combed hair had suddenly become tousled, the way the wool-hat boys liked it.[12]

In 1934 Talmadge became a newspaper owner. On April 1, he ceased to be the associate editor of the *Statesman*, and for $1,000 he became its owner. In a series of letters in 1942, the founder of the *Statesman*, Frank Lawson, described to John Maclean how the transaction took place and the newspaper evolved. A journalist from the North, Lawson had moved south and started the paper in 1930 on "an idea I originally got from *Time* magazine and intended to develop it along the lines of *Fortune*." It would be a reformist paper, a muckraker, and Lawson did succeed in uncovering some political highjinks, but circulation never got off the ground, advertisers weren't attracted, and the little paper floundered financially. Gene Talmadge was looking for a paper that he could use as a platform for his views (as Tom Watson had done), and he sent Breman, Georgia, banker and loyal Talmadge man J. J. Mangham to offer Frank Lawson a $1,000 loan to make Talmadge associate editor. "This constituted a sale of an honest idea for a political mess of pottage . . . but I was already fighting what appeared to be an inevitable financial failure, and I fell for Talmadge's claim that he would immediately bring the circulation up to 50,000 which . . . would give me a monthly profit of $1,000. And so I became a governor's press agent and ruined the paper. I ran the

Statesman as editor with Gene Talmadge as associate editor until the governor split with Mangham. . . . I stood this for a few months, then sold out to Talmadge." [13] Gene bought 51 percent of the paper on April 1, 1934, for $1,000. Lawson was convinced he should sell out after they mailed out 100,000 appeals for subscriptions and got back "less than fifty." Lawson felt Gene was also becoming disillusioned; "Talmadge then began to discover . . . he could not . . . duplicate Tom Watson's *Jeffersonian* for the simple reason Gene CANNOT write." [14]

While Gene was acquiring one paper, rumors were sweeping state press circles that he had inadvertently ruined one of Georgia's great papers, the Atlanta *Journal.* A young member of the Grey family which owned the paper was in jail on a murder charge, and people were saying Mrs. Grey had told editor Major Cohen he would be fired if he printed any adverse news about Talmadge during the 1934 race. She was hoping the governor would pardon her grandson. The paper did back off Talmadge during the race, but no connection was ever publicly proven.

Problems started plaguing Gene before the victory celebrations were over. Unions had been trying to organize Georgia's cotton mills for some months, with violent flare-ups continuing into September. Mill management tried to break up strike lines by breaking heads, and, by the same token, organizers violated the boundaries within which they were to operate. It was rumored that Cason Callaway, textile baron and Talmadge contributor, phoned Gene and said he wanted the National Guard called out, that the situation had gotten out of hand. How much this influenced Gene is uncertain, but almost immediately after the primary election, he moved to break his well-publicized promise to the unions: "I will never use the troops to break up a strike." He had also said in August, "I resent anyone on earth saying they are closer to labor, or a better friend of labor than I. You can look at my hands and the color of my skin and tell it." [15] And, it had been labor that had given him his red suspenders.

Four thousand militiamen were called out in September, and they moved swiftly. Thousands of Georgians were arrested, so many that grass fields were strung with barbed wire to hold the people. When photos hit the pages of the nation's press, showing hapless Georgians being corralled like cattle, the cry went out that Talmadge had created concentration camps. He was stamped anti-labor, and he lost labor's vote forever for his broken promise. But Georgia was far from being

an industrial state, and the huge farmer constituency wasn't concerned
for the strikers. The turmoil ended with the militiamen brutally beating a worker to death in front of his family. Though Gene could not be
incriminated by that incident, one thing was certain: by late fall he had
personally broken the back of the unions in Georgia.[16]

As if the union mess weren't enough, Gene was reported to have
said, "The next President we have should be able to walk a two-by-
four." [17] Given wide publicity, the remark came across as a cruel and
repugnant slam at FDR's polio. Talmadge confidants swore that Gene
either did not say it, or that he was referring to walking a narrow
middle-of-the-road position and not far to the left.[18] Whatever the
truth, Gene had repercussions from all sides for it. He was moved to
write shortly thereafter, in the *Statesman*, "We all have confidence in
our President. We believe his motives are pure as the driven snow." [19]

Gene was actually having a great struggle within himself on FDR.
He told a friend, "I really want to be for the man, but I can't accept his
socialistic programs." [20] The crux of the "Roosevelt problem" with
Gene and other Georgia politicians was that they felt they had been
fooled by the president. Gene had voted for him in 1932 when the man
sounded conservative. But the emerging social activism and expanding government had "scared the hell" out of the Talmadge crowd.
Gene feared socialism and its big government as he feared nothing else.
He loathed welfare as corrupt and saw in it the destruction of the independent man. Philosophy began to clash with Gene's admiration for
FDR, and the contradiction showed through 1933 and 1934. By late
fall of 1934, however, hatred of the New Deal began to shift to the man
who had created it. His praise of FDR in the 1934 campaign and later
were no more than attempts to keep things smooth until the general
assembly met, and to garner votes from FDR's popularity. It was highly
out of character for Gene to be riding coattails. But he was. In November the split was opened for all to see when FDR visited Atlanta, and
Gene went to Savannah.[21] In December Georgians were asked to vote
for the New Deal's Bankhead Cotton Control Act, and Gene went on
a heavy speaking tour to fight it. They voted it in by six to one. Georgians appeared to be making a profound turn-around in their attitudes
toward the function of government and reconsidering which government they would relinquish their power to. Had they, in a sudden
societal reversal, discarded the foundation stones of their heritage?
Were they now willing to embrace big government, with its intrusions
and restrictions? Yes and no. It was a time of ambiguity, dual loyalties,

and two consciousness levels. But it did seem that in Georgia's attitudinal structure, pragmatism was overcoming romanticism and delusion as a base for decision-making. The roots of the past could be heard breaking with undeniable clarity.

Many factors served to split Gene from Roosevelt. The governor knew that when the populace relinquished power to Washington they also weakened the powers of their states. Also, his close circle of friends and many state politicians who detested FDR and the New Deal constantly told Gene so, and many of his banker friends who had hated FDR since he closed the banks pressured him. Equally influential was the growing number of pro-Roosevelt politicians who were joining forces behind the name of the Democratic party in opposition to Gene. And finally, there was Gene's inbred fear of liberalism and socialism, his dogmatic belief that the country was being blindly swept up into a spiritually and economically destructive movement.[22] A man of Talmadge's intensity of belief could not continue publicly to "like" FDR while hating his programs. In Gene's eyes, man and program soon became one. Gene's turn from FDR had involved a two-year process, but once made, it was complete. The incongruities of the 1934 public and private statements were resolved by 1935.

The Georgia farmer in 1934 voted for radical conservative Talmadge on the one hand and radical liberal New Deal on the other. It must be remembered that during the summer campaign of 1934 ideology was not an issue, though Pittman tried to make it one. The voter was not forced to choose between FDR and Gene, for Gene had constantly assured voters that he was backing the president. For those who were aware of the opening chasm between the two, the contradiction was not particularly disturbing, because the votes were made for totally different reasons. The farmer voted for Talmadge because of his personality; he voted for the New Deal, not because he was a budding socialist, but because he was desperate and this seemed the only viable escape from hard times. Gene lifted his spirits; the New Deal filled his stomach. The farmer could enjoy a clean conscience while satisfying his bodily needs. As long as Gene paid lip service to the New Deal and made no real move to end it, he could rave all day about the destructiveness of the welfare system without losing votes. His wiser advisers were worrying, however, about what would happen if Gene tried to push the hand away from the mouth.

Late in 1934 Gene had called his treasurer, George Hamilton, into his office and asked if Hamilton knew the story of Julius Caesar. Hamilton answered "yes!" "George," Gene said, "I believe that a Caesar is born in every century." Hamilton caught the drift of what the governor was saying and said, "Gene, surely you don't think you are the Caesar of this century!"

"Yes, I do think so."

Hamilton left in disbelief.[23]

10

Roosevelt
or
Talmadge

Eugene Talmadge was inaugurated for his second term as governor on Wednesday, January 16, 1935. He would serve two years. On the same date in 1933, in the same assembly hall, he had requested populistic solutions to the depression, asking the legislators to "make a definite stand against the big financiers, economists and wise people who have put this country on the rocks." [1] But in a historical show of incompetence and self-service, the general assembly had done nothing. Gene had stepped into the breach, taken a stand, and become famous for it. The purpose of his whole 1935 legislative program was to get this new legislature to legalize that stand. Gene said events had forced him to pass legislation, and his actions were justified because they had been "voted on by the people" when they elected him. In effect, by asking that his 1933 platform be passed, he was saying he had nothing new to offer for 1935.

He placed passage of his three-dollar tag at the top of the list, asserting with delusions of grandeur, "I believe a step out of our economic depression was gained . . . and this contributed more than any other move that could have been made at that time." [2] Moving down his priority list, Gene asked that his firing of the highway board and the public service commission be endorsed, and he also said the amount that counties could tax property should be limited. He claimed that his economic policies had reduced the state debt from $7,523,835.82 to $5,384,355.24, and as a result, "Georgia is better off than any other state in the Union." [3]

With his platform out of the way, Gene revealed to the legislators that he felt he had done all that was necessary for relieving the depression in Georgia, and now the thrust of his energies and politics would be to save the state from the grasping claws of the federal government. There would be a shift in emphasis. His approach through the legislature was rather veiled, because he saw no value in forcing a confrontation with Roosevelt sympathy before his program passed.

He asked that the state university system be put under the control of the state; as he saw it, recent federal loans to the institution meant it was becoming dependent upon outside forces. His plea for small appropriations was a definitive statement of Talmadge governmental philosophy. "The only way I know a government can help the people is to stay out of business, and be a fair referee between the people, and let its citizens do the business, and then just take as little toll out of their property as you can for government." [4]

The inaugural speech to the general assembly finally ended the arguments about where Gene Talmadge stood on the New Deal programs, and no one got the message better than newly elected house speaker E. D. Rivers. A south Georgia politician and a man who had jumped around the political fence so much he had evaded being cast into any stereotype, Rivers had first run for governor in 1932. In 1933, he had found FDR's coattails, and the Talmadge stand against the New Deal had set him free. Rivers and his close friend, Richmond County representative Roy Harris, would work through the 1935 session to establish a progressive legislative record that Rivers could run on in 1936.

Gene moved quickly after his speech to get his program going through the house. His basic legislative strategy was to rush his bills to the house and senate speakers and other influential members of the assembly, to get their names as sponsors of the bills before the legislature was inundated with the usual pile of local legislation. The Talmadge package consisted of fourteen bills, and they fairly flew through the assembly.[5] The huge Talmadge victory of the past September hung heavily over the lawmakers. Gene expected and received complete legislative support for his platform. The assembly unhesitatingly approved his firing of the public service commission, approved the three-dollar tag, created the lieutenant governor post, authorized four-year terms for governor, okayed his highway department firings, and agreed to divert two million dollars in highway funds to other appropriations. With the passage of these bills, the legislative session moved from one of harmony to one of back-stabbing, quarreling confusion. There has probably never been a more schizophrenic session, and it happened almost overnight.

The powerful voices in the house, Harris, Rivers, and Ellis Arnall,

wanted to give Georgia some of the benefits of the New Deal legislation. But out of deference to the governor they waited until his program
had passed. A six-man committee was then sent to study the possibility of Georgia's participating in federal work-relief programs and to
see that federal posts in Georgia be staffed by Georgians. The group
returned bubbling with enthusiasm. Arriving on Sunday night, they
went straight to the governor's mansion. Rivers later recounted what
happened. He said their recitation of the millions available was met
with a stony silence from Gene. After they had finished, the governor
said there wasn't going to be any New Deal legislation passed. He said
it would destroy the country with its giveaway programs. Furthermore,
in the election year of 1936, there wasn't going to be any more talk
about "Roosevelt and Talmadge"; there was only going to be talk
about "Roosevelt *or* Talmadge." He told the startled group that they
might as well make up their minds right there in that room which side
of the line they were going to be on. The men did not fully comprehend
all that had been said in those few minutes, and their silence goaded
Gene to say that he wanted them to be in his office early the next morning to sign a report that would tell Washington not to send any more
federal aid to Georgia. The group filed out into the night, dazed by the
governor's remarks. Gene was apparently going to openly oppose
Roosevelt for party allegiance and, at the same time, he was asking the
legislature to close down and go home! The battle lines were drawn
very quietly but firmly that night, and Gene's influence with certain
legislative leaders started a precipitous decline.[6]

Talmadge's reaction to federal aid was not consistent. As the New
Deal bills blasted through Congress, the administration came down
hard on the states for their immediate implementation of the programs.
Georgia's first big federal windfall came in the form of nine million
dollars in highway funds. The state Democratic committee chairman,
Hugh Howell, had received first notice of the windfall as a courtesy.
Attached to the use of the money was the stipulation that Georgia
start work on it almost immediately. The deadline was so short that no
time was allowed for legislative, or patronage, handling of the money.
Howell took the proposition to Gene who ordered the state's major
road contractors and their suppliers, the highway department and their
engineers, to meet him and Howell at the Ansley Hotel the next day.

The group assembled in a large room at the Ansley, and a huge map
of Georgia was tacked on the wall. After Howell explained the financial
bonanza and the stipulations attached to it, all in the room shook

their heads in bewilderment. There seemed no way to go through the normal methods of appropriating road money, consulting with every county courthouse gang and legislator, considering who was owed a political favor and who wasn't. Gene then snapped, "We gonna spend every penny of that nine million dollars before we leave this room today. We'll decide right now where the roads will be built." He had two stenographers on hand, and he gave out pencils to everyone. Thus began one of the most unusual allocations of funds in the state's history. Each contractor went before the big map and marked where he wanted a road built. Then the sand and rock men and the asphalt and concrete men started estimating what the roads would cost. The jobs were to be apportioned evenly between the big contractors in the room. The contractors, knowing where their machinery was located, also marked off roads they would like to pave. The stenographers wrote furiously, recording where the roads would be paved and how much mileage was involved, what type paving, and who would pave it for how much. As the millions ticked off through the long day, Hugh Howell remained silent.

When the money neared the nine million dollar mark, he spoke up. "Boys, I'd like to be able to get some of that." Everyone agreed he should and asked where he wanted his road. He sounded almost apologetic: "I don't want but a mile and a half, and if you'll give me that I won't open my mouth again." They chorused agreement. Howell then penciled off a tiny strip that ran through Emory at Oxford College. He had attended school there and remembered the infamous mudhole of a road that wound through it. Countless efforts by school officials to have it paved had failed. Howell then made another request. "I want this road to be the first paved under this money. I want it to be the first money spent. John Whitley can start work on it tomorrow, can't you, John?" Whitley said he would be pushed to get the necessary men and equipment there, but he would try. The benevolent spirit in the room prevailed, and Howell was accorded his road. The group then dispersed, having spent nine million dollars as the obliterated state map that was taken back to the highway department testified.[7]

One of the great political mysteries of the day was just what was going on between Talmadge and Louisiana's governor, Huey Long. They had met a number of times, but neither would ever say what was discussed other than Gene's sullen, "We cussed Roosevelt." National observers and both men's constituents kept looking for an emerging alliance that hinted at surfacing, but never actually did. In February, Gene invited Long to speak about his cotton holiday before the general assembly. Aide-de-camp Henry Spurlin remembers, "Huey was very security conscious and traveled with bodyguards. Georgia law wouldn't let them enter the state carrying guns, so Gene had 'em all sworn in as Fish and Game Wardens and they came armed. Huey was an extremely nervous man. He even paced while he was shaving. He and Gene were great friends at first. They were trying to work out some alliance against Roosevelt where one would run for president and the other for vice-president. The whole thing was being pushed by a rich man named John H. Kirby." [8]

Long spoke on his "share the wealth" philosophy before the legislators; and since Gene was dead against this, the visit was regrettable. Actually a cursory analysis of Long and Talmadge would have revealed far more differences in the two than similarities. Both had risen to power as "champions of the little man," and both had bucked the establishment and become notorious for their iconoclasm, directness, and energy. Both were demagogues and proponents of the Populists. But after that, what they had in common became dwarfed by what they did not have in common. Long was an ultraliberal with his "share the wealth," and Gene was an ultraconservative who thought anything beyond his cotton holiday was Russian socialism. Long was riding ahead of the times, and Gene was falling further back into their wash. Long wanted FDR out of office because he didn't think he was doing enough for the people, and Gene wanted him out because he felt he had done too much.

Other than their dogmatic differences, the men were unlike in their practice of politics once they were in office. Long had erected an incredibly powerful and extensive machine that allowed him almost dictatorial control over Louisiana. Gene, on the other hand, had very little organization except at campaign time. Gene was not an organization or a machine man. He took his case directly to the people and felt he had a bond with them that excluded the need for party or organization.

Long had indicated earlier to Atlanta reporter Lamar Ball what he thought of Gene, "That Talmadge ain't got the brains to suit his ambitions." [9] But this remark did not reach the public consciousness so much as the Long remark reported by the Atlanta press the day after Long's legislative address. Asked what he thought of the Talmadge organization, the Kingfish sneered, "It's a goddamn bush league outfit!" [10] That night over drinks with a small group of Georgia's Washington leaders, the very formal Senator Walter George asked a tipsy Long, "Well, sir, you know we have Gene Talmadge here who is very similar to you in a lot of respects. What material help do you believe he can bring to you?" Long answered, "Senator, have you heard of the man that went fishing and ate his own bait?" George looked puzzled and said he had not. "Well, I'm that man that went fishing and Gene Talmadge is my bait." [11]

These statements seemed cruel and pointless, particularly since Long was a guest of the state and her governor; but he was a blunt man, and he held Talmadge in such low esteem that he was insulted when they were compared. Apparently their great problem was that both men had been thinking beyond a simple southern alliance against the depression or against the New Deal. There were inklings of John Henry Kirby's putting together a national ticket against FDR with Long running for president and Gene for vice-president, and the two had quickly found out that neither was willing to accept the second spot. Whatever their reasons for coming together, their impregnable wills doomed any politically oriented relationship, and they parted as silently as they had come together. Certainly, of the two, Long had a more direct and observable effect on Franklin Roosevelt and national politics, and he thereby escaped the stigma of being seen as a ranting, ineffective southern demagogue—which was the image of Gene Talmadge in the eyes of many northerners and continues to be today.

The members of the legislature began to split badly in February along pro- and anti-New Deal lines. Rivers and Harris knew Gene was holding the veto over their heads, but they moved ahead pushing for a sales tax, old age pension, free texts, and a seven month school year. They also wanted a slum-clearance program, a child labor amendment, and cooperation with the national employment system. But Gene was having none of it, and those bills that his strong influence could not hold back, he vetoed. He later told a staff worker, W. O. Brooks, that he threw every New Deal bill in the trash can without even reading it.[12] Rivers was particularly angered over Gene's refusal to let the old age pension and the sales tax pass.

For the moment, the forces of conservatism held; in fact, a backlash against the New Deal developed, and a states' rights movement and consciousness swept the legislature. As the session neared its close, not one piece of New Deal legislation had passed. While vetoing a bill to sterilize the criminally insane, Gene told Adjutant General Camp, "They made no provisions in here to exempt the governor and the adjutant general. Lindley, you and I might go crazy one day and we don't want them working on us."[13] So adamant was Gene over any type of progressive legislation that he reportedly told a federal agent, "The way to handle a relief program was like Mussolini was handling it in Italy, namely, to line these people up and take the troops and make them work."[14]

The legislature was scheduled to end on Saturday, March 26. As that date neared, no appropriations bill for financing state operations had even come out of committee. Money for the remainder of 1935 had been voted by the 1933 legislature. The events of the last days of the 1935 session would be argued for years to come, but no one would disagree that what resulted was one of the most chaotic and embarrassing situations Georgia was ever forced to endure.[15]

The problem arose around education. E. D. Rivers had built his hopes for the 1936 race on the "education crowd"; and his house floor manager, Roy Harris, was committed to helping Rivers come out of the 1935 session as the friend of education, probably the strongest plank on which a man could run. Rivers' strategy involved getting $5.5 million appropriated for schools. The only way he could guarantee that this sum would be paid in full was to have it placed in behind the "grandfather clause." This was the name given for that point at which all appropriations would be certain of being paid in full. Money "behind" this clause was paid pro rata. Rivers' tactic was to have the education appropriation placed "behind" the clause, thereby assuring full payment with him getting the credit. Gene knew what Rivers was up to and promised him privately that he would see that all $5.5 million was paid before the year was out, but for the time being asked that he "make it $5 million."[16] Rivers refused, because he knew Gene would get full credit if he were allowed to parcel the money out as he wished. The two factions stalemated over the point. House speaker Rivers, as ex-officio chairman of the house rules committee, saw that Harris chaired a joint senate-house committee to thrash out the problems caused by Gene's proposed cut. The group was soon irreconcilably split and could not agree on what course to take. Gene heard about it and sent a spiteful note through Senator Bill Lester from Augusta, saying, "Tell Roy I'd just love the opportunity of running education in Georgia without any appropriations." The fiery Harris retorted, "Bill, tell that sonofabitch he's got his opportunity."[17] Harris went immediately to the floor of the house and announced that the committee was hopelessly deadlocked; he then moved that the general assembly adjourn without waiting for the traditional end of the session. This prompted many solons to accuse Rivers and Harris of deliberately preventing an appropriations bill so that the state would be without money. Therefore, Gene would be embarrassed and politically destroyed. But Harris says this was not true; for in the frantic scramble of those last days, he and Rivers had no way of knowing what would result from deliberately stalling the session. He said, "That would be giving us credit for more brains than we rightly could claim." [18] Legislators who were there would later vehemently disagree. Many others blamed Talmadge for the mess because of his fight with Rivers over who would get credit for the education bill and also because of his defiant stand against any progressive legislation. It was said that he wanted the appropriations bill blocked so that he could take over the finances of the state.

One reason for the breakdown in the legislative processes was the overload of pork-barrel bills introduced in the closing days. The end of the session was the traditional time for lawmakers to indulge one another in getting local legislation through; it was a time characterized by greed and deal making, a time of legislation that was critical to reelections. And in this swirl of self-interest by both general assembly and governor, the appropriation of money for the operation of the state for the next two years became hopelessly mired. The last day of the session was a frenzy of meetings, one fist fight, an appeal on the house floor by the governor, and endless attempts by assembly members to get the house and senate to agree on an appropriations bill. Each had his own version of the bill, with the house version coming closest to what Gene wanted; but they could not agree. A probable factor in the senate's refusal to work with the house was Talmadge's veto of the highly popular old age pension bill on March 22. He had said it would cost forty-two million dollars; but, more influential than that, the bill went against his principles of the family unit and its purpose of caring for its own. "I am opposed to all kinds of pensions, except a soldier's pension. I do not want to see the incentive of the American people to work and to lay up something for their old age destroyed." He concluded, "If the U.S. were allowed to support people's parents, it will take something out of their souls." [19] This veto—coupled with Gene's veto of seven constitutional amendments, of one hundred local measures, and of fifty-two other general bills—helped precipitate the appropriations crisis and diminish Talmadge's influence when it was needed in getting money voted. Legislator Bond Allman observed, "In those last days his influence was crumbling fast." It did not completely crumble, however, as is evidenced by the house vote of confidence for him on March 24, after Representative Verlyn Booth of Barrow County accused Gene of being the cause of the session's problems. This charge infuriated the appropriately named Hellbent Edwards who punched Booth in the jaw. After the ruckus had subsided, the house was moved to pay homage to Gene, saying that he "stood as a symbol of inflexible purpose in the storm and stress of the suffering of his people, and [that he] devised, sponsored, and declared principles and measures which have tended to raise the general level of life in Georgia, and yet stood steadfast to the deep rooted principles of Americanism." [20] The senate accorded Gene similar praise, and he returned the compliments by saying it had been a "history making session," and one of the greatest legislatures since the Civil War. Representative Paul Lindsey from urban DeKalb County inserted a sour note in the unanimous house vote, grumbling, "I'm tired of seeing the state in the hands of that little peewee in the governor's chair." [21]

At midnight on March 24, the 1935 session ended in confusion and turmoil. No money had been appropriated for operating the state. An immediate cry went up for Gene to call the legislature back into session, but he was having none of that. He brushed off the scare-talk that the state would be bankrupt by saying, "The State of Georgia is O.K." When pressed about the matter, he snapped, "There ain't a gonna be no special session." [22]

But to close friends he intimated the real reason he wouldn't call the lawmakers back: "There's a bunch that wants to impeach me. I ain't call'n no session." [23] Actually Gene felt no discomfort over the state being without money, for his friend, lawyer Buck Murphy, had found an old law which said that if the general assembly failed or refused to pass an appropriation, the governor was empowered to promulgate one. [24] When Gene stated this power, Roy Harris said with supreme confidence, "He couldn't spend a penny." [25] Battle lines that had begun to be drawn in February, for and against Gene Talmadge, began solidifying in late March. The thought of Old Gene controlling the entire budget of Georgia had an immediate polarization effect.

Some felt, however, that even more than Gene's taking over Georgia's money, his stand against the old age pension had been the turning point. Rivers and Harris had stumped the state during the session, forming "Old Age Clubs" and seeking to make them a grassroots rallying point for New Deal legislation. Their efforts had gained passage of the bill in the assembly and a veto on the governor's table. Rivers' actions were partly motivated by his seeking a position from which to run in 1936. He had realized the Roosevelt strength for some time and wanted to run on some sort of New Deal platform; but he watched his chance to emerge from the 1935 session as a New Deal champion crumble before the Talmadge votes and vetoes. This had prompted the pivot to the "education crowd" as an issue to champion, and now Gene had outfoxed Rivers on that one also. Talmadge had landed on his feet once again, when even his closest friends had warned of political disaster if he tangled with Rivers and Harris. James Peters had sought Gene out on the last night of the session when it had become obvious that the appropriations bill was caught in a Talmadge-Rivers showdown. Finding the governor "the only calm man in the capitol that night," Peters said: "Gene, what you're fixing to do, you're going to let Rivers and Roy get the best of you. Don't let Ed's political maneuvering get together with Roy Harris' scheming, or they'll beat the devil out of you." Gene, at his indestructible best, quickly shook his head and said, "Aw, naw, they ain't gone do that." And they didn't—primarily because Talmadge was quite willing to accept the consequences of any action he took, though he rarely knew what they would be. He never hesitated because of what might happen.[26]

Appropriately, Gene had closed out the 1935 session by getting laughs out of a veto. It had been proposed that a highway be named for him, and he had vetoed the bill: "I might get on the chain gang . . . or go wrong before I die." He didn't want to be caught busting rock out on the Eugene Talmadge Highway.

11

"Runnin' for President Ain't Like Runnin' for Sheriff"

The Talmadge advisers during his first eight years in state politics were known more for their brief periods of service in that capacity than anything else. He was so volatile and demanded such extraordinary loyalty that he could tolerate few advisers who disagreed with him, and fewer men of any individuality could tolerate a lasting close relationship with him. He had a long list of good friends whom he called on from time to time, and they gladly offered their help and judgment, but only a handful remained in constant service to him.

Gene's gregarious nature and his intimacy with the electorate kept him up to date on the needs and feelings of the people. His mail from the common man was staggering in volume, and he was so available to anyone wishing an audience that bedlam seemed forever to reign around his office door. Because of the way he ran his office, he received enormous amounts of advice. What bothered his critics and many of those close to him was his penchant for refusing to take most of the advice given him, and his unwillingness to change his mind once he had made a decision. Since most of his actions were based on his ultraconservative philosophy, any advice that he sought or accepted had to be directly in line with those beliefs. It appeared that everything he did was prejudged and easily predictable, though some of the actions he took were surprisingly bold.

Since Gene ran his own show, there were no regular or formal advisory meetings; a man might be allowed to contribute to one decision and be ignored thereafter. The few fairly constant members of the inner circle until 1934 included Hugh Howell, Lindley Camp, Tom Linder, Charles Redwine, Judge Eschol Graham, Max McRae, Mrs. Talmadge, Lamar Murdaugh, Henry Spurlin, and John Whitley. Others filtered in and out, but Gene was playing high-risk politics, and few were willing to place both feet on board his wild ride into an uncertain future.

Perhaps no man was closer to Gene during this time than John Whitley from LaGrange. A man of Gene's height, but heavier, Whitley had met Gene in 1922, when Whitley was a struggling road-builder and Gene was a dirt-poor farmer and a sometime lawyer. Their temperaments and beliefs were right in line, and both were frank and dogmatic in their expression of those beliefs.

The science of road building had come slowly to Georgia. Whitley had entered it early and become one of the biggest road builders in the state by the time Gene assumed the governorship. He was a wealthy man because of it, and as such enjoyed some voice in state politics, as roads and politics had become intricately connected. Whitley had also known and been befriended by Franklin Roosevelt when FDR was governor of New York. By the time Gene opened the split between himself and FDR, Whitley shared the confidences of both men, and both thought it amusing. Whitley had built a very large fishing camp and hunting preserve outside of LaGrange which Gene and FDR visited at different times quite often. It was a secluded, unpretentious "man's kind of a place" where Gene spent a great deal of time, usually in secret, when he needed to get away from Atlanta and politics. He would arrive with a driver and a bottle of bourbon, and the word *politics* would not be mentioned for days.

Roosevelt enjoyed the camp for much the same reason, because even at Warm Springs he was constantly surrounded by the press and local townspeople. The president would slip off and make the short drive over to LaGrange with only his secret service men in the car. He was forever trying to get them to "go on back to Warm Springs" insisting that, "When I'm with John I feel perfectly safe." [1]

FDR was very fond of corn liquor and whenever he came to Warm Springs, he would send one of the secret service men over to the camp for a bottle. Whitley didn't make it but his neighbor did. Whitley and Roosevelt rarely talked politics, though at the height of Gene's battle with Washington, Whitley was moved to good-naturedly admonish the president for his spending practices. "You can't spend the country out of debt, Mr. President," he said. Roosevelt laughed and answered, "John, you and Gene have ruined this country; now I've got to do something about it."

Gene's estimation of Whitley was enormous, and he was moved to say of his friend, "He is one of the smartest men not to have an education I have ever met. He has a real good business mind." [2] Gene also felt that Whitley was a man very close to the soil, and he used him as a listening post and sounding board. The two men's beliefs were identical, as were their perspectives and interpretations. Whitley took great pride in his intimacy with the dirt farmer and painstakingly studied his needs. He was one of the few who could cuss Gene out and still call him friend, as he did when the fun-loving Talmadge began hanging out at Atlanta's posh country clubs. "Gene, you stay outta them goddamn country clubs, and them parties! You ain't gonna learn about the working man in them places, and you'll get yourself run outta office if you get too far away from the people what put you in! You better get out in the fields with me and you'll stay in office." [3]

As important as anything in their relationship was Whitley's ability to make Gene relax and laugh. He had a great ability to tell funny stories, and Gene would beg him like a boy to tell them. Whitley's story-telling would make the governor literally collapse with laughter. Many of these stories found their way to the stump.

The Whitleys remember many intimate details about the man. The way he could fall asleep at any time of the day, at a moment's notice, and usually with his big hat cocked low over his forehead. How he had a lot of "hellaciousness" in him; he was forever poking fun with a biting wit and sarcasm that few could match. They remember his refusal to take a drink until after five in the afternoon, and then he would take no more than four drinks of bourbon and ginger ale. He would rise before the sun and be immediately alert and anxious to do something. Gene never suffered from a corn liquor hangover because he generally refused to touch it. His favorite meals were broiled chicken, or steak, and hash brown potatoes with a green salad. He loved hounds and hunting rabbits and bird or deer, which he did more than he fished.

The Whitleys remember Gene with great fondness, as "just being fun to be around," as being a man who desperately needed the quiet of their camp and the uncomplicated, undemanding friendship they offered. Their relationship, however, created a storm of criticism and accusations. Gene was the governor in charge of roads, and Whitley was the state's biggest road contractor, in a state which paid most of its revenue to road building. Critics said that Gene was awarding his friend fat contracts and taking kickbacks. Whitley says the only favor Gene had ever given him was to let him know in advance which roads were going to be paved. This would enable Whitley to do a lot of searching for the lowest bids from the rock and sand and asphalt people who subcontracted under him. No one understood how he could consistently bid so low. His answer: he paid every dime of his bills on the first of the month; therefore, the subcontractors knew they could figure in the discounts. The subcontractors dared not include discounts into bids they gave others, because they knew these men did not have the available capital to pay them until the state had paid the contractor, and then they could not be certain when the contractor would pass on the amount due them. Whitley's was an advantage that no one ever figured out.

Neither Gene nor Whitley felt that an illegality was being performed by Gene's early disclosure of roads to be let. Their rationale was that the taxpayer was the beneficiary because of the money saved whenever Whitley won a contract. Gene pushed his friend to get all the contracts he could and in doing so unknowingly violated an informal agreement that the small group of Georgia road contractors held. Though highly competitive, the contractors knew there was plenty of road work to go around, and they secretly allowed each other a fair share of the work. If one man was not winning contracts, the others would complain of too much work and decline from bidding on a particular road. This would make Gene mad as hell when Whitley would refuse to bid, and he would whine, "Now damnit, John, I know you can win that contract!"

The close relationship between governor and major state contractor caused a continuing barrage of accusation and rumor that Whitley was giving Gene kickbacks. There seems, however, to have been no money passed with criminal intent. Whitley did pay for many of Gene's trips, didn't charge him for the use of his fishing camp, and contributed heavily to the Talmadge campaigns. On one occasion he gave Gene six thousand dollars for campaign expenses, and Gene promptly spent it to increase his cattle herd.[4] Whitley did not make Talmadge rich, if for no other reason than that Gene simply didn't care much for becoming wealthy. He had a couple of farms, which was all he could manage; he wanted a good herd of cattle, and he was improving it; and he enjoyed horses, of which he had plenty. His tastes were more comfortable than extravagant. He was in fact constantly being given gifts ranging from chickens and pigs to cows and cotton bales. What money Gene received from most of his supporters was in the form of pocket change, and that was given at great sacrifice. Country people in faraway corners of the state rarely went into Atlanta, but when they did, they were often going for the purpose of seeing Gene and they would always bring him a gift. Bringing gifts of food and homemade articles was the custom of the country people, and they saw no reason not to extend that bit of sociability to their governor.

It was said he received monies for granting pardons, but he had little to do with actually reviewing the appeals, except in extraordinary cases. His secretary Carlton Mobley handled the flood of requests, studied the cases, and recommended to Gene which ones he should approve. Mobley said that throughout his service to Talmadge no one was ever approached through any persuasion other than legal channels. Gene was very magnanimous about granting pardons and got more of a self-serving feeling of righteousness from granting them than he would have gotten from accepting money. He also knew that it was good for votes, for most of the men he released came from impoverished homes—Talmadge people. All this is not to say that he absolutely never received money or goods for a release, but if he did it was most likely not part of a deal as much as it was the custom of the people to express gratitude in that manner. If he received cash, it was not evidenced in his style of life or possessions.

Herman Talmadge's wife Betty would later remember the nature of the relationship that existed within the Talmadge household. "Gene and Mitt were not demonstrative with their affections. They loved Herman and John and the two girls, but there was not a lot of kissing or hugging. I remember taking our first child to see Gene at the mansion. He would hold it, but seemed uncomfortable when I said he could kiss the baby if he wanted. It was simply not his nature, though he obviously loved the child. Herman meant everything to Gene, more than his stepson, or even the girls. Oh, yes, I forgot to mention, after I had shown Gene our son, he never missed a chance to kiss the child after that." [5]

"We've Got to Find Some Way to Put Gene Before the American People"

Spiritually, and to some extent materialistically, the world had been kept out of Georgia until the third decade of the twentieth century. The industrial age with its plethora of products—its automobile, tractor, telephone, radio, and electricity—had found a home in the state's cities, but had made only intermittent footholds in the isolated countryside. Certainly the new age had failed miserably in these rural areas to alter the allegiances and customs of the people. But what industrialism could not do, economics did. Forming the spear point for the new consciousness, the depression so obliterated the traditional solutions of survival and happiness that the tradition-bound rural Georgian had become eager to grasp any life raft, even if its direction was dead away from his psychological homeland. Reality, that stranger to the southern scene, made its undeniable debut with the depression, ushering in an even newer stranger, pragmatism. The culmination of all this was the arrival of the world in Georgia; and at the head of the invading column rode Franklin Roosevelt. The evangelistic message of the New Deal met in head-to-head combat with the Old Way in the 1935 legislature, and the lawmakers and the electorate began to split as they had rarely done since the decade before the Civil War.

Gene's emergence from the 1935 session as the symbol of total resistance to the new way spotlighted the new way (or the New Deal) as the dominant voter consideration for the 1936 state elections. Gene had also fostered an increase in voter consciousness by making an issue of the New Deal, whereas his previous successes had thrived on a constricted consciousness.

The imposition of the New Deal also signaled new direction in Talmadge's politics. Previously, his energies had been expended in (1) promoting himself; (2) maintaining a poor, but debt-free, status-quo government; (3) giving limited relief to the "little man"; and (4) preaching the positiveness of the Old Way as a solution to life's problems. His was a politics of crises and personality, characterized by an endless series of publicity-gaining confrontations that had polarized the voters—thereby narrowing the choice of candidates, stabilizing politics, diminishing the importance of party and issues. Tremendously successful with this strategy, Gene could have survived on it for years in an older time. He was forced, however, to a change in his strategy. The depression forced it. The New Deal forced it. Mass production, mass communication, mass education, alternative lifestyles, sophistication, the tractor—they all forced a redirection of his energies. And so did his overriding desire to be a United States senator.

The concurrent exhaltation and depression of the session had left Gene exhausted, and he quickly slipped away for the solitude of Sugar Creek. "I rushed off Friday to the farm. I did not begin to feel natural until I walked across the plowed ground and associated with the mules and men at work. Then somehow a calm came over me," he wrote.[6] After a brief stay, he walked from this contentment into an unfortunate interview with the New York *Times*. It was reported he had called

FDR an "extreme radical" and had cruelly abused the stricken president, saying, "The greatest calamity to this country is that President Roosevelt can't walk around and hunt up people to talk to. The only voices to reach his wheelchair were the cries of the 'gimme crowd.' " [7] This kind of candid talk created scorn for Talmadge throughout Georgia and the nation. His friends say he meant no harm; he sincerely felt that FDR was a prisoner of his affliction and was prevented from getting close to the people. Critics say it was another example of the man's propensity for cruelty.

Gene announced he was going on a national speaking tour that fall; and here his motives cloud. Publicly he was trying to arouse the nation against socialism. To close friends, he was doing that while preparing a platform from which to run for the United States Senate. Some northern Republicans wanted him to run for president as a favorite son. But his close friends deny he had any intention of running for president. "Gene knew that no southerner could be elected president," [8] they agreed. From a later vantage point, it appeared he was toying with the idea, but without telling anyone. Certainly he was intrigued by Republican offers of money to help finance his tour, though he cared nothing for the party itself. Certain, also, was the fact that he had failed to stop the New Deal as governor, and his only recourse was to attack it from a national platform. His paper, the *Statesman*, became an anti-Roosevelt sheet, and it marked May, 1935, as the time he unequivocally started his public fight against the New Deal, and his subsequent race for the United States Senate. Typical of his new rhetoric was a Fourth of July speech in which he said, "We are going back to the sanity and the common sense and the honesty of the old horse and buggy days." [9] He laughingly told his friend Henry Spurlin, "If I ever get to be president, the White House lawn will look like Telfair County with all the cotton I'll plant on it."

If Talmadge were to run for the White House he would need big money, the kind neither he nor his rural followers had, the kind of money represented by Georgia's major businessmen. Their support of Talmadge had been scattered until FDR's intrusions into the American economy became known. Georgia's business community and upper middle class reacted to the expansion of government into wage controls, agriculture, and banking by shifting into a rather solid support of Talmadge. He did not go to them so much as they went to him. This is evidenced by a May, 1935, letter written by Georgia Power Company's president, Preston Arkwright, about the governor. "He is perhaps lacking in the elegancies, politeness, and very sensitive refinements, but he is sound and strong, determined and courageous. . . . . I am a great admirer of his and I am for him." [10] Ironically, the rich moved to Gene as the poor left. The first step in his cautiously executed courtship of the presidency was the removal of Georgia's national Democratic chairman and strong Roosevelt backer, Major John S. Cohen. As editor of the powerful Atlanta *Journal*, Cohen had assured FDR a cooperative state party, and he could be counted on to give Georgia's delegates to FDR in 1936.

At the October, 1934, state convention, Gene had replaced Cohen with Hugh Howell, who had long wanted the post and could be counted on to run the party as Talmadge wished. The ouster had created a great deal of concern among Roosevelt's political advisers, and upon their insistence FDR had met in Warm Springs with Talmadge and Cohen to try and save Cohen's job. The meeting failed. Gene had already established himself as a New Deal opponent; and with the power and platform of his state's party under his control, he could project his opposition into the nation's press, the national party, and its 1936 convention.[11]

Shortly after the Warm Springs meeting, assistant to the president, Marvin McIntyre, had sent a memo to FDR saying, "Governor Talmadge wants to come down [to Warm Springs] and bring Hugh Howell with him Monday." Obviously Roosevelt was not in the mood for meeting Cohen's replacement. The note continued, "I don't know whether we can duck this or not, even though I don't see any reason for him to come." [12]

Another example of the cooling of the administration toward Talmadge had occurred in December of 1934, when Gene sent a letter to FDR saying that while the president was in Warm Springs he wanted to "have a little talk with no one present but you and me, before you left the state." An apologetic refusal was sent with an invitation to visit the White House at a later date.[13] The growing private split between the two men was broken wide open in 1935, not over price controls or welfare, but over federal road money.

In 1933, Talmadge had signed an agreement in Washington promising to reorganize Georgia's highway department so that it could competently manage the enormous sum of federal road funding it would receive. The almost comical meeting at the Ansley, where part of the money was divided evenly, exemplified the disorganized state of affairs in Georgia's road department. In January of 1935, the federal government notified highway board chairman, Gene Wilburn, that the funding would start with the construction of a bridge, to be called the Balls Ferry Bridge, over the Oconee River in rural eastern Georgia. It also reiterated the necessity for highway reorganization before the money could be dispersed. The legislature failed to respond, and Gene announced that the bridge was not going to be built because that area was so isolated it would be economically foolish. Furthermore, the federal government was not going to tell Georgia where roads would be built without first consulting with her.

Still in strong opposition to New Deal make-work programs, Talmadge fired off a very succinct letter to FDR in March, briefly giving his reasons for opposing the programs. He explained that his letter had been prompted by "our good old mutual friend John Whitley." Their friend "needed some extra hands to work on his farm. He offered them seventy-five cents a day. . . . He made this offer to men on relief, thinking they would be more interested in getting work. They stated however that they could not take any jobs, if they did they could not get back on the relief work. This is demoralizing the farm labor as you can see, and John says they are all going to have to quit farming if this continues." Gene concluded, "This condition is general all over the state." [14]

In April, Talmadge again stupidly made a public remark about the president's inability to walk around and talk to the common people since he couldn't even walk a two-by-four board. Though Talmadge supporters claimed the statement was well intentioned and taken out of context, many Georgians were repulsed by the brutishness it implied, and telegrams of regret and embarrassment literally poured into the White House.[15] One of the president's backers also mailed along a copy of a sheet titled, "Proposed Presidential Platform for Honorable Eugene Talmadge, Governor of Georgia." Fifteen planks were listed on the typed sheet, including such proposals as 2¢ postage, return of the gold standard, an end to the salaries of the president, all governors and judges, uniform utility and rail rates, removal of government from any controls over business and farm products, and amendments to the banking laws. The purported platform had been obtained by *Collier's* executive George Creel while he was on a visit to Georgia.[16] Whether it actually came from Talmadge is unknown, but it did add credence to the all-out fight Talmadge was waging against FDR. If there had been any doubts in anyone's mind about where the governor stood, they were erased on May 7, when Talmadge traveled to Washington to deliver a long and bitter attack on the New Deal and its creators. Carried over the CBS network, Gene called the National Recovery Act (NRA) "a mixture of Communism, frenzied financing, and wet nursing." [17]

The road controversy came to a head in July. Gene realized he had forced the administration into an embarrassing corner over their insistence on building the locally unpopular Balls Ferry Bridge, and he was stumping the state blaming the government for holding up Georgia's federal road money. It was a states' rights issue to Talmadge and one that could be projected nationally: could Washington build roads at will within a state, whether they were needed or not? Two of the president's close political advisers, Harlee Branch and Marvin McIntyre, had become increasingly concerned over the storm Gene was raising, and over the increasing pressure they were getting from Georgia's congressmen about releasing the funds. On July 11, Branch wrote McIntyre that he had come to two conclusions about the "Georgia road fund controversy." First, he said, "There is no need for haste." Secondly, he was afraid for the United States to take action against Talmadge; that would make it look like the United States had capitulated to him. "It would simply add to the political strength of Governor Talmadge and strengthen his hand in his fight on the President." Mr. Branch also continued to feel that Georgia should be made to comply with federal laws or lose the road funds. He concluded his letter saying that Talmadge was "adroitly misrepresenting the situation" over the bridge.[18]

On July 15, Gene's old classmate and friend John Monaghan arrived in Washington to meet quietly with United States road chief Thomas McDonald. Apparently Talmadge had sent him there to look for compromise. Failing to find any federal flexibility, Monaghan went over to the White House, this time as a secret emissary of Atlanta *Constitution* editor Clark Howell.

FDR had obtained the support of Georgia's two most powerful newspapermen, Howell and Cohen. The president's advisers, however, suspected that Howell was not above dual loyalties. Nevertheless, they had appointed him chairman of the Federal Aviation Committee, and he maintained a strong line of communication with advisers from his Washington office. Howell had also been a backer of Talmadge, though the relationship was straining badly because of the Talmadge-Roosevelt split. Trying to become peacemaker in the road fight, Howell had sent Monaghan to try to arrange a meeting. A note was sent into the president's office stating that Monaghan was outside and had said,

"Clark Howell has an idea that it is getting about time for Governor Talmadge to see the President and straighten out the whole situation. I am close to Talmadge personally and can get Gene in a conciliatory frame of mind better than anybody else." [19]

Monaghan returned to Atlanta with Roosevelt's agreement to meet on July 17 at the White House. Howell then called Gene, told him what had been done; he said the meeting had been set up without anyone else's knowledge, and the governor agreed to go. The meeting, as it turned out, played into Talmadge's hands and became an embarrassment to Branch and McIntyre if not to FDR. Talmadge received assurance that the funds would not be spent without Georgia's consultation, but road chief McDonald said that nothing would be spent until the Balls Ferry Bridge had been built—whether Georgia liked it or not. This was all the fiery governor needed. He emerged after the White House meeting in the lobby of the Mayflower Hotel and loudly berated Roosevelt before gathering newsmen as a "damned communist"; he proceeded to get into a shouting match with Howell, assuring everyone that it was "Mr. Howell's own arrangement and no notion of mine that I came," and that if Washington ignored Georgia's wishes and needs on the bridge construction, her highway department might as well move to that city and be a puppet. Branch, who witnessed the whole affair, memoed McIntyre that the visit had "intensified" the issue and gotten Georgia's congressmen "somewhat excited." [20] That was an understatement. The Georgia delegation, including her two senators, was shocked to find out through the press that Georgia's governor had met secretly with the president over such a hot issue as the road funds. Senators Russell and George made personal visits to the White House, and George suggested that the bridge be put aside and the rest of the funds released. The representatives sent a letter to FDR on July 22, urging a "speedy adjustment of differences" and asking the president to intervene and remove the bridge as a "condition precedent." [21]

During that period the White House was receiving conflicting reports from Georgia on the impact Talmadge was having and just what he was really up to. On July 16, James Farley sent a letter he had received from an H. T. McIntosh of Albany, Georgia, over to Harlee Branch. The letter read, "It is my candid opinion that not only has Governor Talmadge failed to draw away from the president the latter's friendly following in Georgia, but it has had the effect of breaking the Talmadge grip on the state." He concluded, "Counties in which Talmadge was practically invincible have turned away from him as a result of his bitter attacks on the president." [22]

Reflecting far more alarm, Clark Howell wrote Marvin McIntyre on July 30, that withholding the funds was a bad mistake. "This delay is very harmful and very threatening," Howell warned. In an interesting assessment, he wrote that "Talmadge has all but announced his candidacy" [23]—presumably for the presidency.

A third and conflicting report on the Georgia situation came through a letter from Atlanta Coca Cola executive J. L. Edmondson to Lawrence Robert, Jr., then assistant secretary of the treasury, a 1932 Talmadge-backer, and a successful Georgia businessman. Robert had sent Edmondson's letter to presidential assistant Marvin McIntyre. The letter stated: "There is a lot of feeling against the New Deal and since the Supreme Court and other court decisions have been rendered the New Deal has become more unpopular," but he concluded that the president would "have little or no opposition. It is well conceded that Governor Talmadge will not offer again for Governor, and as I see it his efforts will be to get himself in line so if there was a change in the administration he would try to secure Secretary [of Agriculture] Wallace's place. I think this belief is pretty well shared by all of his followers." [24]

It is obvious that no one agreed on exactly what Talmadge was up to, and it is probable that he didn't know himself. The one certainty was that Roosevelt's advisers were losing patience with Talmadge. On August 5, Branch wrote McIntyre that he thought Secretary Wallace, whose department was in charge of the national highway program, should demand that highway chairman Gene Wilburn reorganize Georgia's highway board in ten days or the federal government would sidestep both the governor and the highway board and disburse the money through county and city officials. Having moved from his position of July 11, Branch wrote, "I also think the time has come for us to consider the political situation in Georgia and would like the opportunity of going over this matter with the president. . . ." He said he thought Gene was planning on calling a presidential primary before anyone else in the nation in 1936, and he was concerned that it would be sprung so fast that Roosevelt supporters would not have time to organize. A quick Talmadge victory could look bad nationally. Branch advised that the "President's friends in Georgia be authorized to effect a state organization so as to combat any move that may be made by the Governor." To add weight to his request, Branch said that James

Farley had urged him to talk with the president to discuss the situation.[25]

On August 15, almost three weeks after he received their urgent message, Roosevelt wrote Georgia's congressmen a calming letter. He said the issue was "a simple one. The sole question is the adequacy of the state highway organization to provide plans and to supervise the expenditure" of these millions. He suggested that the Balls Ferry Bridge issue could be decided later. If the highway department would only organize satisfactorily, the money could be released.[26]

Sensing that he had backed the federal government down, Gene said he had every intention of reorganizing the highway department and now that the bridge would not be built, he would do so. The struggle had given him confidence in his ability to mount a national movement against the New Deal, and he assumed a degree of leadership by default when Huey Long was shot to death in September.

Although not known as a letter writer, Talmadge had communicated with Roosevelt often enough to broaden the split between them. One angry Talmadge note over the federal relief work program said, "I wouldn't plow nobody's mule for fifty cents a day when I could get $1.30 for pretending to work on a DITCH." Roosevelt fired back under Harry Hopkins' signature, "I take it you approve of paying farm labor forty to fifty cents a day. Somehow I can not get it into my head that wages on such a scale make possible a reasonable American standard of living." [27]

In early December, 1935, Gene announced he was going to New York to give a radio speech entitled "Georgia Answers Roosevelt." This sent Roosevelt Democrats in Georgia into a fury of protest. Gene was giving the appearance of speaking for all of Georgia's Democrats, and this speech caused the coalescing of a state movement to defeat him. On December 3, the Atlanta *Journal* noted that the speech would cause the Talmadge-FDR split to become wider and deeper. It was rumored that Gene's challenge had caused the national party to consider refusing him his seat on the national committee.

The speech was a carefully planned attempt to start a national movement to stop FDR; the movement was to emanate from a southern convention to be called the Grass Roots Convention. The purpose of the convention would be to create a ground-swell of support against the 1936 reelection of Roosevelt. The result would be to split the solid South away from the national Democratic party. Gene Talmadge would be the wedge. Its sponsor would be the Southern Committee to Uphold the Constitution. This whole affair read like a study in political frustration. The movers behind it were seventy-five-year-old John Henry Kirby, Texas oilman and old Long backer; the Reverend Gerald L. K. Smith, termed by the New York *Times* a "semi-fascist" nut;[28] and national organizer of the Share Our Wealth clubs, Thomas L. Dixon, author of *The Klansman*. Forty-one thousand dollars was coming from the Raskob and DuPont families, Al Smith backers; other monies and support were coming from Alfred Sloan of General Motors, from chairman of the board of Coca Cola, from the president of the big West Point Manufacturing Company, and from various major Georgia businessmen. None of these names were prominently mentioned, aside from those of Talmadge, Kirby, and Smith.[29] Though still claiming a vague allegiance to the Democrats, Gene was in December, 1935, joining in a strange coalition of conservative Republicans, liberal Democrats, and just plain dissident Independents. All had come together to fight Roosevelt, and they were putting their money on the one southern politician who was willing to stump the country trying to drum up support for the anti-Roosevelt drive—Gene Talmadge. Gene promised nothing but his energies and his commitment to their shared aversion to the New Deal. He cared little for the group or their parties beyond their contributions and support. No one was even hinting at Talmadge for president, yet it is difficult to believe that anyone else was expected to emerge from this coalition to run for that office. It can be said with certainty that the Republicans weren't going to back Gene, but they would probably have offered him an office if they won.

The big question with most Georgians was not whether Gene would run for president, but how he was going to finance his state in 1936. On December 27, he met with lawyers from the major Atlanta banks and found them solidly against allowing him to borrow money, unless the funds had been allocated by the legislature. They reported him visibly shaken by their refusal. The bankers had traditionally backed Gene, and he was disconcerted by their "turning" on him.[30] Without the ability to borrow, he had only unspent allocations and gas taxes for funds.

While the rest of the state enjoyed the New Year's holiday, Gene holed up at his office in the capitol. Reporters, hearing he was there, found him alone in the huge building, calm and reflective, smoking a thick cigar, wearing his hat, with one leg propped up on his desk. He said there was no need for alarm; "The State of Georgia is spinning like a top." Others saw it differently. State senator Frank Dennis issued a statement that day saying, "The old year carried out the state of

Georgia and ushered in the state of Talmadge." On January 4 Gene heard that a $2,500,000 surplus had accrued from 1935, and he resolved to divert these funds to pay state operation for January and part of February.[31] He received another bit of good news the next day when the Supreme Court ruled the AAA farm program unconstitutional. He praised the court for endorsing him and intensified plans for the January 29 Grass Roots Convention. Traveling to Washington in the middle of January, Gene was allowed his seat at the Jackson Day Dinner. FDR was the main speaker. Following his talk, a vote was taken in support of him for the 1936 nomination. Gene cast the lone nay vote. *Time* magazine described Gene: "By the coldness of his eye, and the hostile tilt of his cigar, national committeeman Eugene Talmadge . . . stood out like a skeleton at a feast." [32]

Preparations for the convention in Macon began gearing up in late January. On the twenty-first Gene asked the Federal Communications Commission (FCC) to let them "pipe" the convention to Mexico. The Roosevelt appointees on the FCC were afraid to grant approval, knowing that the convention would crucify their boss. The networks refused to carry it, the convention sponsors filed suit, and CBS later agreed to carry the convention.

When reporters asked Gene if he was running for president, he snapped, "It ain't so!" Then he added, "Any sane man would like to be president . . . and I am a sane man." To those who asked why he just didn't go ahead and declare, he answered, "Runnin' for president ain't like runnin' for sheriff." Then very truthfully he told reporters, "If you boys find out what I'm going to do let me know. I would like to know myself." [33]

There is a real possibility that Huey Long had been the presidential candidate many hoped would emerge from this convention, and his death had left a reluctant and apparently confused Talmadge trying to determine whether he wanted to take Long's place. Invitations to the convention had been sent to Democrats in seventeen southern and border states, printed in red, white, and blue with the flag of the Confederacy at the top. The Southern Committee to Uphold the Constitution was listed as sponsor.

Gene announced before leaving what he was seeking: "To save the nation and the Democratic party by blocking Mr. Roosevelt's renomination." He was not seeking a third party: "We will nominate a Democrat." Gene said he was sympathetic with New England Republicans, but "this is exclusively a southern fight within the party." [34]

Ten thousand persons were expected to jam the Macon auditorium, but arriving parties noticed at the outset a definite emptiness for a major convention to be in town. They knew they had come to the right place, however, when they entered the auditorium. A giant confederate flag hung heavily behind the podium, and an issue of *Woman's World* magazine could be found in every seat. On the cover was Eleanor Roosevelt talking with a Negro. Inside were articles on how FDR had appointed blacks to office. When the last delegate had taken his seat, there were thirty-five hundred people in the place; the majority were Georgia farmers.

The speeches attacked the New Deal as an ideological danger and an economic fallacy. Once the problem was stated, the solution evolved as no more than a call to return to an older America. The irony of this appeal was that FDR had only been in office four years and mass production had only been in high gear for about thirty years. Perhaps it was a tribute to the impact of the New Deal that the antagonists in Macon, Georgia, would talk about a long-departed older America that in fact existed only a handful of years before.

The platform committee, consisting of delegates from seventeen states, agreed that FDR was not a Democrat, that a return to strict constitutional construction should be made, and that Eugene Talmadge should be nominated for president on the Constitutional Jeffersonian Democratic ticket. The man of the hour, Eugene Talmadge, took the podium amid a roar of applause. Strange indeed was the appearance and performance of the man from Sugar Creek. Almost overdressed, pressed, neat, clean, he refused to remove his coat, or loosen his black necktie, or pop his suspenders, if indeed he even wore any. The speech was just as stilted. He called for a tax cut, local self-government, payment of the national debt, tariff reform, and an end to bureaucracy. "Rewrite the platform of 1932! Nominate men on the platform whose word is so good that the best test of it is to have the New Deal call *him* a liar." [35]

When he finished, a throng of overalled men rushed to carry him out on their shoulders and the meeting turned into chaos. Gene had not said whether he would or would not run, and incredibly the convention adjourned shortly thereafter with a very weak platform, no candidate, no final vote on a party, no plans for the future, and a lot of confusion about just what it had all been about. There had been no organization, no credentials committee; no one knew exactly who was a delegate. The result of it all was that the thirty-five hundred delegates who had come "united to oppose Negroes, the New Deal and . . . Karl Marx" dispersed never to be heard from again. The whole thing had been an enormous embarrassment. Meeting with his adviser Hugh Howell during the convention, Gene had agreed that the convention had failed before the first speech began. Gene's secret drive, if that's what it was, had floundered in the grass roots at Macon. Gene's old opponent, J. J. Brown, scoffed, "It was just a plain old fashioned crab grass convention." [36]

Though Gene realized that the convention had failed, he remained determined to carry his fight from "coast to coast." He had squelched all talk of the presidency and was apparently motivated more by commitment than by a quixotic search for office. Gene said in announcing his tour, "I talked to enough real farmers . . . yesterday to know how they feel about the New Deal. If you want to know which way the wind is blowing, don't ask a city man, get the opinion of a rube." [37] Hugh Howell was heard to say almost hopelessly, "We got to find some practical way to put Gene before the American people."

Trying to drum up some interest over the disaster, Gene called the Macon platform, "the greatest ever written in history." It was a melange of dogmas and fears, colored with a number of old southern political philosophies: states' rights, populism, isolationism, know nothingism, and supporting tariffs and more silver.[38] Timid as an assertive document, it was neither thorough nor analytical, but a gut platform written in anger, apparently more to blow off frustration than to propose viable solutions. It creaked dangerously with age; its planking had been trod over many times before. But it was Gene Talmadge. It was desperation in the face of an unstoppable history—a cry to the past to give help for the future. It represented an historical southern fear of "becoming 'indistinguishable,' of being submerged under a national steamroller," with nothing less at stake than "the survival of a southern heritage." [39]

Liberals descended on Gene, saying he "rose to power entirely on the ground swell of bigotry and ignorance." His advisers were described as a "collection of a dozen dreary heels—shabby, inept, corrupt, and Ku Klux-minded." One reporter said, "Talmadge is the most brazen and cheapest of these post-war demagogues, and hence the most transparent." Another wrote, "Talmadge is no Hitler. But he is a symptom which should be disturbing." [40]

Roosevelt Democrats in Georgia, thinking Gene was on the verge of political destruction, began pressuring state democratic chairman Hugh Howell to call a presidential primary that would pit Gene against FDR. Howell, with good judgment, refused them.

12

Treasurer
Talmadge

Anticipating the day when the state's money would run out, Gene appointed Samuel D. Hewlett his lawyer on February 5. He had drawn a rough draft of an executive proclamation explaining how he planned to handle the situation. His ability to get Treasurer Hamilton to sign checks on unappropriated money would be essential to the success of his plan. On February 10 he asked Attorney General Yeomans to read the rough draft and give an opinion on the same day; Yeomans stated that both the treasurer and the comptroller should issue checks on warrants the governor issued.[1] The opinion seemed to close one eye to a constitutional limitation of the ways the governor might draw money, that is, the provision which stated: "No money shall be drawn from the Treasury except by appropriations made by law." [2] Gene had said he could stretch that to include monies appropriated in 1933, but which had not been paid in full. He said, "These appropriations have never been repealed, altered, or modified, but remain in full force and effect." [3] He reasoned that they had not "lapsed" because they had not been placed in a department budget. The revenues would make further legislative action unnecessary; in other words he had found a way to avoid calling the legislature back.

In addition to these monies Gene felt he could get at the constant tax revenues collected by various departments on licenses, cigarettes, gasoline, and numerous other goods and services. He suggested that the departments simply keep these monies and never turn them over to the treasury; or he himself could take money directly from the departments, or even from the sources, and thereby avoid the treasury. Gene figured he could run the state with the old money plus the tax collections, and Yeomans agreed that he could ask for and get checks on these monies. Armed with this endorsement, Gene had the executive proclamation typed up.

The crisis in state financing made its long-awaited appearance on

February 13. Several departments reported that they were running out of money. Without consulting Talmadge, Hamilton ordered the various state departments to start turning over their collections to him. This was exactly what the governor had not wanted. Hamilton's order initiated meetings between Gene and Hamilton—their offices were only steps apart in the capitol. Though their relationship had never been intimate, it had been friendly, but the cordiality quickly crumbled under the rising pressure of events. Hamilton felt Gene was tinkering with the integrity of the state constitution, and Gene quickly found out he was dealing with a man of iron determination and conviction. They were obviously headed for a showdown. Gene reconsidered his position on Sunday, February 16, and on Monday moved to exert his powers. On the seventeenth he issued a proclamation fixing state appropriations for 1936—the budget for state government. He had taken over the government's disbursements. He said appropriations would be the same as those of 1935, not a penny more; with a bit of circumlocutory reasoning he was saying that because these amounts had been appropriated before the legislature, the same amounts were approved indefinitely. His source of revenue would be the unspent monies of that year, plus the collections of the state departments.

The constitution had said he could only spend appropriated money —and that was what he was doing, even if that money was two years old; and by letting the departments keep their collected monies, he would never have to handle it. All eyes then turned to the treasurer and comptroller for their reactions. Both men said they would give their answers in a few days. Privately Gene was meeting with both men in the capitol in long and heated arguments over their refusal to cooperate. Both men had told him earlier, after reading the proclamation, that they would not accept it. Gene finally ended the discussions by telling Hamilton. "There ain't no point arguing any more. We've both made up our minds." [4] When the talking stopped, Hamilton knew that action would follow soon.

Both men figured Gene would fire them and then attempt to get the cash the state kept in banks around the state. If the governor ever physically got hold of the millions, only a revolt would have gotten it back. Harrison had heard that Talmadge was going to test him immediately by getting the state school superintendent and the warden at the Milledgeville mental institution to make requests for money to run their departments. Gene would then issue warrants based on the requests, thereby calling for Hamilton to issue checks. If he refused to do so, Gene would claim the treasurer was denying funds to teachers and the insane—difficult accusations for the treasurer to explain away without losing public support.

On hearing of the plans, Hamilton contacted school superintendent M. D. Collins and found him to be against Gene's plans, but confused about what to do when Gene called him. Hamilton reminded Collins that the governor had to have the superintendent's signature on the request before a warrant could be issued. Hamilton advised Collins to go into hiding and made very secret arrangements for him in an Atlanta hotel. Talmadge was angry and dismayed when he couldn't find Collins. With the governor temporarily stymied, Hamilton made plans to get the state's money out of the governor's reach. He knew he had only a few days before announcing his intentions, and he used his time judiciously. He called Senator Walter F. George and asked him to have Roosevelt order the Federal Reserve in Atlanta to reserve space for the collateral bonds Hamilton held on the state depositories. Possession of the bonds amounted to a crown of authority, for unless they were in the physical possession of the state, no cash could be exchanged between state and bank. If the bonds were locked in federal vaults, Gene couldn't touch them. FDR agreed to the request, and the United States government joined forces against Gene.

Comptroller Harrison was an old man and had been ill. He told Hamilton that he could not physically stand against the oncoming Talmadge and that if asked to leave office, he would have to comply even though he bitterly opposed what he considered the gross illegality of Gene's plans. Hamilton would have to go it alone. Accepting this, the treasurer carefully drilled his staff on what to do in the event he was thrown out of office. They were to remove all collateral bonds and cash from the state vaults, set the eighty-hour time lock on the empty vault, and run for the federal reserve and the local banks, where they were to deposit both bonds and cash. Speed was essential because of the closeness of the treasurer's and the governor's offices.

With everyone steeled for battle and Gene wondering where in the world M. D. Collins was, Harrison and Hamilton on February 20 publicly announced that they would sign no checks for the governor under his proclamation. They insisted that the proclamation was voided by the "grandfather clause," which voided old unspent appropriations. New appropriations, they said, had to be made by the last legislature. Claiming they stood on constitutional grounds, they said the question at issue was "whether the constitution of Georgia was a living document, or a worthless piece of paper." [5] Throughout that day, Gene sent his secretary, Carlton Mobley, back and forth to the two finance offices, trying to get them to sign a warrant for funds for the board of control. Mobley was consistently refused.

Washington's birthday closed the capitol on February 22 and stilled the guns. The Atlanta *Constitution* headlined that day: "The Governor's Illegal Attempt at Dictatorship." The Atlanta press was hard after the governor.

On the twenty-fourth Gene made his move. "It appears from trustworthy information," he wrote in an executive order, "that the comptroller general, William B. Harrison, grossly neglects his duties, and is guilty of conduct plainly violative of his duties, and demeans himself in office to the hazard of the public funds and credit of the state." [6] Harrison was therefore released from his duties. In his place Gene appointed G. B. Carreker. An identical order was delivered to Hamilton, and J. B. "Tobe" Daniel was appointed treasurer.

Both men sent word that they would have to be physically thrown out of office. The tactic was designed to make Gene appear militaristic —a bully, a dictator who ruled not by law but by force. Since Gene's martial-law order from September, 1934, was still in effect, he had the national guard at his disposal. Upon hearing that the men would not leave, he ordered his adjutant general, Lindley Camp, who had been waiting for this, to take a couple of plain clothesmen and get Harrison out of his office. It was still early morning. Camp was not a violent man, and he asked Harrison politely but firmly to leave. "You're no longer comptroller, and you will have to leave this office," Camp said. Harrison, seated behind his desk, looked disappointed that no armed force had shown up. He asked, "Where are the soldiers?" Camp leaned long over the desk and drawled, "I'm some soldiers!" Harrison got up and quietly left.

Gene then told his aide Henry Spurlin, "George won't open the safe, so go over there and tell him he's fired and to get out." Spurlin said, "I went in and found Hamilton sitting at his desk, and I told him he would have to leave his office at once. He pulled a large pistol out and placed it on the desk, and said, 'I am constitutionally elected to this office, and I have the means to protect it.' I turned around and went back across the hall to the governor's office and told him that George had a big pistol on his desk and was refusing to leave. Gene blew up, and started yelling at the top of his lungs, 'Lindley, Lindley, Lindley!' About that time the adjutant general came walking through the door, and said, 'Keep quiet, governor, I heard you all the way across the street.' " [7]

At 4:00 P.M., Camp and six men entered Hamilton's office, lifted him from his chair, and carried him out of the capitol to the street. As they carried him out he yelled to his assistants who dashed from the office with the treasury's cash and bonds. Everyone thought the men were fleeing in fear. Hamilton then wired the banks and said that he was still the legal treasurer, that he was holding the collateral bonds, and that the banks would be liable for any money they paid out. He would sell their bonds if they signed any checks. He also asked the United States Post Office not to send any mail directed to the treasurer to Daniel, and it complied. [8]

It had been a long and busy day in the state government, a day which ended in total confusion about who controlled what. Hamilton was seen just before dark tacking his name plate and title on a door across town, and Gene prepared to move on the state vaults.

Tobe Daniel made a routine visit to the vaults on February 25 and found them locked and sealed with an eighty-hour limit. Furious, Gene ordered locksmiths to open them. They said nothing but gas torches would open them; Gene then ordered the locks burned open. [9] The Atlanta *Constitution* wrote that day, "God save the state." The *Journal* that night condemned the governor's action, saying the men had been "ruthlessly thrown out" under "absurd pretexts." But thrown out they were, and if Gene was left standing with an empty vault, he at least had his own men guarding it. The scene of the men furiously working to open an empty safe left the governor with a red face, and he vowed to move hard on Hamilton to get back the money.

Gene's first order of business was to send his new man out for money, but he received a stunning shock when Daniel presented a $100,000 check to the Fulton National Bank; though it held $900,000 in state funds, the bank refused to cash the check. When Daniel returned to the capitol without the $100,000, Gene wrote a letter to Fulton National Bank President Ryburn Clay, telling him the bank would have to pay 7 percent interest on the $895,199.69 it held. He also said that his executive secretary, Carlton Mobley, was now authorized to accept the money and bring it back to the capitol if the delivery to Daniel bothered the bank. When young Mobley handed the letter to Clay on February 26, the prominent banker jovially asked, "What are you going to do with the money if I give it to you?" Mobley, dead serious, answered, "I'm going to take it and put it in the Treasury." The banker smiled and said he could not release the funds. In a return letter Clay said, "The problem of state deposits in this present situation has been the subject of long and anxious discussion" by clearing-house banks. It was the "unanimous opinion of the counsel of all the clearing house banks that they can not feel entirely safe" in giving the state its money "until there has been some judicial determination." [10]

Hamilton's strategy had worked. Gene exploded in anger, turning his fury erroneously on the legislature and the federal government. He said a clique in the House of Representatives had hatched the plot a year earlier in Washington, trying to force the state to call an extra session to drain off money and force Gene to raise taxes. He said the mess was "deliberately brought on by the New Deal."

Gene received another unexpected blow on February 26, when Attorney General Yeomans, who had been away sick, suddenly let it be known that he had never ruled in favor of what Gene was doing and that he was furious with Gene for saying that he had. Simultaneously, Talmadge was faced with the fact that Georgia's constitution required that the treasurer be bonded before he could assume office. But no bonding company in the state would touch Daniel. They were as afraid of the situation as the banks were. They didn't know Tobe Daniel, and if he had run off with the state money, they would have been liable. A frantic search of the nation for someone to back the bond then ensued, with calls going out all over from the capitol. There was no getting around it: Daniel had to be bonded, and money had to be found to back the bond. Gene turned to his friend John Whitley for help, and Whitley located the Western Casualty and Insurance Company in Fort Scott, Kansas, which was willing to go $300,000, if money could be found to back it. Whitley actually went to Fort Scott and negotiated the matter. Gene asked that he and Gene Wilburn, chairman of the highway board, put up the money. Wilburn was known as the tightest man in the state government and was given much credit for enabling Gene to keep his economic promises. Gene and Whitley used to laugh and joke about what a skinflint he was. And when Talmadge went across the street to the highway building to ask his friend to put up $65,000 of the money, Wilburn stalled and whined and mumbled, putting up every argument he could think of. Gene later laughed, "I never saw a man go to the bathroom so many times in such a short period of time." But finally Wilburn agreed to put up the money. There was no problem getting the rest from Whitley.[11]

The Atlanta *Constitution* editorialized on February 27 that Georgia was in a condition of confusion and chaos. The next day it was reported that as many as fifty legislators had signed a petition agreeing to attend a special session whether the governor called it or not. They would, in effect, wrest control from him. There was also the inevitable talk of impeachment, only this time there was reason to believe it. State senator Allen Chappel said the governor was mentally incapable.[12] And a survey of newspapers from across the state reflected the shock and repulsion many felt for this latest example of Talmadge enforcing his will. The Albany *Herald* said that Gene had invoked "lynch law." The Cordele *Dispatch* worried: "He is getting to be worse than Hitler or Mussolini." The Columbus *Inquirer* scathed that he is a "paper-mache dictator" and "a sort of amusing political clown who slipped into the governor's office during the storm of depression." The Athens *Banner Herald* called his actions "a disgraceful spectacle," and the Macon *Evening News* termed it "this impudent usurpation." The Brunswick *News* asked bitterly how long Georgia would have to be "misruled by this crazed governor who suffers hallucinations of grandeur and imaginary greatness?" [13]

Gene's answer was that it was all a political plot to keep him off the campaign trail. "This invasion of states' rights can hold me in Georgia; but the New Deal is going to be defeated this year." [14] The fires of his critics were further fueled when it was heard that $17 million in United States road funds were being held up because Gene had taken $2 million in earmarked road funds and spent it elsewhere. The laws said that interdepartmental diversion of funds could only take place if the money were going to teachers. On February 29 the *Constitution* reported that Gene had quietly taken $3 million in highway money to pay state bills. On February 29 the Atlanta Post Office was ordered by its superiors to start sending Daniel and Carreker their mail. Gene's suit to have that done was dropped. On that same day, it was reported that Gene had fired board of regents chairman Marion Smith, because he learned that Smith was representing Hamilton and the Fulton National Bank as attorney.

At 11:00 A.M. on March 1, Gene went before a meeting of the clearing-house banks and asked the officials to release the state's money. It was the kind of request he did not like to make, particularly since they refused him. He stormed out, saying he would scorch the bankers. His plan was to write checks to pay for school bills; then if the bankers refused to honor them, public pressure would be directed away from Gene. It didn't work.[15]

The Atlanta *Journal* came out that day with a long list of state papers which were highly critical of the governor. Of forty-four papers sampled, thirty-seven were critical, angry and uncompromising. The Gainesville *Eagle* wrote, "He has out herolded Herod in a despotic dictatorial action that transcends the throttling of Louisiana by . . . Huey P. Long." The Newnan *Herald* wrote, "We're getting the kind of government we asked for when we elected the wild man from Telfair." And the Donaldsonville *News* commented, "The more rope given a jackass, the more he kicks, cuts up and brays."

Bad news appeared to be coming in avalanches on March 1. A news story from the farming community of Barnesville said that ninety-two names were signed to a petition in less than an hour calling for Gene's impeachment. The story said that only three people refused to sign.

It is doubtful that Gene would have read the many attacks on him had they not been reprinted in the two big Atlanta papers, the only ones he read regularly and thoroughly. His office received few others, since most newspapers in Georgia at that time confined their reporting to church and social news and crop information. The Atlanta *Journal* and the *Constitution* were without parallel for their influence and their political reporting. They were *must* reading, and no man read them more carefully than did Gene.

Carlton Mobley spent March 2 scurrying over town delivering letters to the major banks, demanding 7 percent interest on money they refused to relinquish. To those who worriedly asked, Mobley said the state of martial law which had never been voided since September 14, 1935, had been dissolved. This was announced to dampen the cries that military rule was again impending. Gene's office was beseeched by business leaders worried over what the crisis would do to the economy. They asked for a special session. Gene heard that afternoon that some of Georgia's congressmen were asking Washington to circumvent the governor by paying road funds directly to the counties. That night George Hamilton capped a miserable day for Talmadge by promising to "fight to the last to see that the law shall rule and not a tyrannical despot who has gone mad with egotism." [16]

With Gene having "fired" those banks which held state money and refused to turn it over, an impasse had been reached. Attorneys for the banks sought to break out of it by asking the Fulton Superior Court to rule which treasurer could legally sign state checks. Three judges agreed to hear the case the following Saturday morning. [17] The next day

Tobe Daniel brought suit against Hamilton in a lower court to force release of the collateral bonds. No one yet knew where they were.[18]

To add to the pressure, Roosevelt supporters were pressing state Democratic chairman Howell to call a presidential primary. Howell claimed he knew of no one who wanted to run. Marion Allen, Roosevelt's chief supporter and organizer in Georgia, was trying to use a primary to embarrass Gene during the money crisis and thereby take over the state party. Gene and Howell knew this and refused Allen. The reports coming in from straw votes indicated that Howell was correct in his refusal. From Seminole County, where Gene had received 882 votes to his opponents' 109 in 1934, Roosevelt outpolled him 661 to 120. Seminole voters were quoted as saying they were "through with gourds and red suspenders." In Harris County, which Gene had won 423 to 96 in 1934, he lost to Roosevelt in the straw vote—991 to 34, a 17 to 1 ratio. And in Whitfield County, Gene got only .02 percent of the vote for president.[19]

Practically every friend and adviser urged Gene to forget his feud with Roosevelt. The straw votes were a confidence-draining factor. But characteristically Gene shrugged the votes off, saying they were given without notice and to known Roosevelt supporters. He had "heard from some of the boys" that they didn't know a vote was being taken until the voting was over. He termed it desperate tactics and said he would not allow his name to be placed on any county primary. Gene had a point about the tactics used, but the total one-sidedness of the votes in former Talmadge strongholds gave credence to those Georgians who had been saying the state wanted Roosevelt more than it wanted Talmadge. The irony of it was that those who seemed most to want FDR for president, also wanted Talmadge for governor. This was partially true because of the fact that Gene's constituency was the group receiving most of the benefits of the New Deal.

The Atlanta press was less interested in primaries than in breaking up the financial mess. The *Constitution*'s editor, Clark Howell, discreetly asked Talmadge's man Hugh Howell (no kin) to drop by his office. The editor told Howell that he ran the most powerful newspaper in Georgia, one that was looked to for direction by the state's other papers, and that he could dictate in a fashion what the papers wrote. Clark Howell also said that if Gene would call a special session, he would guarantee a written promise by a large number of legislators that they would leave the session after having passed an appropriation bill. If Gene would do this, the *Constitution* would stop attacking him and publish a nice editorial. This would encourage other papers to do the same, and Gene would emerge from the mess in good standing. The editor said further that if Gene refused to call the session the *Constitution* would do all in its power to see that he was impeached.[20] Gene exploded at hearing the offer, and he tried to embarrass Howell by giving the episode wide publicity. Gene answered, "Your threat to impeach me has fallen on deaf ears." Howell replied that if Gene was muleheaded enough not to call the session he *should* be impeached.[21]

Talmadge was crushed on March 14, when the court ruled that neither Hamilton nor Daniel could sign checks on money that had not been appropriated. They did not rule which man was legal treasurer but offered to do so.[22] Gene said he would ignore some of the order and pay teachers. To his supporters he said, "You boys out in the country be not disturbed. The steel had to hit the rock. You are going to see some sparks fly." [23] He would appeal.

Secret meetings by members of the legislature were reported all over Georgia as everyone sought a solution. Out of these meetings a petition emerged, signed by a majority of the senate. The petition pleaded for a session and said the legislators were not trying to coerce the governor. But Gene responded with equal formality, saying there was no emergency and thus no reason to call them back. "Georgia has the money," he asserted; then he praised the house and senate and extended to "everyone of you an invitation to come out to the mansion and let's eat some ham." [24]

The oil companies told the governor on March 18 they would stop their monthly tax payments of one million dollars unless Gene removed any liability from them for what happened to the money. He angrily agreed to do so. The next day Hamilton asked the courts to adjudge him treasurer, and the state's labor leaders sought an injunction against Daniel. On March 23 the state revenue commissioner suddenly quit, and Gene made his new comptroller take on the extra duties. When Carreker tried to write a check on the gas money, Rome judge Claude Porter enjoined any monies being paid to Carreker. The Atlanta *Journal* wrote dismally that things were going from bad to worse.[25]

Gene apparently agreed with the press. By the end of that week he had bought radio time to defend his actions and explain his reasons for fighting FDR. On the air he said he was no dictator, but that he had had no alternative but to run the state's finances in order to feed the sick and insane. To those who had called his northern speaking tour a quest for the presidency he said, "Georgia is an integral part of this Union" and "wishes to share the responsibilities and duties" of being a member. Justifying his trips, he said, "Georgia feels that she can help the Union in formulating policies." He specifically felt that he "owed it to my country to resist certain tax-mad policies" and "owed it to the Democratic party to make a fight for our national platform." He gave himself credit for being the only man who had stuck by that platform.

The long financial crisis reached a sudden and dramatic conclusion on April 11. Four of the six members of the Georgia Supreme Court disqualified themselves from the case the banks had brought against Treasurer Daniel. The four said they had affiliations with the banks and could not judge on the case. This came as a windfall decision for the hard-pressed governor, because it was his responsibility to name replacements for the disqualified judges on the court. Two days later Gene put four of his trusted friends in, and it was all over but the judgments which would come on May 9.

Gene was also enjoying a temporary victory over Roosevelt Democrats who were trying to get the party to call a primary. The executive committee met on April 15, and FDR's people were routed. Gene said he wanted no more presidential primaries with his name on the list; thus the committee resolved that no man could run in a primary who did not come forth in person and sign his name. This was done "to protect Talmadge from being entered . . . by his enemies." They also tacked on a $10,000 entrance fee. If no one entered the primary which was then set for June 4, Gene and Howell could name Georgia's delegates to the national convention. Obviously a tool for Talmadge strategy, the committee met again on April 28 and announced that entries for state races that year would be accepted up until 11:30 on the morning of July 4. This meant that Gene could delay his decision on which office he would seek until after the national presidential primaries. He hinted that he was considering running as a favorite son if FDR received a low vote in that race. This delayed qualification date also caused some embarrassment to Talmadge politicians who were eager to run for the senate or for governor, depending on which office Gene didn't run for. But they could not declare themselves until he did so without risking running against him. It also confused Gene's enemies who either did or did not want to run against him, but who didn't know which, if any, office he would seek. A condition of chaos resulted while Gene relaxed. Talmadge had followed the old Georgia tradition of using the state's only party to the advantage of the incumbents. The one-party system had become a license for selfish action long before Talmadge came along. Actually, Georgia's one party had been split into two by the emergence of a strong federal government, and the battle was announced on April 29 when Marion Allen reported that FDR would enter the June primary. This meant that the only way Gene could retain control was by entering the primary against Roosevelt; and with reports coming in daily indicating a national Roosevelt landslide, Gene was increasingly reluctant to do that.

The conclusion to the financial crisis, which had for all purposes ended with the appointment of the new judges, came on May 9. In a five-to-one decision, the court upheld Gene in his suspension of Hamilton and Harrison and declared Daniel the legal treasurer. The court said the suspension was subject to the review of the legislature and until that could be done, Daniel should remain in office.[26] The decision caused the release of federal road funds and the cashing of checks by the Atlanta banks; and Hamilton returned the collateral bonds to the state. Talmadge supporters were ecstatic. His secretary Carlton Mobley said later, "The man was unbelievable. We all used to worry like hell when he'd get into these situations. There would seem no possible way he could come out on top. And then at the darkest moment, he would land on his feet." [27]

13

Gene and Junior

The Telfair *Enterprise*, which had managed to maintain some journalistic integrity despite Gene's influence, reported a simple poll taken in May, which, as these things sometimes do, proved uncannily prophetic. Five farmers standing around a country store had been asked whether they would have Gene or Roosevelt for president. Four answered Roosevelt. But when asked who in Georgia they preferred for governor all five said Gene. The paper concluded: "They seem to think that he is their governor and that is where he ought to stay." [1] The consciousness of the Talmadge supporter could not project him beyond the state's boundaries. Perhaps he had oversold his "Savior of Georgia" image.

Talmadge lost control of the state Democratic party on May 15, when the entries for the presidential primary closed and the only name on the list was Franklin Roosevelt. This meant there would be no primary. FDR had won by default. Gene quietly left town that day for Sugar Creek. But Marion Allen was spoiling for the last word. He called Gene a coward: "After creating the issue, Talmadge could not muster the courage to test it before the Democrats of Georgia." With delight and much truth Allen proclaimed, "Governor Talmadge has acknowledged his first political defeat." Allen proceeded to move the state party back into the national Democratic fold. What had seemed a year-long camouflaged chase after the presidency came to a sputtering end. Ed Rivers, preparing for his governor's campaign, said of Gene, "He has deserted the people who put him in office; he has knifed his own friends in the back; he has deserted his own party." [2]

Georgia's Democrats, already suffering from schizophrenia, split themselves a third time—into a small group called "free Democrats." Intellectuals led by former university chancellor Phillip Weltner, their aim was to create a movement against Talmadge, but not necessarily on the basis of a pro-Roosevelt stand. Their uniqueness was their detachment from political allegiances and their commitment to conscience. The political pros also saw them as unique in their naivete in thinking that they could draw supporters from the Talmadge power base whose lifestyle had generally been the antithesis of the Weltner group's. They held a mini-convention in Macon and asked the respected Judge Blanton Fortson to be their candidate for governor. Their formula for success was an absurd request that all opposed to Talmadge unite behind Fortson, a man with no political base. Ed Rivers blew their plans all to hell a few days later by announcing his candidacy, as did three other men. Gene cast a bemused eye on the Weltner movement. "Something funny about this primary that was held in Macon— and the funny part does not do the people any good." [3] The movement never really moved, though it did fractionalize the party a bit more.

On Wednesday, June 17, the state executive committee met at the Ansley to choose Roosevelt delegates for the national convention and to witness the political death of Gene Talmadge. Not to be upstaged, the corpse came striding briskly through the lobby, grinning broadly, shaking hands and slapping backs. As he moved through the crowded lobby one man refused to shake his hand, saying sullenly he didn't want to meet any new acquaintances that day. The explosive Talmadge called the refusal an insult and ordered the man to remove his glasses. Gene's instant fury betrayed his real feelings over the meeting. A melee ensued between the man and Gene's entourage, scattering people over the lobby. Gene was pushed away from the scuffling and it ended quickly. He then entered the meeting to present news only slightly more shocking than the lobby battle. He would give his complete support to Roosevelt. The eighty-four delegates sat loose-jawed as he said, "I will support whatever candidates and platform are adopted at Philadelphia. I am a party man. I stand for the principles of my party. My fight has been within the Democratic party, and it is there I intend to stay." [4]

Some there believed him; those better acquainted with him knew that he didn't mean a word he said, but they also knew him to be unusually flexible and munificent to his enemies when he had been defeated. He did not dwell on a loss; however, the smokescreen politics he was playing that day appeared to be more making up with old enemies than resignation or defeat. Suspicions were proven correct on June 22, when he flip-flopped back to his old anti-Roosevelt stand. He shouted after the deaf ears of delegates as they left for Philadelphia, "I think the party would make its greatest mistake to nominate Roosevelt." [5]

Unknown to the public, an embarrassing and stubborn battle was being waged between Gene and one of his oldest supporters, Hugh Howell. Howell knew that Gene had decided to run for the senate, and he wanted to run for governor as Gene's handpicked man. He felt with a great degree of truth that Gene owed him at least a hearing. As the July 4 qualifying deadline neared, Gene offered no support to the hint-dropping Howell. This forced the lawyer to try and force Gene's hand by publicly saying on June 21, "If the people should call me to succeed Gene Talmadge, I shall preserve these principles of Democratic government that he and I fought shoulder to shoulder to maintain." [6] Talmadge said nothing, but he did get mad as hell, because he had no intention of backing Howell. He was forced to say this to the man's face when Howell, unable to continue the cat and mouse game, asked Gene if he would back him.

Howell couldn't believe the refusal and asked why not. Gene said only that he was backing his close friend Charles Redwine. The two argued, and Howell listed the many loyal jobs he had performed for the Talmadge career; but Gene was adamant. Deeply hurt, Howell vowed, "You'll live to regret this, Gene." [7] Gene would say very little of the matter publicly, but intimated to friends that he thought Howell was too young and inexperienced to be governor and that he also seemed unable to say no. The truth was closer to Gene's owing Redwine more and being a better personal friend of the legislator.[8] Howell was forced into the humiliating position of having to remain publicly within the Talmadge circle or be defeated by Gene if he tried to run against his wishes. Still wanting office, he stubbornly hung onto the facade of friendship.

With FDR's renomination on the twenty-sixth, politics returned to the state, and Gene was again at center stage. Reports from McRae predicted another huge Talmadge kickoff. Two hundred hogs, fifteen cows, five hundred chickens, fifty lamb, and four thousand gallons of Brunswick stew were being prepared for the mass turnout, as the Talmadge spectacular would once again launch the man into another hell-for-leather roadshow. Lamar Murdaugh felt moved to warn Gene about running against Russell. "It's Dick's job, Gene; he's there and he's doing a good job. There's no reason to run against him." [9] A lot of Gene's friends agreed, but the commitment had been made. He had spent a year chasing all over the North and all over his own state establishing his platform and his reasons for seeking office in Washington.

And the office held by Richard (Junior) Russell was the only open door through which he could pass. There was no turning back.

The roads to McRae had been crowded all day Friday, July 3, and the campsites and rooms for rent had gone quickly. The Barbecue King had been at work since Thursday, slaughtering and cleaning and preparing the donated animals. All day Friday and into the night the coals and logs hissed at the rivers of grease that splattered into their slow, unrelenting heat. Twenty-three extra hogs and five hundred extra chickens were killed when word came that all of Georgia appeared to be on the move to McRae. Friday night a supper was held for Gene and Mitt, with two hundred guests out on the Ocmulgee at a clubhouse; it was a big supper—informal and festive—with lots of tea, and some whiskey outside by the cars.[10]

July 4 dawned clear, camps broke, and hotel windows were sleepily peered out of; thousands of women awakened thousands of husbands and children, brushed and scrubbed them, cooked them eggs and grits and ham and gravy and biscuits, packed apples and fruit and drew jugs of water, climbed in the car, or aboard the wagon, and headed for one of the best orchestrated political rallies of any era. They arrived over the flat south Georgia dirt roads to a tight mass of white-shirted men and formally dressed women who were standing talking, gossiping, laughing, arguing, and sometimes drinking in a pine grove in a park in the middle of McRae. Fiddlin' John Carson was picking his cacophonous sounds that were carried by three large black speakers thrust rudely above the pine planking and the bunting the ladies of McRae had so carefully tacked onto the soft pine. For once Gene arrived early for a speech, because of the 11:30 qualifying; he even brought the qualifying committee from the secretary of state's office. He mounted the platform in a white suit split by a red tie, red handkerchief in the coat pocket, and blazing red suspenders. Fiddlin' John struck up a furious rendition of "Hot Times in Georgia," and the crowd gave a tumultuous roar for their man. The platform was jammed with hopefuls, notables, and local politicians all trying to get close to the searing Talmadge magic.

Talmadge opened, as he always did, by patting himself on the back over his accomplishments. He said the people had been trying to get him to run for governor because "somehow they believe what I tell them. Somehow they know I feel their troubles." He then cried, "I am not a candidate for governor!" Twirling dramatically he thrust his finger at Charles Redwine preening behind him and shouted, "Here he is!"

Redwine rose to a roar and gave his acceptance speech which was distinguished for its unnoteworthiness. His four-plank platform was blatant Talmadge: (1) work for states' rights; (2) anti-union; (3) ratification of Gene's manipulations of treasury; and (4) continuation of Talmadge economic principles. Like a well-trained boy he kept his remarks brief, then turned the show back to Gene, who bellowed, "I want to go to the United States Senate and protect Georgia!" He then gave one of the longer platforms of his career. Typically the planks included: (1) creation of a law to prevent a national debt; (2) stopping the issuance of federal bonds; (3) cutting the national budget to under one billion dollars; (4) strict constitutional construction; (5) removing "every cabinet officer who endeavors to change our form of government"; (6) limiting taxation power to Congress and not bureaus; (7) reducing the price of a stamp from three cents to two cents; (8) taking government out of competition and letting it act only as referee. With a touch of hypocrisy, Gene then demanded that the federal government give Georgia every penny it had coming to it under the New Deal.[11]

Ceremoniously, Talmadge put his red suspenders on the man he had chosen to succeed him as governor. The galluses were no sword or crown, but they were just as good for annointing the gee-haw boys. Those suspicious that Talmadge had become a living political party were interested to see if voter loyalty could now be so manipulated. Could Gene project his authority onto others?

From Gainesville on the same day Ed Rivers opened with the most liberal platform in Georgia history; he called it a little New Deal. Rivers had latched onto Roosevelt's coattails with fingers, teeth, and toes, promising total emulation of the big New Deal.

Finding out definitely that Gene was going after his office, Russell had bought radio time, to begin as soon as Gene's announcement was over. His speech proved a timid, off-target rebuttal, chiding Talmadge for his courtship of the Republicans—"an abortive and ridiculous campaign"—and exposing Gene's quixotic effort to be someone's favorite son against Roosevelt. But it was a start and the campaign was off. Russell later said of the 1936 race: "The Talmadge campaign was the bitterest I was ever in. It was a very bitter campaign. It tore the state to pieces; it had brothers stop speaking to brothers, and partners dissolving partnerships." Russell said he bought the radio time to "denounce him for having used the committee that way; and the campaign got off on that foot and it went from there in all directions. It was a very hard campaign." [12]

When Roosevelt's man Marion Allen announced that he was managing Russell's campaign, Gene said that he would not only not have a manager, he would have no headquarters. He was running alone, which seemed stupid when one realized that it wasn't Old Gene against a field but Gene against the state and national Democratic parties: organization, big money, machines and deals. But Talmadge, as supremely confident as ever, loved the martyrdom of it all. Me against them. It was his game.

So fearsome had the Talmadge legend of campaign mastery become that the Russell staff came into the race scared and tight. Gene stirred men's souls and left them howling like dogs. Russell appealed to their reason and left them in quiet discussion. Neat, clean cut, respectable Dick—the kind of man you might think Gene would eat alive. The Russell staff soon concluded they would play up Dick's cooperation with the New Deal, avoiding any rubber-stamp relationship, while attacking Gene's record and his disloyalty to the party. Democratic loyalty as exemplified by one's stand on the New Deal was the issue.[13]

The Russell organization, quivering before the thought of battling Talmadge, was particularly disturbed over the refusal of senior senator Walter F. George to endorse their man. Russell described his early problems: "I had troubles to start with . . . some of my friends came in weeping . . . at my headquarters at the outset, saying what bad shape things were in. I never was really concerned though . . . because although Governor Talmadge was a very strong man politically, I just didn't see anything that he had to run on. I thought I could make that clear to the people." [14]

While Gene's was the politics of style, Russell's was the politics of respectability, and this soon attracted Rivers and agriculture commissioner candidate Columbus Roberts. They sought a coalition against the Talmadge slate, but Russell refused them. Nevertheless the phrase "Roosevelt, Russell, Rivers, and Roberts" emerged to represent a slate of men with similar goals. It became the catchword for the 1936 campaign.

Overconfident as usual, Gene announced that he would make only one speech a week. In the meantime Russell was conducting one of the most intensive campaigns ever waged. He seemed indefatigable as he dragged his weary workers up one end of the state and down the other. At the same time, his speeches sounded defensive and timid compared

to the Talmadge rages. Russell continued to suffer from a staff mes-
merized by the Talmadge legend. They were also wary of the degree of
commitment Georgians had made to the New Deal. They realized the
profound issues reflected in the race—and the rejection of older values
they were asking the voters to make. The voters weren't saying anything—just listening.

Postmortems always look for those singular events in a contest that
could dramatically be called turning points. The entry of Senator Walter F. George into the Russell race on August 1, in a crowded tobacco
warehouse under a driving rain that crashed onto the tin roof so that
those crowded among the leaves could barely hear the speakers and
feared the downpour might crush the roof momentarily, was said by
the Russell people to be their turning point. They desperately needed a
boost that would slow the rampaging Talmadge. What they didn't
say was that George had the slickest political organization in the state
and that a little energy from that machine would guarantee defeat.
George wanted no part of the Russell race, but he saw a Talmadge
victory as an endorsement of all Gene espoused. If Gene won, it could
hurt George, because George was a lot more New Way than he was
Old Way; and if Gene proved that the people wanted the Old Way back,
his power in the state would be vastly enhanced. He would be in a
position to run Georgia politics from state house to Congress. So Walter
George came out on a very bad day, with all of the conviction of a man
talking to his dentist about the value of pulling teeth, and endorsed Dick
Russell by endorsing the good deeds of the New Deal: "I can't see how
any Georgia farmer can fail to realize that . . . Roosevelt has been the
greatest friend of southern agriculture since the War between the
States." He said, "No one with decency and honesty would wipe out"
what Roosevelt had done. Every Georgian had reason "to remain loyal
to President Roosevelt and the New Deal." And then Dick stepped forward and latched onto the New Way, so there would be no mistaking
that if George was for the New Deal he was also for Dick Russell. "I
have no apologies to make for supporting President Roosevelt in his
efforts to relieve economic distress. On the contrary I am proud that I
have been able to be of some assistance." The Atlanta press called it a
"gratifying hour." [15]

As Gene prepared to move his campaign into Monroe in central
Georgia, he received reports that mill workers in the area, men he had
had arrested the previous September, were planning to throw eggs at
him. Gene's reaction to those reports created a second critical event in

the campaign in two days—one which the powerful press of the *Constitution* and Russell's astuteness turned with disastrous results against Talmadge. Before Gene arrived in Monroe, a large group of plain-clothes national guardsmen cordoned off the area around which he would speak. Not even the press was allowed within the area. The show of force was not in itself much of an event, but it did have the seeds of vulnerability within it; and the scandal-conscious opposition grasped at the affair and exploited it with uncanny skill. The local Walton *Tribune* called the security force an outrage, and the *Constitution* said Gene was "a governor gone dictator-wild." [16]

Rumor had it that 125 armed men had come down from Atlanta. Local citizens had seen them emerging from their cars carrying pistols, but from the capitol Lindley Camp said he had sent no guardsmen from Atlanta, that the men in question were from the Monroe area and had volunteered their time to direct traffic and guard against any trouble. The Monroe police chief said many of them were from Atlanta. The mayor contradicted this story by agreeing with Camp that they were local boys. Whatever the case, the story that finally got to the people was that Gene was stumping the state with carloads of armed toughs—that he was once again using the state military to have his way.

During the campaign, Gene found new reason to hate the Atlanta newspapers. The *Constitution* had promoted its talented sports editor, Ralph McGill, to the editorial page, where he began throwing very pointed and effective barbs at Talmadge. McGill did not dislike Gene personally, but felt that this type of Old South demagoguery and staunch conservatism was tragically out of place in the twentieth century. His editorials were a little too glamorizing in Russell's behalf, but his criticisms were well researched and telling to the point that Gene for the first time became angry about a specific writer instead of the paper. The air became very tense between the writer and the governor, and the charge of the rift was quickly picked up by Talmadge's friend John Whitley. McGill had been hinting that there seemed to be some payoff going on between Gene and the road contractor, and this was the type of innuendo that the fiery Whitley did not take too lightly. During one speech that summer he had been standing behind McGill when the writer went into a long harangue about how old Gene and John were getting rich through their under-the-table dealings. He had hardly started before the enraged Whitley was upon him. "You been writin' lies about me and Gene long enough. We ain't never done nothin' to hurt the taxpayers of Georgia. I'm gone teach you a lesson you ain't gone soon forget!" With that Whitley attacked McGill, knocking him down, kicking him, and literally dragging him all over the area, to the amazement and amusement of the crowd. When he was finished he stood over the dusty bleeding McGill and proclaimed for the crowd to hear: "You goddamn sonofabitch, McGill, if you ever say anything about me and Gene Talmadge, I'll kill you!" McGill was not badly hurt in the fracas, and he returned to his typewriter with a vengeance. Ralph Mc-Gill was no coward, and he knew he had hit home with his barbs. He did not, however, reckon on the temper of Whitley. A few weeks later he again found himself face to face with "thin concrete" John—this time in the lobby of the Henry Grady Hotel. Whitley, who seemed to suffer from a limited vocabulary when he was angry, screamed at McGill, "You goddamn sonofabitch, I told you I'd kill you if you didn't quit writin' lies about me and Gene. Now I'm gone do it!" With that the hapless McGill (who was about the same size as Whitley) was punched all over the hotel lobby. Whitley even beat his head against the columns in the lobby. "I beat the lyin' bastud 'till I got tired. I'd rest, then beat him some more 'till he was bleedin' good. Then I told him, 'McGill, the next time I see you I'm gone have a pistol, and I'm gone kill the hell outta you!' " [17] The stubborn McGill—again, not badly hurt—went right back to his typewriter, but took care to avoid the violent Mr. Whitley. McGill had found out that Gene was literally building his campaign platforms with materials and labor belonging to the state, and he bore down heavily on this as another example of the corruption that was going on in the Talmadge administration. It was good investigative reporting, the best that had ever been done against Gene; but the materials and the incident were really weak pap from which to make the generalizations of the kind that McGill was making. His writing, so superior in competency and style to anything before it, did become an effective force in the campaign in criticizing the name and administration of Gene Talmadge during that very hot summer.

The new Russell aggressiveness came out strongly at Royston on August 7. "When a politician runs out of arguments, when he hasn't any more soap and knows that in the minds of the people he is convicted of pure cussedness in keeping the old people of Georgia from getting their pensions, then he comes hollering, 'nigger, nigger, nigger.' " It was a memorable accusation and one of the most effective political phrases of the campaign.[18]

In the 1936 campaign, the increased use of radio, newspaper advertising, posters, automobiles, and electrical amplifying equipment had created quantum leaps in political communication. Young men could easily remember when politicians rode into town by train or on horseback and were forced to bellow every word. Although Gene still rode into town on an ox- or mule-drawn cart, when the place was small enough for that to still be appreciated, he had quickly become a devotee of mass communication, utilizing the best of both worlds in which he lived.

With the campaign going tooth and nail, Griffin, Georgia, sent out a statewide invitation for everybody to meet there on August 26 for a showdown. And everybody accepted. Russell thought he already saw the tide turning when farmers began taking off their red suspenders at his speeches and symbolicly laying them at his feet. Exhibiting the new look of his campaign (since Senator George's endorsement), Russell announced that he too would be traveling with a bodyguard. On cue, thirty high school girls would march forth and lead Russell off stage through a highly appreciative crowd. It was devastating sarcasm, the type that had Gene in a defensive posture for the first time in his career.

"You hear false interpretations of my service to you," he pleaded. "Junior says I go around yelling 'nigger.' Well I don't believe in sending Negroes down here to rule over white people." [19] But Gene couldn't deny his desertion rate. By mid-August Hugh Howell was refusing to appear again on a Talmadge platform.[20]

The schedule for the Griffin speeches had come out a few days early and had terrified the Russell staff. Ed Rivers would go first in the morning; he would be followed by Russell at 11:25. A barbecue lunch would then precede Talmadge-man Redwine at 1:10, and Gene himself at 1:55. It was considered disaster to speak first and have no time for rebuttal. Gene would have the last word. The Russell staff met in somber discussion about strategy. What emerged was a masterstroke of planning, designed to force the Talmadge record to be recognized and to out-circus the great ringleader.

The twenty-sixth dawned blast-furnace hot; and as the sun climbed, forty thousand people made their way into the little town. The crowd talked through most of the morning speeches, cheered loudly for Ed Rivers, and then hearts pounded as Dick Russell strode toward the stand. Suddenly a loud blast of trumpet and drum shattered the quiet as the thirty-member Monroe Drum and Bugle Corps escorted Russell in a mocking swipe at Gene's toughs. Drawing cheers when he announced this was his bodyguard, he tore into Gene, calling him inconsistent and a liar. Mocking Gene's rural delivery, he drawled, "Old Re-

publican Gene. He ain't changed, He's a liar still." [21] Holding up a list
of questions, Russell demanded that Gene answer them when he came
on. He said they were critical questions that Gene had been dodging
all over the state. With great determination he read them. The first dared
Gene to show where his platform offered help to the farmer or to the
old, or where there was anything of a humanitarian nature. The second
asked how Gene would help the farmers if he didn't borrow money
from Washington. The third asked how he would finance the many
programs then helping the farmer if he killed the federal income tax
bill. The long list continued in detail, pinning Gene on every major
question of the day. "I am now going to tack these questions to this
podium," Russell said, in closing, "so that nobody can throw them
away, and when Gene comes up here to speak, I want you to demand
that he answer them." [22]

Continuing to bore in, the senator produced a copy of Gene's *Statesman* dated July 1, 1933, in which Gene had called the Construction and
Conservation Corps (CCC) boys bums and loafers. He then pulled
out a copy of the *Congressional Record* which showed that Russell had
voted for the soldier's bonus, thus taking away one of Gene's major
attacks against his opponent. Placing the *Record* over the other papers,
he closed his speech with an embarrassing accusation. "By what right
do you criticize anybody's war record . . . [Talmadge had said Russell
had never fought in World War I] when you hugged the banks of Sugar
Creek so closely during the war." [23] He left the platform to the brassy
sounds of his "bodyguard" which he said was "prettier than Gene's
soldiers." Gene had been drawn and quartered—his style and stomping, his demagoguery and showmanship all pared away; and the record
crowd stood blistering down the sloping high school grounds, humming with excitement over what they had just seen and heard. This
wasn't the Dick Russell of July.

After the barbecue it was Gene's turn. He found the thick pile of papers still lying on the podium. Picking them up with great disdain and
searing them with an icy stare, he scowled, "I'm not going to answer
these questions. It'd take a Philadelphia lawyer all day to answer them!"
When he moved into his own speech, the Russell staff felt a significant
point had been breached, and they felt Griffin confident of victory for
the first time in the campaign. They had seen the second turning point.[24]

The last two days of the race proved to be the most violent, and probably the worst of Gene's career to that point. He would finish up in mill
country, the stronghold of his opposition; and the "lint heads" were

waiting for him. At Dalton, on the eighth, a great free-for-all fist fight broke out at the start of Gene's speech. He tried vainly to talk to the combatants, but the throng was seized with the pent-up fury of a long and bitter race. Finally Gene yelled down to some who would break up a particular fight, "Don't pay any attention to them. The Talmadge boys can whip them. Let them fight it out." Gene then ignored the swirling battles before him and nonchalantly continued his speech. Half of the crowd was watching and racing after the fighters; the other half was listening to Gene. Surely it was one of the most unusual speeches in Georgia politics. Many were hurt in the melee, including a local deputy sheriff who was beaten severely by five national guardsmen from Atlanta. He had them all arrested. Gene finished his speech while the fighting continued to rage, then quickly left Dalton. The ride off the platform on someone's shoulders would wait for another day. Probably half the people didn't know he had left since they were still being knocked down or were running after a new battle. Russell was having a calmer time of it at distant Sandersville, where he stated what the 1936 race was all about: "The farmers are awake to the fact that my opponent is promising them nothing except to cut off their checks . . . while I stand for larger benefit checks." [25]

On election day, it quickly became apparent that Russell had crushed Gene Talmadge in one of the biggest landslide victories in Georgia history. In the final count Russell carried 143 counties and got 256,154 votes; Gene carried only 16 counties with 134,695 votes. Similarly, Rivers received 230,184 votes to Redwine's 122,048 and Fortson's 33,438. Columbus Roberts continued the sweep of the "Four R's" by beating Talmadge-man Tom Linder for agriculture commissioner; and the unstoppable George Hamilton got his revenge by running up the biggest margin of any victor when he beat Tobe Daniel so badly that Daniel even lost the street that he lived on in LaGrange.[26]

Gene was stunned by the defeat, but wrote a long congratulatory message to Richard Russell anyway. He said, "The policies that I have advocated and carried through in state government are diametrically opposed to the policies of the New Deal," and he predicted an eventual victory for his ideals. In what sounded like a promise to return, he said, "I am in good health, and in the prime of life . . . and stand ever ready in the future to help in any way." Wearing a dark suit with a rose in the lapel, he said, "I am going down to Sugar Creek and get a drink of water." [27]

Upon reflection Gene said, "Ya'll leavin' them questions on the table at Griffin was a smart thing. I should have answered them. I think the campaign turned there." [28] There were critical points in the campaign, and Griffin was one of them, but more important were Senator George's endorsement and Russell's campaign strategy and ability. Russell had been and appeared to be uncertain whether to come out whole hog for the New Deal until George gave his backing. At this point the Russell campaign seemed to bolt with new life and determination. Russell became aggressive, assertive, and his precise attack on the highly vulnerable Talmadge record was devastating. Gene had started the campaign too casually and then let Russell get the jump on him; and his organization was too skimpy.

But it can be argued that the race was predetermined from the start and all of the battles of that summer were fought in vain. An alternative tide had swept America, and the Georgia minds had been profoundly affected by it. A new America had been born, a new turn in the road of history taken. It had been in motion since 1932, and in four years it had wrought vast psychological change. Perhaps none were more affected than the wool-hat boys who constituted the heart of Talmadge's support; and yet, ironically, he seemed to have kept that core. It had come to be said that Gene Talmadge had a guaranteed vote of 100,000, and the statement rang true. Certainly if he could draw support from the chief beneficiaries of everything he was against, he could draw from it any time. To 100,000 Georgians, Gene Talmadge was almost a diety. His hold was hypnotic and unshakable on this core constituency. But while his stand did not affect the vote of his own constituency, it lost the election because of the effect it had on the swing vote.

It has been said earlier that by the 1934 election Gene had created a bifactional polarization in Georgia. He had destroyed localism and factionalism as a voting factor. This statement demands slight qualification with the 1936 race. For though the bifactional electorate (either for or against Gene) seemed stronger than ever, an undecided 100,000 or so votes swung the election. This swing group was not polarized for or against Gene, and these voters could not be placed in a particular group that had a predictable behavior. Most of them were simply convinced that the New Deal was helping them more than hurting them. Another influential factor was the high voter turnout, the largest in Georgia's history. Gene drew from a hard-core group, and the numbers did not fluctuate much above 140,000. But the other two opponents were so terribly weak, and Russell so strong, that they were unable to break up Russell's vote. It was, to the voter's mind, a two-man race; and in a two-man race Gene could be beaten.

The location of the votes follows the 1934 pattern in one respect; Gene drew heavily from the rural areas. He won only one deep south county and took an angular line of north Georgia counties and a rambling and more heavy group across the center of the state. The count defies the north-south delineation that would suggest a conservative-liberal break; a geographic breakdown cannot be given. Populations and town sizes, along with occupations, incomes, and economic mainstays of the counties must be studied. Here one would find a voting pattern along rural-urban lines, particularly if the people were very isolated, dejected, and dispossessed. But even this is a generalization that cannot be made without qualification, for Gene received heavy support from businessmen who feared the high New Deal taxes. The wealthy and the very poor had once again combined for Gene. He had lost the labor vote, which was growing, and also much of the middle class.[29]

One interesting aspect of the race was Gene's attempting to pass his power and constituency along to Redwine. It could be argued both ways —that he did succeed and that he didn't. Redwine did receive over 120,000 votes, the Talmadge hard-core number, but he was defeated badly. It is probably safe to say that Gene did successfully pass his power through the hard-core supporters, but he failed with the anti-Talmadge 100,000 and failed where it really counted, with the big swing vote. The true test of Gene's ability to pass on this power was prevented from being made, however, by the one great issue which for all intent had predetermined the results of the campaign. Russell only had to wage a good strong campaign to fulfill destiny, and this he did. The people of Georgia had reaped huge rewards from the New Deal. It had lifted them up in their hour of greatest need, and neither the Georgia government nor Gene Talmadge had ever offered anything comparable. The proof was in the food on the table. It is interesting here to interject that Gene did "give" the people money in 1932 with his three-dollar tag and his utility rate cut, and the people responded by giving him an overwhelming victory. By 1936 he had been outspent by the New Deal. There was no way he could offer bigger checks or more assistance than the United States government. His 1932 savings to the people were drops in the bucket compared to the millions from the federal government in 1936. To tell a starving people they should no longer receive these benefits was whispering into a hurricane. But the people did not leave him eagerly. In June there was an agonizing decision made by a lot of Georgians over whether to desert this man who represented their heritage and to step off into an unprecedented direction, a path that ran counter to everything they had ever believed in. They were moving in the new direction, however, and needed only the gentle prodding of Dick Russell to turn it into a stride. Gene Talmadge was defeated by the times.

All of his activities for the last nine months of 1935 had been political suicide: foolishly allowing "Republicans to wine and dine me"; [30] insulting Roosevelt's afflictions; running alone in the nation against an obviously popular president; and failing there, running against a popular and good senator. Gene had covered all the wrong bases.

14

"Sold Out"

Old-time Talmadge supporter Lamar Murdaugh had drifted to Ed Rivers side during the 1936 race, and he had become a trusted adviser. Soon after Rivers' victory, the governor-elect had called Murdaugh and asked him to an early morning meeting at the Ansley Hotel. Arriving, Murdaugh found Rivers lying in bed shaving with an electric razor, a new invention Murdaugh had never heard of and couldn't believe. Lying beside Rivers was a book titled *Call of the Aged*. "Lamar," he finally said, "I got elected because I said I was going to provide for an old age pension and a lot of other welfare programs, but I don't know a damned thing about it. How about fixing me up a welfare program."

"Good God a'mighty, Ed, I don't either," exclaimed a startled Murdaugh. As they began to talk over what could be a monumentally embarrassing situation, Murdaugh remembered a Dr. Ash from Birmingham, Alabama, who had done a lot of work on the original old age and welfare programs. They agreed that Murdaugh should enlist Ash's aid, which he did, and this led to much of the writing of Georgia's welfare programs. Perhaps, if nothing else, the incident was prophetic of how much the office-hungry Rivers knew about his own platform and how well he would administer it.[1] His tenure in office—four years—would prove to be a fiscal disaster, though it brought unprecedented social reforms to Georgia. The only thing Rivers understood less than his own programs was the enormous amounts of money that implementing them would require. He would nearly bankrupt the state.

The concomitant social advances and economic misfortunes of the Rivers administration convinced the irrepressible Talmadge that all he had warned about had suddenly come to Georgia, and his only recourse in halting the New Deal was to run again for the senate. Senior senator Walter George would be up for reelection in 1938, and Talmadge, showing absolutely no political shrewdness, determined to take on the highly respected George. It must have appeared that Gene Talmadge had become possessed. His friend-turned-enemy, Hugh Howell, said it was all ego. "Gene was for Gene first!" But the man was no fool. It appears that more than simply wanting the fame of higher office, he had become more committed than ever to slowing the impetus of the New Deal. He had succeeded in stopping its adoption at a state level in the 1933 and 1935 legislatures, but he had been powerless to stop the big federal programs. This could only be done from a national platform, a stage now occupied by the very large figure of Walter F. George.

Gene wandered back to his farms—a politician out of work, a lawyer with still not much of a practice, a farm owner who wanted to be a cattleman. He knew cows; he knew horses and good rabbit and bird dogs. "I never could like a man much who did not like either dogs or horses," he once remarked.[2] And he spent the winter and spring of 1937 trying to build his cattle herd, bird hunting, a little lawyering, and doing a lot of talking about 1938. Mitt was left to all she had ever cared about, the McRae farm. The old house had burned down, and they had built a big two story red brick home with columns on the porch. They planted the place in pine trees. "That Mitt was the most independent woman I ever met," remembers a female neighbor. "Gene knew about as much about what she was up to as she knew about him. I don't think he ever did know she was working convicts from the state prison out at Sugar Creek. A lot of people in McRae worked them, but nobody ever knew about it. I would think a lot of people across the state were doing it since it came so easy to us here. Mitt worked the cheapest niggers she could get. I never knew none of them that could read or write. That's one of the reasons she made such good money out of the farm. Like I said, Gene, to my mind, never knew about it. He was fair to his niggers."[3] This accusation, though sworn to, is denied by others close to Talmadge who said he kept a very close eye on the McRae farm and would not have allowed the illegal use of prison labor.

Talmadge made all the stops in 1937, from veterans clubs to county fairs; and every Sunday the reluctant agnostic preached in a different church. His newspaper, the *Statesman*, became his voice and mass platform. The paper reflected his new strategy of avoiding personal attacks on Roosevelt. Instead, he became more populistic— moving against big interests as represented, he said, by none other than Walter George. Gene proved he was a politician by backing off from the president, proved he knew when he had made a mistake. His problem was that he could not or would not foresee that he was heading in the wrong direction. He was a man of great hindsight.

Once it became known that Gene would run against George, those who had questioned his good judgment in 1936 questioned his sanity in 1938. Walter George—erect, properly greyed, obviously educated, tremendously powerful, supremely organized, and the essence of establishment—was regarded by state politicians and most of the voters as a true statesman, a man with the aura of greatness. George's base of strength was the business community—money and position and the same people who backed Gene, with the exception of some bankers who had strongly supported Roosevelt from 1932 on. And to further test the Talmadge-George loyalists, Gene threw away his 1936 anti-New Deal platform and took a Populist one. He had learned his limitations. He could not ignore what the people had indicated they were for and expect them to vote for Old Gene. No longer could the vague defeat the obvious, or the myth defeat reality. So he found his platform in the consequences of the New Deal as he saw them, *i.e.*, the creation of dehumanizing big business and the conversion of the individual to subjugated masses, big government and big spending, everything so huge that the little man became lost. Gene would stress the basic southern characteristics of independence and individuality; he would pursue that pioneer who was out there on the isolated farm, who knew best what he wanted and cared for no man telling him what to do, that man who hated "big." Although Gene had not attacked Russell much personally, he planned to go after George and the way he had personally served the interests of the privileged.

On May 13, 1938, surrounded by a grinning bunch of the boys, Gene qualified for the senate race. His platform was short but startling to Talmadge observers. There was actually some practicality in it, very little Old Way rhetoric and some real progressivism. It was populistic, primarily serving the "little man"; and it indicated that Gene had not only felt the mighty whack the New Deal had given him, but that he had learned from it. His platform was : (1) to give free land to any American that would work it; (2) to offer vocational education that would not educate people in things they would never use, but give them practical job-oriented training; (3) to improve the CCC camps and make them teaching grounds for vocational technical schools; (4) to stop federal waste by taking money designated for relief and spending it on land, then giving that land away. He called it a platform for the "common people, the laboring people, the Christian people," [4] and he said it would save the nation. The platform was basic Talmadge economics—hard, honest labor as exemplified by the farmer. The platform, this time, would offend very few. Even Gene could be a little flexible. The Atlanta press immediately endorsed both George and Ed Rivers, who was running for a second term to remain "100 percent loyal" to FDR. Lawrence Camp also announced his candidacy for the senate and was expected to run as another "100 percenter." One W. G. McRae also announced as being 100 percent for FDR, but he felt the New Deal should be financed by a 2 percent gross sales tax called the Townsend Plan. Of the four candidates for the senate, all neatly in order of preference for the policies of the federal government, one sees: Camp 100 percent for everything; McRae almost 100 percent; George maybe 50 percent; Talmadge close to 100 percent against everything.

The first speeches said it as it would be. Gene was a protectionist, isolationist, nationalist, populist. Gene said that George had proved himself against the American farmer by supporting oleomargarine, a coconut derivative, over United States dairy products. In his first speech Gene detailed his free-land plank: "You place thousands of people on small tracts of land . . . and you will help them to get on their feet, and they will go to work." Gene felt that this migration back to the farm would generate a new need for farm implements and equipment; and from that need, a manufacturing base would be established as well as the attendant industries of farming. It became apparent that while the Talmadge planking and rhetoric had become more complicated, his solutions to problems retained their famous naive simplicity; they were in the best tradition of the Old Way. The revamped Talmadge campaign approach also involved an incredibly heavy speaking schedule, established before the race started. And Gene even announced a campaign manager, a man who would become increasingly important and influential in the Talmadge political life—his twenty-five-year-old son Herman.

George established his tone with his opening July 4 speech. It was in stark contrast to the Talmadge style. Appearing almost pained and embarrassed to be asking for votes, George opened with a formal, detailed, and erudite rhetoric that simulated a lawyer presenting a brief. But the Atlanta press, reminiscent of its anti-Talmadge bias of 1936, gave the George speech enormous coverage. However, this and anything else the paper or the candidates did that summer would prove of little relevance, for events had been occurring that would predetermine the outcome of the race.

Tensions between old- and new-line Democrats, increasing since 1936, had erupted in 1937 when FDR tried to pack the Supreme Court. Old-liners held the Court to be a last defense against the more radical New Deal program. These programs, and the decline in influence of conservatives, had made the southern Democrats stubborn and afraid, even though they sometimes found themselves obligingly following FDR because of the huge patronage his New Deal involved. The dissension erupted with the death of United States Senate Majority Leader Joseph Robinson in 1937 and FDR's appointment of a "militant" new leader, Hugo Black. This was construed as a "deliberate policy on the part of the president to encourage and foster the growth of liberalism in the southern wing of the . . . party." [5] Pressure from southern leaders like Talmadge only heightened the split within the national party. As the congressional opposition grew, FDR decided to take his case to the people and get dissidents voted out; Walter George was so marked.

Georgia businessman Chip Robert had been part of a coalition of Jewish and Catholic businessmen who met in Atlanta in 1932 to raise money in support of Roosevelt's candidacy. The establishment group included lawyer Jack Spalding, merchant Morris Rich, John Price, and the owners of the Atlanta *Journal*. They often referred to themselves and their kind as Goldbug Democrats, which meant they were as close to being Republicans as Democrats could become. As a result of this group's efforts Roosevelt had come to know and respect Chip Robert; he asked Robert to head up the wage commission under the Wage and Price Administration (WPA), telling him and the other commission members: "We don't want a dole system. It's been the damnation of England."

One of the first wage levels the commission set was that the head of a Negro household in the South should make $6.50 a week, and a white family head should make $12.50 a week. No sooner had this decision reached Atlanta than Gene was on the phone to Washington: "My God, Chip!" he fumed, "you give a nigger $6.50 a week and he won't never work!"

Robert told Roosevelt that Gene Talmadge was furious and was pressing him to change his mind. Roosevelt laughed, knowing that Robert was caught between loyalties, and quipped, "Chip, you go

Campaign photograph of Gene in late 1920s. Photo courtesy Atlanta
Journal/Constitution.

Gene riding in to speak before a typical Talmadge following. Photo courtesy Atlanta *Journal/Constitution*.

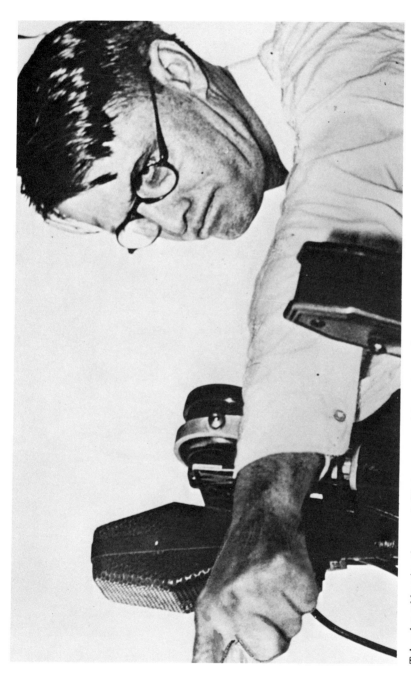

Talmadge addressing the crowd. Photo courtesy Atlanta *Journal/Constitution*.

Talmadge at a Fourth of July rally. Photo courtesy Atlanta *Journal*/*Constitution*.

Typical military dress for a Talmadge outing. From left to right: Lindley Camp, Gene, and Hugh Howell. Photo courtesy Atlanta *Journal/Constitution*.

straighten Gene out." Gene called again and exploded, "Goddamn ya'll! You went and elected Roosevelt, now the country's going to ruin!'"

The next phone call from Talmadge came four months later and was strangely different. Gene had found out that blacks in the North were allowed a higher minimum than in the South. He had also been pressed by Georgia merchants to get more for local blacks because they were spending the money as fast as they got it and it was good for business. Gene said, "Chip, I want to come up and see you." Robert saw no point in the trip and suggested they talk it out over the phone. Gene then sang his different tune: "Goddamn, all my friends and supporters around Macon are mad as hell because you're giving niggers here $6.50 a week and they're spending it all, and you're giving niggers more in Ohio. Hell, give 'em as much as you're giving everybody else!" Gene was sounding unusually political.

By 1938 Robert had been appointed both assistant secretary treasurer of the United States and treasurer of the national Democratic party. He had become very close to Roosevelt and his family, often breakfasting at Hyde Park with Mrs. Roosevelt, and numbering himself among a small group of men intimate with the president. One day, early in 1938, Roosevelt called Robert in Washington and invited him to Hyde Park. He wanted to talk over some matters that would not lend themselves to phone conversation. Robert traveled to New York the next day and spent all Friday visiting with FDR's mother, but did not see the president until the next morning when the two had breakfast.

"Chip, I've got a job for you to do." They had barely started their meal before the president had gotten to the point. "We've got to beat Senator George in Georgia and you're the logical one to run against him." The news hit Robert like a sledgehammer. Walter George was one of his best friends and a man considered by the Georgia business establishment to be of inestimable value to the state.

Robert stammered, looking desperately for a way out. "My God, Mr. President, I couldn't be elected dogcatcher in Georgia. I'll back you 100 percent, you know that, on anything you need, but why do you want to beat Senator George?" Roosevelt, perfectly relaxed, seemed amused over his friend's shock. Understating, he said, "Evidently you don't want to run against George." Robert answered meekly, "People would laugh at me," but Roosevelt refused to let him off the hook: "Well then, you're going to have to pick out the man to beat him."

Robert continued to balk "as politely as you refuse a president" and asked again why George should be removed. Roosevelt answered. "It's as simple as this. Senator George's position in the Senate is such that anything he advocates, you can count on at least forty senators going with him. I can't pass legislation without him and I cannot depend on him being with us. We've got to get somebody in there who'll think our way. I want you to talk to our friends in Georgia and get their support in beating George."

Robert was dazed. He saw it was fruitless to continue arguing with the president, and the breakfast ended with his saying he would do what he could. The news he brought back to Georgia hit the establishment like a thunderclap. Calling a select group of powerful Roosevelt backers, who also happened to be staunch George backers, Robert was summarily cursed, called a fool, laughed at, and hung up on. Roosevelt be damned. Their loyalty to George would not be betrayed. It was a soul-wrenching request the president had made to the backbone of his own and Senator George's organizations in Georgia. Yet he was the head of their party and he was asking for their loyalty to him. So traumatic was the request that upon hearing he would be asked to help defeat George, Richard Russell suddenly departed Washington for an extended trip to the remote woods of Panama. Feeling he was committed to do something, Robert picked Russell's 1934 campaign manager, Lawrence Camp, as the man Roosevelt Democrats should support for senator. He then lay very low while the air filled with verbal buckshot.

In June of 1938, with the race just beginning, Roosevelt began his cross-country barnstorming for congressmen who would support him. On the train to the Pacific Coast rode Chip Robert. Just out of Reno, after dinner and cigars, the president said he was retiring to his private car for the night. As he left the group he told Robert, "I want to see you in here a minute." Alone in the president's car, Robert was told that it was definite—that George would be fought and that Camp was acceptable. Robert began a last-ditch attempt to change his mind. "Mr. Roosevelt, are you really going to do that?"

"Well, what's your suggestion?" Roosevelt asked.

"If you will not come to Georgia, you will win the state. You are 85 percent strong there. If you do come and use your influence to beat George, Gene Talmadge will beat him."

The president smiled at the mention of Talmadge's name.

"I can't conceive of your wanting Gene Talmadge to come to Washington as senator," Robert said, thinking he might have a pry.

But Roosevelt called his bluff. "Listen that sounds all right, but if I don't come down there and face the issue in Georgia, you damn rascals will get together and elect George."

Robert pleaded, "You can't let Gene Talmadge put on the show he'd put on. He'd be a menace."

"Yes, I'd prefer that."

"But he'd be another Bilbo. He'd just make an ass of himself. And Georgia couldn't stand that!"

The president smiled. "It wouldn't be the first time you all had a fellow who made an ass out of himself."

That ended it. Roosevelt did not fear Talmadge as a senator, thinking just as Robert had said, that he would make an ass of himself and garner the support of no one. He would much prefer Gene to George. As Robert sat dejected, FDR told him of his plans.

"I'm going back and landing at Pensacola. No use in your coming there to meet me. I'm coming straight to Atlanta and making a speech in connection with the REA." [6]

Lawrence Camp, Roosevelt's new man in Georgia, issued the invitation, as instructed, for Roosevelt to come to Georgia. No one knew outside a small group of depressed Democrats that the whole thing was planned in advance, nor did most people know for sure to whom Roosevelt would give his support. A few days later, under heavy questioning, Senator George said he would welcome the president to Georgia, even though a lot of people were speculating that a purge was in the offing. George went so far as to call the president a great and good man as though he were trying to dampen the rumors.

Camp was picking up the bludgeon against George, saying that he was "the most subtle and adroit enemy of President Roosevelt and the Democratic party in the United States." A lot of people started putting two and two together as Camp continued by saying, George "has been the Senate leader for the forces of entrenched greed, big business and its millionaire owners in the country." [7]

Gene thought the whole thing humorous, mainly because he was confident of emerging the winner. With a four-man race, and three of the men running in the liberal camp to varying degrees, he felt the county-unit vote was all his. He became obsessed with this strategy and adopted the theme "Hold tight your lines," meaning that if the loyal 100,000 would just stay with him he saw no way to lose. The whole race seemed destined for a profound vote splitting and that's where Gene came on. He determined, "This is not a good year for coattail riding." [8]

Richard Russell's father told the press that he had asked Gene (whom he was supporting against George) why he was running for the United States Senate again. Gene had answered, "I am not running against your son this time for he is a real man and I have never made any complaint of the fact that he defeated me. This time I am running against a man in tailor-made clothes, full only of wind and broken promises." [9] The *Constitution*'s Ralph McGill heard Talmadge speak in July and found him hungry for victory. He concluded, "It's dangerous to underestimate him." [10]

Senator George seemed to be floundering in his own rhetoric from the outset. He had been severely criticized for proclaiming that he stood for "liberal movements" and "liberal leadership of the party." The word *liberal* had been anathema in the South, though the New Deal had created a more flexible attitude toward the philosophy. George soon found himself qualifying his remarks, saying that he was a "liberal within the Constitution." [11]

The late July and early August speeches were a wasted effort. Attention had begun to rivet on the tiny community of Barnesville and the day of August 11, the place and date of the president's speech in Georgia. The village was fifteen miles from Forsyth and just east of Warm Springs, and almost embarrassingly small for a presidential visit. The shiny copper wire being strung would supply electricity to all of 357 families. Washington had supplied the loans which enabled local people to build the lines. Significantly, it was the federal government and not the state that was bringing the modern world to isolated Georgians. Gene said he would not attend the affair but would listen from Atlanta on the radio. "The predictions," he said, "are that the president will discuss Senator George's record, but I don't know whether or not he will annoint Camp. I know one thing; he will not annoint Gene Talmadge." [12]

The big Roosevelt barnstorming campaign rolled into Georgia on August 10 and settled at Warm Springs. The political air was electric as the president's intentions began to unfold. Staff members began leaking word that he "would crack down hard on George," and rumor became fact when Camp and Rivers came driving into Warm Springs to dine with the president. Columnist Stewart Alsop said there was no doubt that FDR was going to back Camp, and he called this attempt to purge George "a rather sordid, slapstick comedy." Alsop knew Camp would not be a strong candidate. His organization and campaign strategy had made New Dealers wince. Incredible as it seemed to Alsop, it appeared the president would risk having Talmadge elected so that he could have his revenge on George.

Alsop and his fellow reporter Robert Kinter, in Atlanta for the speech, dropped by Gene's law office. It turned into more of a clash than a visit. Gene was at his redneck best, and he disgusted the two writers who made the mistake of taking him seriously. The office was described as cheerless, and of the man Talmadge they wrote, "Besides demagoguery, the outstanding talent of Georgia's former governor is hitting any spittoon, at any distance, at any time." Gene boastfully told the men, "I'll make America another Garden of Eden." [13] Alsop feared he was talking to the next senator from Georgia.

One old fence sitter in Warm Springs told a reporter that he was voting for Talmadge, Rivers, and Roosevelt. "Talmadge is promising 40 acres of land . . . Rivers promises to exempt it from taxation, and Roosevelt will rent it from us. . . . Why not vote for 'em all, and sit on the porch . . . and collect a steady income?" [14]

Finally the long train bearing the president and George and dozens of dignitaries steamed into Barnesville. As the president's big party piled off the train and into waiting cars, Senator George suddenly found himself without a ride. Only half of the scheduled cars had come out to the station, because the drivers were afraid they would miss something if they left the Gordon Institute Stadium where the speech was to be held. After walking the length of the train the solemn-looking, grey-haired senator hitch-hiked to the speech. Roosevelt sat in his open car, surrounded by townspeople and admirers from across the state. Rarely had a president earned such devotion from the Georgia people, but whether the independent southerners would turn on their own for the president's political ends was another question.

Roosevelt told the assemblage that he had never been fully aware of the total lack of electricity in rural areas until he started visiting Warm Springs; he had never appreciated the poverty of the South until he came into its midst in rural Georgia. "It is my conviction," he said, "that the South presents right now the nation's No. 1 economic problem," and he felt this and other problems could be cured by senators who would vigorously support him. He then dropped his bombshell: "Because for many years I have regarded Georgia as my 'other state,'

I feel no hesitation in telling you what I would do if I could vote here next month." His gentlemanly attack on George proceeded with great amicability, but there was no mistaking that he was in Georgia to block the renomination of George. "My friend the senior senator . . . cannot possibly . . . be classified as belonging to the liberal school." This contradicted all of George's precampaign rhetoric and the base he had been trying to build. Roosevelt continued, "I trust that Senator George and I will always be personal friends even though . . . on most questions he and I do not speak the same language." He then brushed Talmadge's candidacy aside with one of the few public statements he ever made about one of his more stubborn detractors. "I have known him [Talmadge] in Georgia for many years. His attitude toward me . . . in 1935 and 1936 concerns me not at all, but I have read so many of his proposals, so many of his promises, so many of his panaceas that I am certain . . . his election would contribute little to practical government. That is all I can say about him." Roosevelt then moved on to Camp, praising his record in state government, calling him a successful man, and "a man who honestly believes that many things must be done now." Then the purge: "If I were able to vote in the September primaries in this state I most assuredly would cast my vote for Lawrence Camp."

Applause was formal, almost confused. Friends on the platform rushed to George's side as Roosevelt finished and took his seat. George rose, shook hands with the President, and in his scholarly way told the hushed gathering, "Mr. President, I regret that you have taken this occasion to question my democracy and to attack my public record. I want you to know that I accept the challenge." And with that the day that was characterized as "the greatest and most thrilling political spectacle in Georgia history" was over. As the big cars and the long train moved away through the hot summer afternoon, hundreds of people stood in disbelief, arguing over what they had just witnessed. Only the setting sun removed their numbers. Gene Talmadge yawned from Atlanta, "It concerns me not at all." [15] He refused to accept the event as anything more than a further fractionalization of the vote.

George's staff was uncertain of what the impact might be, but felt their backs against the wall with little recourse but to come out fighting. Camp's staff considered that their man was either now the front runner, or, at worse, that the race had been narrowed to Camp and George. They felt Talmadge had been knocked out, for the issue was support of Roosevelt.

The speech had a jolting effect on the 1938 race, which had plodded all summer with vague issues and little interest. All that changed after August 11. Just as George's speech had sparked the Russell campaign in 1936, the Roosevelt speech gave impetus to the dull George campaign. The only parallel historians could find had occurred twenty years earlier, almost to the day, when Woodrow Wilson sent a letter endorsing the candidacy for senator of William J. Harris.

Gene was back on the trail on August 12, using an interestingly inaccurate interpretation of the Roosevelt speech. Twisting the president's intent, Gene, with a straight face, was trying to use the address to his own advantage. It became a major part of his campaign strategy and rhetoric. He said in Gainesville—after driving into town behind a team of mules—that FDR had a right to say what he had said. "The President reminded me of a bucking horse. He threw George clean over the Gordon Institute." Gene said Camp was just another "coattail rider." At Jonesboro Gene said, the attack "will destroy his [George's] candidacy and elect me on the first ballot." Patting himself on the back, Talmadge said FDR had not attacked the Talmadge record because "he knew that that record could not be successfully attacked." [16] This was astonishing news to those who had heard Roosevelt totally reject Gene's candidacy on the basis of his record, one so irrelevant the president would not address it.

Senator George came out saying, "I am going to fight to the last dying ditch." [17] It was strange rhetoric for this normally taciturn, urbane senator, but no stranger than his playing martyr to the hilt. Suddenly it was Walter George against the insiders, the man alone. He wisely avoided going against Roosevelt personally, choosing instead to condemn what the speech represented—an attempt to destroy the political integrity of the people of Georgia. Oddly enough it was the old Talmadge standard George was now carrying. Old enemies of George had left Gene alone with his sword while they joined forces with the unlikely George. A Gallup poll published in the *Constitution* on August 17 showed that while most Georgians supported FDR, 75 percent felt he had made a mistake in trying to purge George. This factualized what the George staff already knew: their man's candidacy had been instantly romanticized by the speech.

Gene's strategy had also been transformed by the speech. Besides somehow twisting what Roosevelt had said about him as a politician, he also began to attack George through the words of Roosevelt. Gene had entered into a very odd and deceptive alliance with the president, despite the president's intent. It was the height of irony that after years of fighting Roosevelt, Old Gene would now be found sidling up to the Roosevelt camp. To those who say politics is the art of compromise, it must be said that Talmadge reached political maturity in 1938. Franklin Roosevelt for the second time had become critical to the Talmadge fortunes in a campaign, proving once again the profundity of the impact Roosevelt had wrought on Georgia.

With a very subtle usage of Barnesville, Gene announced from the stump, "Now, I'm not mad at anybody. I have no complaint, no criticism." An Atlanta reporter covering the speech wrote, "tousling his hair over his eyes and looking his fiercest," Gene closed with his memorable phraseology: "Now three of the senate candidates are polished gentlemen. . . . I am the only rascal in the race." [18]

A Gallup poll on September 13 reported that the senate race had ended in August in the dust of the Gordon Stadium. It predicted that George would get 46 percent of the vote to Gene's 28 percent. That same day Gene was found exulting in his "cheerless" law office over the heavy flow of contributions that had continued to come in. "Four hundred dollars in the mail yesterday," he grinned to a reporter, "and not a contribution of more than $5." Emptying his bulging pockets of fists full of change, he said, "Tell 'em that Talmadge will be nominated in a landslide. I know my Georgia and I know my politics. I am deceived by neither." He ceremoniously predicted, "On Wednesday night the wool-hat boys will come to town." [19]

On election day Gene arrived early at his office in the William-Oliver Building. His tiny staff, other lawyers, and close friends drifted in throughout the day until they numbered about twenty-five. That was almost too many for the small offices; the room clouded with smoke and the smell of men too close. Gene sat back in his chair, a soiled Panama resting loosely on his head. When the polls closed, he stood and said, "Come on, boys, let's go over to the Ansley."

They had to push their way into the hotel that had become famous for the politicians who headquartered there. As the sun set, the crowds grew thicker; the boys had returned for another expected Talmadge celebration. When Gene took an early county-unit vote lead, he mounted a table in the ballroom his supporters had rented and shouted, "I'm tired, I'm broke, and I'm happy." He was then carried about the room on the shoulders of supporters as pandemonium broke out.[20]

The enthusiasm at the Ansley was premature. As the votes continued to come in through the night and the next day, it became painfully apparent that Gene had again been defeated for the senate of the United

States. Walter George polled 141,235 votes to 103,075 for Gene—44 percent to 32 percent. George also beat Gene badly in the county-unit vote—246 to 148. Roosevelt's man Camp finished a poor third, with 78,778 popular votes.[21]

The unusual thing about the results was the high incidence of close county races. There were five counties which George won by less than 20 votes and four which Gene won by less than 20 votes. A little addition showed that a change of 210 votes in the right counties would have given Talmadge the election through the county-unit system. The vote also reflected the erosion of the Talmadge base because of the migration of people to urban areas. While he won almost half of the smaller counties, George was winning all of the large urban counties and twenty of the thirty medium-population counties. Even a decade earlier these numbers would have shifted into the Talmadge column because of the rural preponderance.

Political observer Jim Peters, a Talmadge man, attributed Gene's 1938 loss to three factors: (1) the powerful George organization; (2) Gene's weak showing in county precincts because of his inability to establish a base of support with the courthouse gangs; (3) heavy contributions by the utilities for George.[22] What this basically said was that Gene's traditionally weak-to-nonexistent state organization had been beaten by a very finely tuned organization. Gene's habit of running a campaign out of his back pocket was no longer pragmatic in Georgia in 1938.

But Gene Talmadge was not giving up easily. He surprised a lot of people, and disappointed a lot of others, by announcing the day after the election results that he would contest the vote in thirty counties. He said that if his suspicions were proved correct, a re-count would "clearly give me the election." The Talmadge office had been literally flooded with phone calls and letters complaining of voting irregularities. Many were sworn affidavits. People claimed that dead people, children, and nonresidents had been voted for George. Payoffs had been made, counting falsified, and ballots premarked.[23] Such was the weight of the complaints, and such was the desire of Gene Talmadge to be senator that he proceeded to file complaints with the Democratic committee in thirty-four counties. Simultaneously, Gene started a quiet campaign with Hugh Howell, who had run for governor and been defeated, and with Rivers who had been elected governor. The Neill Primary Act of 1917 had said that any candidate for governor would be awarded the delegates from every county he won, regardless of who won the primary. Those delegates would be committed to that candidate at the October Democratic convention. Gene knew that if he could get Howell and Rivers to pledge their delegates to name him senator at the convention, the popular and county-unit votes would be voided and he would be elected. This was a desperate tactic since his relations with both men were strained. [24] Gene knew the county contests would be crucial to his persuading these men to award him their delegates. And the first results were damaging. Coweta County rejected Gene's charge of foul play, and the county officials rebuffed him angrily. He had insulted their county, they asserted; furthermore, he was being billed $76.50 for their trouble. This was bad publicity, and Gene began firing out letters to friends in the contested counties asking that further confirmation of wrongdoing be sought. In a letter to one R. C. Grace, on September 21, he wrote that he knew several counties were going to "decide the case against us. We will then appeal it to the Convention at Macon on October 5th." Talmadge went on to say, "Get all the evidence of irregularities in the election that you can. If you can get any evidence of money being used, get this in affidavit form." [25]

The rejections continued. By September 25, fifteen of the thirty-four counties had refused him. The next day the state Democratic committee notified him that he would not be a delegate to the convention. The county rejections were so unanimous that Gene appealed to the state executive committee on Friday, October 2. He asked the sixty-five members to overrule the county committees, but they too rejected his appeal by a vote of sixty-one to four. After the poll Gene told them, "The very resistance of the executive committee to a recount bears out our contentions that something was wrong."

Talmadge was too politically wise to become overly angry with these party functionaries. He knew the allegiances to power and loyalty reserved for the man in power. And he was not only not in power, he had been beaten in every conceivable way. Walter George was in power and had been asked by the people to stay there. Gene had always turned up his nose at the party. He had been inattentive to the county power structures. And now when he needed these ignored power sources, they were delighted to refuse him. The anti-machine man had been run over by machinery. Characteristically magnanimous in defeat, Gene told the gathered state committeemen, "I am not mad. I enjoyed running. I didn't take cold and I am in good humor." But he could not resist warning, "From every stump in Georgia in two years the people will be asked if they are in favor of a recount." [26]

Gene was no sooner out of the meeting than he was planning a last frantic stand on the convention floor. It was at this point that his fight took on the air of vindictiveness. He seemed to be carrying the thing too far, particularly when he asked his supporters to march on Macon and demand that his contests be heard. Gene arrived in Macon the day before the convention and came under great pressure to stop fighting George. His friends feared he was hurting his future, and they pushed him so severely that he appeared to be wavering on the night of the fourth. A large group had assembled in his suite at the Lanier Hotel; led by Brick Miller of Madison, the group was telling Gene he had been beaten, that he was making everybody angry, and that he ought to admit he had lost. Alarmed at Gene's apparent wavering, a supporter ran from the room, sought out Gene's old Forsyth friend James Corley, and told him Gene was giving up the fight. Furious, the wiry Corley ran to the room, barged through the door, and rushed to Gene's side. His voice quivering, Corley said, "Now let me tell you something, Gene. I have voted for you in every election, and thousands and thousands of Georgians have too for one reason or another. You ain't a quitter. If you quit now, I'll never vote for you again!"

Gene's eyes sparkled, and he snapped, "I ain't gone quit!"

With that, someone in the crowded room handed a glass of clear liquid to Gene; without asking what it was, he took a deep gulp. Suddenly he lurched forward in his chair, spit the liquid in a wide spray, and smashed the glass against a wall. In a rage he screamed, "They say I'm a drunkard, and now they're tryin' to prove it!" Someone had tried to slip him a glass of corn liquor and as Corley remembers, "The air was blue with cuss smoke." [27]

Hugh Howell claimed that later that night Gene sent Tom Linder to say that if Howell would release all of his delegates to Gene, he would get Gene's support for governor in 1940. Howell no doubt remembered the letter still in his possession that Gene had written a friend of Howell's after refusing to back Howell for governor in 1936. It read, "He cannot say 'No' and stick to it. He jumped into the race without talking with me or anyone of our close friends." [28] To Howell this had been a cruel lie that he had never forgiven or forgotten, and he refused Linder's offer, snuffing out Gene's last hope of victory.

The convention exploded with a frenzy of activity, most of which was engineered by Rivers' floor manager Roy Harris. Rivers wanted New Deal-type programs nailed all over the Democratic platform that came out of the convention. Gene and his supporters were seen scurrying all over the hall in a pointless attempt to bring Gene's fight to a roll-call decision. Rivers confidently allowed the request, knowing George could not be harmed; and the convention delegates added flowers to the Talmadge grave by soundly voting down his request for reconsideration of the vote.

Gene reacted bitterly toward Howell. "I believe that 95 percent of the Talmadge supporters in Georgia voted for Hugh Howell. . . . I first thought they were making a mistake and forewarned them. Now they know Hugh Howell won't do!" [29] He answered letters asking him why he lost at Macon by blaming it on Howell. Typically, he wrote a Mrs. M. W. Gonzales: "We had stacks of evidence at the Macon Convention, but they refused to even look at it. The great trouble there was that Hugh Howell sold out the Talmadge people, and appointed George men as delegates in the counties he carried in the governor's race." [30] It was a rare hurt that Talmadge showed.

Georgia's power sources, normally fragmented, had again been pulled together because of the impact of Franklin Roosevelt; and again they had pulled together against Gene. Perhaps it was again preordained because of Roosevelt that the race would be determined by some reaction to him. Georgians thought highly of Walter George, and neither Roosevelt nor Talmadge gave them good enough reasons for ousting him. Gene's initial allegation that George was a servant of the rich was never satisfactorily substantiated. Worse, Gene's plank on giving away federal land had an air of unreality to it; besides, people were moving off the land. It must also be said that Gene's candidacy was also overshadowed by the growing wars in Europe.

Roosevelt made two mistakes in his attempted purge. One was to underestimate the independence of the southern people. It was just common sense to students of southern people that these isolated until recently and still partially rural voters would resist a blatant power-play by an outsider. Roosevelt's second mistake was to back a weak candidate against an exceptionally strong one. The Georgia electorate had no intention of backing Camp. Nor did it appear that they wanted Gene Talmadge ever to be any more to them than their governor.

15

"I'm a Minor Dictator"

Talmadge had bought parts of his father's old farm, the place of his birth, in 1934 and 1935, and a little bit more (five hundred acres in all for $5,000) from other landowners. The farm sat for three years, until Russell beat him so badly and then Walter George walked all over him. By 1938 he had spare time to walk over the place and think of crops. Gene hired a black man named Buster to be his foreman, and got his old supporter from Forsyth, James Corley, to tend to a cattle herd Gene wanted to build. Corley remembers Talmadge as a farmer:

Gene wasn't married to farming. Not the way people used to be. Farming was their life. Politics was Gene's life. But he understood farming real good. He was a tough boss. He didn't put up with no foolishness. He was the boss and he made sure you knew it. In 1938 we planted sorghum and peas and 135 acres in peppers, but the peppers started to die and I asked Gene if we could plant butterbeans while the season was still on, and he agreed, and me and him went into Forsyth and bought 600 pounds of butterbean seed. The 1939 crop was good, and Gene made a little money and got all excited. When it came time to plant again, Gene called me and said "let's go buy them butterbean seeds." But I had to tell him we weren't planting beans, or no other row crops no more. He said, "Why ain't we?" And I told him the niggers wouldn't pick row crops no more. They said it was too hard work, and I had to agree with them. It was backbreaking. A nigger woman named Lillie Mae Davis that lived in a railroad shack used to bring us all our laborers. We'd pay about 75¢ a day, a little better than anybody else. Gene paid his help fair and treated them fair, and any nigger that knew Gene liked him.

When we couldn't find laborers to work the crops anymore, Gene started to buying up cattle. I remember he wanted to set up a cattle auction on the place, and he built a huge shed and invited a bunch of farmers and had a big barbecue. Well, everybody got to eating barbecue and drinking and nobody cared to offer Gene much for his cattle, so he got up and said, "The auction is off. I can't sell my cows for these prices, but that's all right, boys, go ahead and eat my barbecue." Well, everybody got to feeling bad about eating the barbecue and before you knew it, they was starting the auction back up. That Gene was smart like that.[1]

185

Gene had announced that he would run for governor on the day Walter George defeated him, and he had fought to the last in the October convention partly to let the politicians know that Old Gene was still around. He was flexing his muscles, and though it did him no immediate good in the convention, it more or less prepared the people for his next race. He was "a politician to the marrow born," and he considered politics his life's work. He was a worker out of the only work he knew, and 1939 had hardly dawned before he was out knocking on doors trying to get back in. He would launch his career's most carefully planned assault on the governorship.

In January of 1939 he telephoned fifteen of his close friends and advisers—as usual this group was not the one which had served him in his previous races. He asked that they meet with him in Room 441 of the Ansley Hotel. The group included three brothers named Morgan from Savannah; Carson Smith; Zack Cravey, old-time friend from McRae; a lawyer from Cartersville, Wes Culpepper; Sam and Gene Wilburn; a Judge Butler from Macon; roadman Johnny "Cowboy" Goodwin; Charles Redwine; a Judge Dunn; Arnold Ansley from Thomaston; and Jim Peters from Manchester.[2]

The meeting was a serious, businesslike gathering, where each of the men was given an assignment or post and general strategy and probable opponents were discussed. The conversation was rambling, with Gene doing a lot of listening. Every man expressed what he thought to be the pressing issues, and before the day was over, broad general agreements had been reached. It would be a loose organization, with Jim Peters as chairman for the next meetings. Gene, as always, would be the center of the effort and would in fact "run the show." Gene told the men to pick workers carefully in their areas, but not to set up a structured and formal state organization. He said the "better plan is to wait and let the organization set itself up." He felt that "if you select a certain man to run your campaign in a specific county, he won't do anything until the election is over." When Peters asked why that was so, Gene answered, "They'll tell you they are going to work for you; they'll tell you they are working for you, but you'll lose the county and wonder why until you find out they were sitting on their ass the whole time, waitin' to see who was going to win the election, then they'd rush to you asking for all sorts of jobs and tellin' you how hard they worked for you. And if you won the county and had not checked up on them, you wouldn't know the difference." There was no point trying to convince this man that he should have a well-structured statewide organization.

The members of the meeting resigned themselves to working within a weak structure.

Jim Peters, who chaired the meeting, was, like everyone else, often baffled at the impulsive responses Gene would give, responses that no politician in his right mind would make, the consequences of which were often obviously disastrous. He had brought the subject up, hoping to suggest some moderation to the fiery Talmadge. He said, "Gene, if you would not be so hasty you wouldn't be in so much trouble all the time." Gene looked at him and said, "You know what I think? I think that's what's gotten me where I am." [3]

The fifteen men spent the year promoting Gene in their areas and quietly soliciting the support of their respective courthouse gangs and politicians. There was no more talk of senator; Gene was going to run for governor again. Talmadge spent the year working on the *Statesman* and doing law work in Atlanta, hunting and fishing on his farms, raising cattle and dogs, and making speeches to anybody who would invite him—no big stuff, just local city clubs and organizations. He seemed to be all over the state in a quiet sort of way, visible but not ruffling any feathers. He made nice, friendly talks with the veterans or the ladies' clubs; attended chicken dinners and barbecues at small gatherings; went to church socials, the all-day "preachin' and eatin'" on the grounds variety. By 1940, he could look at a firmly developing grass-root movement and a coalescing organization.

Talmadge would leave no stone unturned. He even committed himself to carrying Fulton County, something he had never done. Having no organization within the county, he planned to go after the local bosses with an offer they could not refuse. Gene called four of his most trusted aides to his suite at the Ansley and ordered them to very quietly round up the madames of Atlanta's whorehouses. These operators were well known, and Gene furnished names and addresses to the men. The madames were brought one by one to Gene. He asked for their support and asked that they encourage their patrons (who included some of Atlanta's most respected citizens) to vote for Old Gene. The ladies were astounded and flattered that their support had been sought; and undoubtedly foreseeing good times ahead if Gene won, they became ardent Talmadge supporters in some of the most compromising positions in Atlanta. In 1940 Gene would carry Fulton for the first time. [4]

A number of factors made the return of Talmadge possible. One was the scandalous debts run up by Rivers; the state was almost bankrupt.

Another was the shadow of a world war and the anxieties that fear produced. An air of crisis was created; there was a need for strength, a desire for the simple solution in a complex and confusing world. A future that no one wanted made the past a psychological crutch. Gene Talmadge, the iron man of action, would once again ride onto the political stage to save the day. He saw no way he could lose, because there simply were no other strong candidates to run. His estranged friend, Hugh Howell, was going to try for a third time; and old campaigner from Athens, Abit Nix, offered up again. Rivers could not seek reelection, and there were no new faces—just the same old one from Sugar Creek.

Talmadge had been out for four years, rejected for office twice, humbled by Roosevelt the first time and inadvertently beaten by him a second, ironically stripped of power by his arch enemies—new times and new ways. He had in two elections been recognized as a man disjointed from the times. That fact had been his strength in earlier races, but it became his weakness; and now, again, it would be his strength. Unsettled times had thrown the people out of step. With war threatening, they began to look for that well-worn path. And they dug back in their past and found the certainty they had been seeking—Old Gene. He was their crutch in a way, only this time, it was war and needless bankruptcy that demanded an aura of toughness. And Gene was the man with the sword.

It was rumored in late spring that throngs of "the boys" would swarm the capitol to pay Gene's qualifying fee, then march over to his office in the William-Oliver Building where they would have him address them from an office window. Gene felt this window speech would make him look like Mussolini, and he opted for a more conventional height. A fourth entry came onto the scene during that week—Columbus Roberts from Columbus. Roberts had been politically ambitious since serving as agriculture commissioner, but members of the Talmadge staff felt his strength lay in his pocketbook and not in his ability to politic.[5]

On Wednesday, June twelfth, the Great Talmadge Show hit Atlanta, complete with a throng of a thousand sweating, swearing, wool-hat boys, spitting their huge, juicy tobacco wads on the streets and in corners of the capitol rotunda. The *Constitution* said that "Gene brought his circus to the capitol." [6] The qualifying fees had to be paid there, and that seemed a symbolic place to hold the first Talmadge rally, probably the first political rally ever held in that august city. Gene was tanned, his hair long, his white shirt starched, and his suspenders a blaring red. After paying, he stood on a chair under the rotunda, quieted down the two fiddlers who were sawing madly on their instruments, told the grinning gee-haw boys who were doing jigs all over the floor to step aside, and launched into a romanticized speech about why he was running. He said his suspenders were "the insignia of a red heart and hard work" and that he was prepared to run again because in his heart he loved Georgia and "because the silent monitor within me tells me to." He made a rather vague appeal for unity, said in effect that he would cooperate with the New Deal—adding, however, that his record bespoke his stand. The speech did not reveal much of his platform, but that was not its purpose. It was designed to say that personality politics were back, and he was off to a mighty roar. His approach had, in fact, begun early that morning at the rooftop restaurant of an Atlanta hotel. One of the staff had taken the floor to say that "the only two things that could get this many people out of bed this early in Georgia were a dove shoot and Gene Talmadge." The breakfast showed how well Gene's staff and workers had done their jobs over the past year and a half. It was estimated that influential people from half of Georgia's counties were in attendance. This, far more than the razzle-dazzle at the capitol, reflected the strong initial thrust that Gene was getting. He had good support early.[7]

It became increasingly difficult to find news of the impending campaign in the state press and over radio. The smashing legions of Germany and Italy were beginning their destruction of Europe; and Georgians, like the rest of the world, were riveting their attention to that conflict. Also, Roosevelt was up for a third nomination, and this was also drawing interest away from state politics.

To liven things up, and to show the electorate that the old entertainer was back, Talmadge headquarters announced early in July that a song had been written for the campaign and a record made of it. It would be played before every Talmadge speech. Gene's son Herman predicted that "all Georgia will be humming it before long." Probably no cornier piece of doggerel ever graced a campaign; the song was entitled "An Apple for the Teacher," and its lyrics painfully read: "An apple for the teacher is very fine indeed,/but, sad to state, an apple is not all the teachers need./The needless state employees, and government so wild,/ had a very marked effect on every Georgia child." Gene thought the boys would probably like it, and they probably did.[8]

The platforms of the 1940 race were very similar. They were big on education, big on making the state solvent again, big on retaining some of the social consciousness begun by Rivers, and big on bringing the lavish expenditures of the highway department under control. Because of the assured 100,000 Talmadge base, the other candidates were forced to make Talmadge the major issue. Actually the fact that Gene had been successful in his precampaign groundwork made his candidacy as awesome as his base. Herman had brought a freshness and a flexibility to Gene's campaign. Relatively unencumbered by the dictates of the past, Herman recognized the social reforms that people had come to expect, and he respected the muscle that organization and machinery could exert in a campaign. Gene was still his own man, but he had been taught by experience that perhaps there was sagacity in the opinion of others. He found Herman willing to go into the camp of the enemy in search of support, and it was a tribute to the Talmadge resurgence that they would invite him in.

The New Deal Democrats who had taken control of the state party in 1936 and engineered Gene's downfall had been split badly by the attempted purge of Walter George in 1938. Having found a home in the programs of Ed Rivers, they were further dispirited by his total inability to handle money and avoid scandal. Ironically, in 1940 they realized that their only hope lay in an alliance with Talmadge. His victory seemed a foregone conclusion, and continuing to fight him would have spelled the end of their effectiveness as a political group. Loosely headed by the old 100 percenter Lawrence Camp, these New Deal Democrats offered Gene their support in return for his promise to push several of their programs, thereby maintaining their credibility as a political unit. Gene was not overjoyed at their offer. He didn't need them. And he cast a skeptical but amused eye at their floundering condition before deciding to see them.[9]

Herman was sent to the state Democratic council where he asked for support in return for a more liberalized Talmadge platform. An agreement was worked out on June 29, but was not publicly announced by the council until July 11. The council, comprised of old New Dealers, shocked a lot of people with their humble-pie rationale for backing their arch enemy. "Gene was on the wrong side of the fence . . . but he's okay now." [10]

The Talmadge campaign initiated a tremendous early impact that had sent state power sources scurrying to Gene's side in hopes of aligning themselves with the man who had the smell of victory. Those who had scorned him found him ready to receive them, and they credited some of this pliancy to Herman. The platform that emerged from these alliances contained six major planks and one gimmick plank: (1) to maintain schools and pay teachers; (2) to enforce economy in government; (3) to protect the counties; (4) to veto a sales tax; (5) to encourage the development of natural resources; and (6) to cooperate with the federal government as war approached. The gimmick plank, which had become a standard part of any Talmadge platform after the huge success of the three-dollar tag, was a single auto license for the whole family. The "family license" was supposed to save Georgia's large families money. The 1940 platform was the strongest and most farsighted of Talmadge's career. It was practical and it was political; it accepted the realities of the day. Gene had covered all the bases this time. A Talmadge victory was so certain that the race took on a great degree of boredom, Fistfights at the speeches, a common occurrence, began getting as much press coverage as the speeches themselves. One of the most uproarious meetings of the race occurred on July 27, when all gubernatorial candidates met at Warm Springs. A large Howell crowd was there cheering wildly as their man said Gene was backed by the rich, and Abit Nix's people hoorahed when he said that Gene "boasted he had read Hitler's book seven times, although he said he was too busy to read many other books." While Nix was speaking, Gene arrived— late as usual, creating a loud disturbance among his supporters as he walked through them shaking hands. Once on the platform, he walked to one edge and began shaking hands and talking with supporters, while Nix, who had been drowned out, tried to draw the crowd's attention back to his speech.

Nix had been badly upstaged, and his infuriated supporters started a wild fistfight below the platform. The fight subsided, but then exploded out of control when Gene got up to talk. The fiery Talmadge shouted above the din, "That's a Nix man that started that fight. That's the type of people he brought over." The fight became so furious that a cripple who was at Warm Springs for treatment was set upon when he heckled Gene. The Nix crowd had been angered all day because Gene's loudspeaker system had been installed and wired to the platform so that only his "An Apple for the Teacher" could be played, and it had been played endlessly, drowning out the prespeech music of everyone else.

When the fighting finally subsided, Gene explained that he had just had an operation (hemorrhoids) and that his doctors had asked him to come late and leave early. He did not mean to interrupt the others.

But the crowd was now full of devilment; and while supporters spoke for Gene, a car was set afire at the back of the crowd and the people swirled to watch it burn. It was just like the old days.

About the only punches Gene's opponents were able to land that summer were in regard to Talmadge's early admiration for Europe's rising dictators. They all honed in on Gene's propensity for militaristic action and pointed to where that type of action had gotten Europe. Gene ignored them.

On the night of September 11 the votes pouring into Atlanta indicated a gigantic Talmadge victory. His supporters were jammed into a swank rooftop restaurant in a downtown hotel. Delirious with excitement and drink, the crowd roared enthusiastically when Gene finally arrived at 10:30 that evening. He looked old. His eyes were glazed, but he gamely smiled and shook hands as he worked his way through the press. His neck had thinned, and there was a hawkish look to his nose. The campaign had etched itself onto his features. He finally made his way to the orchestra platform where he waited for the din of noise to stop. When it did he thanked his supporters briefly and said with a weary smile, "Come . . . to see me, boys." As the crowd resumed its clamorous noise, Gene sneaked out and went to his room where he fell exhaustedly to sleep.[11]

The returns were not all in, but the contest had been over long ago. Talmadge's victory was resounding. He had received 179,882 popular votes and an astounding 320 county-unit votes. Columbus Roberts had gotten a strong 124,858 individual votes and 78 unit votes. Abit Nix finished weakly, with 42,534 popular and 12 unit votes.[12] There had been no high or low points, no critical issues or events—just a giant rushing wave for Gene Talmadge that had started in that January, 1939, meeting and peaked with his election for a third term as governor. He had offered a good platform, had admitted his mistake in fighting Roosevelt, and had even agreed to work with FDR's supporters. He was a confident, a mellow Talmadge. So completely had Gene been returned to power that even his old nemesis Ralph McGill had to admit the man had something. He said that no matter where Gene was, "he is always . . . Talmadge." Gene had a "direct honesty" the journalist admired. And about his hypnotic ways: "Talmadge has something only a few men have. He has that quality that makes men want to follow him, to fight for him, to defend him." [13]

To insure a harmonious legislature, Gene had appointed his old friend from Tom Watson's hometown, Randall Evans. This post had

actually been promised at the 1938 convention. Rivers had ordered a
recount of votes in Evans' race for the house in 1938. An angry Evans
had immediately announced that he was a candidate for speaker of the
house against Roy Harris. He also accused the Rivers-Harris people
of trying to eliminate him as a representative—which they were. In
the recount Evans lost by 3 votes, but he kept running in the general
election and won by 115 votes.

"Then I went to Talmadge," Evans said, "and told him that I had
no real chance of being elected [speaker] and the only thing that could
result therefrom would be embarrassment, but he was anxious for me
to run to see just how many friends he had in the General Assembly
[in 1939] that he could depend on," even though he was out of power.
"I told him that I would run for speaker against Roy Harris if he would
shake hands with me on the proposition that he would support me the
next time if he was governor and I were a member of the house . . .
and we did shake hands on it. Two years later I ran for representative
unopposed." And Gene won big. "Thereafter, a great deal of pressure
from corporate interests and people in high places who had contributed substantially to . . . Talmadge's election sought to get him to oppose me for speaker, but he told them he had shaken hands with me
and he intended to live up to that handshake and he did." [14]

The Democratic convention that year was termed a "Talmadge
orgy," as 4,300 near-hysterical red-suspendered supporters jammed
the Macon auditorium to pay homage to "the man who came back
from Sugar Creek." [15] One giant banner hung behind the platform. It
read, "Sugar Creek Welcomes All Democrats." Admiring supporters
were heard to exclaim, "I'd go to hell for Old Gene," and "Look at
him. Damn if he ain't a peach." [16]

The October 1 Atlanta *Journal* reported Gene's campaign expenses
as being $40,000, in sharp contrast to the $12,123.64 he reported for
his 1938 race.[17]

Gene sent Herman to see Roosevelt to promise him that the Talmadges were burying the hatchet and would cooperate fully in the war
effort, and the 1941 legislature opened to more soothing words than
had been heard in years.

A cautiously optimistic state press seemed to think that possibly
Gene's time as a leader had arrived. The normally vitriolic Atlanta
press said, "He has the gift of brevity in public statement. His words
are few but they carry a punch. In a sentence he can state a political
philosophy or summarize a situation, and the sentence sticks in the

mind. He has color and an amazing vitality." [18] *Collier's* magazine described Talmadge to its national audience: "A stout fellow, the Wild Man from Sugar Creek. Make no mistake about that. Sublimely self-assured, utterly without doubt as to the justice and wisdom of his own judgment, decisions and actions, he drives to his goals with a headlong, headstrong impetuousity that takes no heed of obstacles or of the consequences of defeat. To use his own expression, 'He goes the whole hog.' " [19]

The Nazi devastations in Europe brought out the isolationism in Talmadge. He saw the conflict as a potential drain on America's economy. There was, for him, little value in foreign aid taking money from the hungry farmer's pocket. Talmadge singled out FDR as the main force behind America's growing involvement in the war, and this increased his hatred of the man. He felt that if the United States remained strong, the country would be left alone. He said in November, "If you lead a bulldog around with you nobody is likely to jump on you." And in the same breath he warned, "America cannot take the stand of being permanent guard for Europe." [20]

Some thought Gene's isolationism had gotten out of hand when he wrote some highly favorable editorials about Japan in the *Statesman* after that country had just killed thousands of Chinese. Japan thought it had an ally in Gene and invited a member of the *Statesman* to "witness the real life and scenic beauties of Japan so that you may represent them to the American people through your newspaper." Gene was an innocent dupe who was so desperate to keep attention from leaving the poor farmer that he would even try to sanctify warmakers.[21] Others saw this as indicative of the dark side of Gene. When told people were calling him a dictator, he said, "I'm what you call a minor dictator. But did you ever see anybody that was much good who didn't have a little dictator in him?" [22] Gene's early admiration for Hitler, the fact that he had read Hitler's book seven times, and his tendency to surround himself with huge military staffs and nonchalantly call for martial law gave an eerie backing to his words.

16

"One Hell of an Incident"

The great social changes of the 1930s had done little to lift the burden from the black man's shoulders; he remained a second-class citizen. Disfranchised by the white primary, he had to pay when he did vote and was discouraged, often brutally, when he tried to register. His place was at the back of every line, and he was directed by signs not to eat next to a white, or pray next to him, or go to the bathroom next to him. Georgia remained a segregationist society in 1941, and Gene Talmadge remained its greatest advocate. Prior to 1941 he had not made racism a major part of his politics, because he had no reason to. Practically every white Georgian was a racist to some degree; every candidate could be expected to treat the black about the same, which was poorly, and any issue of race had previously been overridden by the New Deal, or by personality. Depending on how far back in the country and how poor his white audience was, Talmadge would allude to the black in the most patronizing or derisive terms. Racism had been a part of his career, but it was far from crucial prior to the 1940s.

It was inevitable that the issue of race would follow close behind the urbanization and sophistication of the South, the profound liberalism and mind-altering effects of the New Deal. Self sufficiency, frontiersmanship, isolationism, and narrow perspectives had been crumbling since 1917, and with geometric speed through the 1930s. Big government had emerged where there had been no government. The culture had eroded. Change appeared to seek change; and in the feudalistic South, this trend had to explode eventually onto the shores of segregation. Southerners could no longer retain their schizophrenic liberal-conservativism. They would find it increasingly difficult to eat from the fruits of an expanding consciousness, while retaining a mental block about the most basic of rights for the race that lived around them.

One of the traditional criticisms of the South was the inadequacy of its educational facilities, both for the white population and for the Negroes. The state university system had been making moves to improve itself, and in doing so had begun hiring teachers from outside Georgia. The infusion of these new perspectives and the attempts by the university administrators to upgrade their system in the late 1930s put them on an unintentional collision course with Gene Talmadge. It would be a classic struggle between a conservative, domineering leader and the liberalizing educators. With Talmadge's ideals on the virtue of the work ethic and weak government destroyed by the New Deal and welfare, he had been backed into an ideological corner. All that remained of his cultural armament, all that remained of his revered heritage was its cornerstone—segregation. The educators were about to bring that cornerstone into sharp focus.

In 1937 Dr. Walter D. Cocking had been hired from out of state to reform and rebuild the University of Georgia's dismal College of Education. He brought impressive credentials and attacked his job zealously. The Board of Regents asked him to do a study on higher education of blacks, which he did and which reported the pathetic state of their schools. He recommended that the state give them more money and suggested that blacks might separately use some white educational facilities.[1] The study was financed by the Rosenwald Fund, a philanthropical foundation established by a northerner who recognized the backwardness of southern schools and did a great deal to change that condition for both whites and blacks.

Another study by the faculty of Cocking's school came out at this time, recommending that a school for rural white and black teachers be built near Athens. Integration was hinted at.[2] News of this reached Gene through some graduate students. At the same time, a Mrs. Sylla Hamilton who taught in a high school operated by the College of Education was fired. She partially blamed Cocking, and she began firing off reports of the black studies program to Talmadge while making inflammatory statements about Cocking. Soon thereafter Talmadge supporter in Athens, I. M. "Bull" Bray, began spreading a rumor about Cocking having an affair with his colored cook. So much attention was given the rumor that university president Harmon Caldwell had it investigated, and Cocking was cleared.[3]

The unfolding scene expanded to the Georgia Teachers College at Statesboro over another progressive educator, the president, Dr. Marvin S. Pittman. In this case the "Sylla Hamilton" was a sixty-nine-year-old professor, R. J. H. DeLoach, an economics teacher only because "it was felt he could cause less harm teaching that subject than some other." [4] Angry about Pittman's aggressiveness and jealous over the promotion of a younger professor, DeLoach began a long correspondence with Gene, making slanderous accusations against Pittman.

Little was known publicly of these events until the May, 1942, Board of Regents meeting. Chancellor S. V. Sanford routinely recommended that all administrative heads be rehired for the next year. Gene, who was a member of the board because he was governor, agreed to all the names but Pittman's. He vaguely accused Pittman of engaging in "local partisan politics." The motion was then passed. Gene next attacked Cocking, opening the whole affair, rumors and all. He said that he had been informed that "Cocking . . . had made a statement that he wanted to see the time when a school for Negroes would be established at Athens so that Negroes and white boys could associate together." Gene said he would remove "any person in the university system advocating communism or racial equality." [5] His motion again passed. President Caldwell heard of the votes and angrily submitted his resignation. [6] This caused the board to meet again in a tumultuous session that called for a hearing before a new vote could be taken. The meeting was on June 16 in Gene's office. The place was packed with school faculty, there to back their men. Gene only had Sylla Hamilton who said Cocking was trying to integrate Georgia. Dean Cocking swore he was not. The regents then voted eight to seven to reinstate Cocking. [7] Gene bellowed from the *Statesman*, "I'm not going to put up with social equality. We don't need no niggers and white people taught together." [8]

He then went after Pittman with a vengeance. Pittman's hearing was to be held on July 14, and it would not be in the privacy of Gene's office, but for public viewing in the general assembly chambers. Gene also told Cocking to show up to hear new evidence against him. This mainly involved his association with the Rosenwalds. He called their fund "Jew money for niggers." [9] Gene had the Statesboro library searched for "Communism or anything else except Americanism." [10] Prior to the hearing he began mounting a public campaign that painted the two men as Communists financed by Jews and bent on destroying Georgia's culture. Privately Gene was working to remove those regents who opposed him: his old classmate and lifelong friend Lucian Goodrich and *Constitution* editor Clark Howell, Jr. Goodrich resigned by letter. "I will not resent nor think any less of you," he wrote, "for withdrawing an appointment which I did not solicit . . . a friendship of forty years cannot be broken." [11] But he concluded, "There was the shadow of a doubt in my mind as to the falsity of the charges."

Gene personally went after Howell in the *Constitution* offices. He told Howell he wanted his resignation. Howell said he would send it by letter. "Get your secretary," Gene snapped. He stood while the letter was typed and left with it in his hands. At 2:00 A.M. he called Jim Peters in Manchester. "I want you in my office at 7:00 sharp in the morning. That's room 444 in the hotel."

Peters sleepily protested, "That's mighty early. Can't you make it later?" Manchester was two hours from Atlanta.

Gene barked, "I've been up all night, an' I'll be up the rest of the night working. If I can do that you can be here."

Arriving an hour late, Peters found Gene seated, giving his secretary Howell's resignation. Goodrich's had already been written. Another classmate of Gene's, John Monaghan, was also there. When Elsie Ray finished the last letter, Gene read them to the two men for their reactions. Peters was concerned. "You can fire Lucian 'cause he's your classmate, and he won't get mad or do anything, but if you fire Clark Howell he will be your political enemy as long as he lives."

"Oh, no. He offered to resign."

"I don't care what he offered; he does not like to be removed in the manner in which you are removing him."

Then Talmadge said, "Jim, I want to make you a member of the Board of Regents in . . . Goodrich's place and Chip Robert in place of Howell, so I can undo what they did in the elections."

"Let's talk about it a little bit," Peters answered.

"We can talk about it as long as you want, but I already know what I want to do."

"Let the elections stand, Gene. You can go all over Georgia from now to election time, cuss Cocking and Pittman and fan the racial thing and get elected. You have these regents and university officials backed to the wall. This racial issue will reelect you overwhelmingly, because the people are with you. But if you accept these resignations, Clark Howell and the *Constitution* will fight you with all their power and influence, and the university will lose its accreditation and the two will result in your defeat."

Monaghan nodded his agreement, but Gene glared at Peters and said, "You know what I think about what you just said?"

"Tell me."

"This accreditation you're talking about is just an incident."

Peters shot back, "It'll be one hell of an incident before you get through with it!" [12]

As news of what Gene was up to filtered to his friends, they, almost to a man, advised him to back off. No one was more relentless in her arguments than his wife. "I begged him to drop the fight or it would ruin him. The school crowd had become too powerful. Education was too important. He told me, 'You ain't my kind of politician.' And I said, 'No but it takes a devil of a lot of my kind to elect you!' " [13]

The public hearing was a public spectacle. The hall was packed, mostly with Talmadge people; and down front—stage center, white suited, smoking a huge cigar, and wearing a ten-gallon hat—sat Gene. His face was locked in a fierce glare that made him look almost wild. It was all show. Flashbulbs sparkled the air, people cheered, police swarmed, and Jim Peters opened the show by reading excerpts from *Brown America*. The book, written by Rosenwald chief Edwin Embree, had been found in Statesboro's library. "Throughout this book," said Peters, "the thought runs: erase the feeling of superiority of the white man. . . . They want them to pull the white man down and draw the races together. They want them to use the same schools, ride the same trains. It means they want intermarriage, that's what it means!"

Gene shouted, "They won't do it," and the galleries rocked with laughter and applause.

Peters was by nature a rather calm speechmaker, and when Gene thought things were slowing down, he would whisper, "Hit the chair and holler, Jim!" It was a phrase that would forever follow Peters.

The purpose of reading the book was to find Cocking and Pittman guilty by association with the Rosenwald fund. Cocking rose, gave a brief denial of the charges, and noted his shock at the circus hearing: "That such tactics could be employed in any country on earth is hard to believe; that they are employed in Georgia has all the earmarks of a terrific nightmare."

The gallery shouted, "Yankee teacher!"

Gene had one witness; Cocking had thirty, but his attorney was not allowed to use much of his material. The new Board of Regents voted ten to five to fire Cocking. The whole affair had been like a bad movie about southern demagogues. Following the Cocking vote, Peters attacked Pittman. DeLoach testified that five Negroes from Tuskegee Institute had toured the Statesboro school and eaten in the cafeteria. There were no whites on campus at the time. Another book dealing with minorities, *Calling America*, was read from, and the Board of Regents voted again ten to five for firing. Gene had had one witness; Pittman had thirty-six.[14]

News of the shame reverberated throughout the state. The Cobb County *Times* wrote, "Justice was publicly raped under the very dome of the capitol." This type of reaction was countered by a deluge of congratulatory mail from the wool-hat boys. To those who asked that he reverse his decision, Gene wrote, "Dr. Cocking favored the teaching of white and negro children in the same classrooms. I am opposed to social equality and so long as I am governor of Georgia, no such teaching will be permitted in our school system. Dr. Cocking, as you know, was reared in Iowa where white and colored are taught in the same classrooms. His conduct since being in Georgia is proof of the fact he retains the views and ideas gained by him in the State of Iowa. I am not in favor of such foreign ideas . . . being taught in our university system." [15]

The school officials and the regents had been overwhelmed by Gene's bold attack. They had massed against him—organizing meetings, firing out petitions, showing up to defend their men; but so long as Gene was able to manipulate the Board of Regents, their fight was temporarily hopeless. The University of Georgia faculty was outraged by the affair,[16] but powerless.

And then the thunderbolt hit. The Southern Accrediting Commission on Institutions of Higher Education announced that it was investigating the Talmadge takeover of Georgia education. Rumors that the state's schools would lose their accreditation swept over Georgia. The governor's office was besieged with frantic calls from parents. Gene scoffed, "We credit our own schools down here." [17] Under intense pressure he went on radio to defend his stand. It was a highly racist speech, which he concluded by saying, "The good Negroes . . . don't want any co-mixing of the races." [18]

The crisis was creating problems for Gene that the public was generally unaware of. Georgia's attorney general, Ellis Arnall, a long-time Talmadge supporter, felt the governor's removal of the regents was outside the law. Gene knew he felt this way, and when Arnall left town for a few days, Gene got one of Arnall's subordinates to write an opinion saying that the governor was correct. When Arnall returned he countermanded this opinion, thus projecting the two men into open opposition. As Arnall said, "I had always wanted to be governor, but to do this, I had to have an issue and seize it. Academic freedom was the issue here and I seized it. The Talmadge dynasty had been built on segregation and he was trying to make that the issue in 1941 when academic freedom was the real issue."[19] Arnall would announce for governor against Gene on December 6, but from July on, Gene would refuse to have anything further to do with his former floor leader.

According to Talmadge aide Henry Spurlin, the break became so bad that in January of 1942, Gene would try to have Arnall arrested. "The legislature was in session, and Gene needed an opinion. He asked his executive secretary Carlton Mobley to check with Arnall, and Mobley said he was in Florida on vacation. Gene blew up and told Carlton to fly down on his own money and get the attorney general, that he should never have let him go while the legislature was in session. Carlton protested, saying Arnall would be in on the morning train anyway. Gene told me and Carlton to go down to the train which got in at dawn and arrest Arnall and bring him to the governor's office. We met him and he said he wanted to get some breakfast at the S & S Cafe, and we said Gene was waiting in the capitol, and he ought to come along. He wasn't really under arrest, because we couldn't do that, but we did take him in, and I heard Gene tell him he was going down a one-way street the wrong way." Arnall says this whole story is a fabrication, that it never happened—and so go the contradictions that surrounded Talmadge.[20]

On September 1, a committee from the Southern Accrediting Commission suspended ten schools in the Georgia system, for "unprecedented and unjustifiable political interference."[21] On October 14, the Southern University Conference dropped the university from its membership. The regents called a November 1 meeting at the capitol to discuss how they might approach the accrediting committee and clear up the mess. Gene appeared, acting strangely recalcitrant. To the board's shock and relief, he said, "I have inadvertently run afoul of the great higher educational system. I here now heartily concur in every proper and logical safeguard that has and can be made to 'protect' the system." He said the whole affair had become a "verbal cyclone" and a "red herring [that] developed into the size of a whale." He appeared to have buckled under the enormous public outcry to save the schools regardless of the cost in integration. Certainly, the regents had had second thoughts since the hearing. The pressure on them individually had been as intense as it had on Gene, and they had relented. Gene told the regents that they could "without qualifications and reservations . . . make whatever changes to my suggestions and actions in the past six months affecting the university system of Georgia that might properly dispel for all time any idea that I . . . would have this system thrown into a political quagmire." He asked that they take his message to Louisville and give assurances he wanted the university system to be of the very highest standards.

Armed with what appeared an appeasement from Talmadge, the board organized a committee of five to "confer with the investigating committee of the southern association and to do whatever the committee deemed proper to protect" Georgia's accreditation. The board then voted to be "honor bound" by whatever the committee of five did in Louisville, thereby protecting any deal they made against Gene.[22] The two committees met shortly thereafter, and upon returning to Atlanta, the five called a regents meeting for November 19, to "secure formal ratification" of what had been agreed upon in Louisville. Only eight members showed up at the meeting, and Gene appeared up to his old tricks when he said the meeting would have to be called off because eight members did not constitute a quorum. When he was informed that the bylaws said that seven made a quorum, he refused to budge. His actions were a slight jolt after the sounds of compromise he had made on the first of the month. He was now trying to block the board, though they had agreed to be "honor bound" by any decisions. Probably the reason Gene didn't want the board to meet was that the committee had decided to recommend that Pittman and Cocking be rehired at their old salaries in return for appeasing the accreditation committee. Member Sandy Beavers assured the board there was not the "least possibility of Cocking returning."

Beavers was a Talmadge man, and he was deeply concerned over what Gene's actions had done to Georgia's colleges. Because it was felt the accreditation people would respect what he said, Beavers was selected to go before the committee in Louisville in December to seek a reinstatement. The committee of five's efforts, filled with promise, had failed because of Gene. Beavers knew he must go to Louisville with more than a vague "honor bound" pledge and Gene's verbal promises to cooperate. He felt he needed written documentation from the governor and every member of the board.

On November 25, he wrote a letter for Gene to sign in which Gene admitted that his powers in controlling the university system were limited. He followed up delivery of the letter to Talmadge with a telegram: "As soon as you have approved or revised that letter to me I suggest you give copies and favorable comments to the press in as much as it answers satisfactorily the Georgia Alumni and everyone else at the same time. The more concessions and the stronger you can make the letter, the sooner it gets into the papers, the better will be the effect here in Georgia now and next week in Louisville." [23]

On November 26 Gene wrote back: "I think it is a mistake for a governor to write any letter which might limit his authority as governor. I think the less said about it in the papers . . . the better. In fact the only case they have against the university system is newspaper 'blah.' " [24] Beavers had subtly tried to give Gene some good political advice and get the man to show some flexibility. But Gene wouldn't.

Beavers would not give up. Writing Gene again, he asked that he re-read the letter and "you will find that it does not limit your authority except as far as you desire. I am sure that such a letter would do more for the university system and for you than any other course." Beavers said the state could get off with a "warning." Continuing his argument, Beavers wrote, "As it is, those people in Louisville know that you and the other regents agreed unanimously that you were 'honor bound' to back the five-man committee, and they also know that you not only have not done so, but that you have caused other regents not to do so." Beavers kept pushing, "Unless you arm me with a letter along the lines of the one I submitted to you yesterday, the least we can secure in Louisville will be 'probation,' and this means a long, hard political fight from now until next summer with most of the newspapers and several thousand students and their families against you." Beavers closed with a hint of warning, "Think it through, old fellow."[25]

Gene still refused to budge. He believed the issue was not the loss of accreditation by a bunch of "two-by-four professors." The issue was whether Georgians wanted their whole society altered by social acceptance of the Negro. Gene felt the implications and the threat were of far greater magnitude than even the New Deal had been, though he saw them both as a common conspiracy by "outsiders" to take over the lives of Georgians. He did not believe the voters wanted integration; he did not believe they gave a damn about an accreditation association. He believed that their opposition to Negro equality was so strong they would risk almost any loss. Although his best friends and his wife told him he was wrong, letters kept pouring in from the wool-hat boys saying he was right. He felt, as he would say a year later, "When the people speak on September 4, those credits are going to come running back so fast that a Greyhound bus couldn't catch them." [26]

Beavers wrote the other regents on November 27 with a candid admission of his motives. He said he had only two: one was to protect the university system, and the other was "to assist my life long friend Talmadge" to reelection. He said that despite the current mess, Gene's "financial policies" would reelect him. Beavers also asked each member to send him a wire promising to back any agreement he might make at Louisville.[27] Beavers failed in his efforts for reinstatement.

On December 4, after appeals had been exhausted, the Southern Accrediting Commission had voted to end the accreditation of Georgia's ten state-supported white schools. The fight for academic freedom seemed lost. Gene's attempt to control the educational system brought contempt from the nation's liberals. Typical of the image the governor was projecting was an editorial in the St. Louis *Post-Dispatch*: "Here in the heart of Dixie has developed a prize specimen of full-blown American fascism . . . the dictatorship is just as effective and just as vicious as the . . . Long dictatorship." [28]

17

"The Negro's Place Is at the Back Door with His Hat in Hand"

Liberals thought the elections of 1942 represented a landmark, a show of conscience, and a blow to racism. Conservatives would say it seemed that a crack had appeared in the white supremacy cornerstone, but it was not serious, because all of the candidates were racists at heart. The myth was that white Georgia would be asked to choose between the Negro and education, and they voted for education. The truth was that two racists (Talmadge and Arnall) opposed each other; one identified with closing the colleges, the other with keeping them open and accredited. Most Georgians felt the issue was not segregation, but education—or to the theorists, academic freedom.

Arnall, emerging as Gene's only opponent, said that the issue was not the black man, not the mixing of the races, but whether Georgia's children would be denied quality education. Gene kept saying he was not against education. But he was having trouble shaking the suggestion that he was, as voters formed their initial opinions about the candidates and issues.

This would also mark the first time in the state's history that students could claim an impact on state politics because of purposeful efforts on their part. University of Georgia students made themselves heard throughout the fall of 1941, putting on anti-Talmadge skits at football games and joining the Arnall campaign in substantial numbers to canvas for support. Theirs was to be the generation freed from the tragic cycle imposed by the one-crop agricultural economy. Education was their way out. Their parents, who had not had college, were proud of the young people for getting it. Higher education was becoming more than a luxury of the rich; it was becoming a source of pride and a necessity for all income groups. And Gene, they said, was taking it away.

Arnall felt that the only way he could beat Gene was to be his only opponent. The racial issue was dynamite, and Arnall knew that thousands of voters would back Gene to the hilt on it. He also knew he could not compete against Gene in a "nigger-hating contest." Gene had the market on that. That left only education as the platform on which Arnall could stand. It was also the only platform any other candidate could stand on, and that could mean a split of the county-unit vote and a victory for Gene. When Columbus Roberts let the word get around that he wanted to run, Arnall sent Roy Harris to talk him out of it. He had become so committed that it took Harris a week to wear Roberts down. Roberts had thought Gene would run for the senate and back him as governor, but when Harris convinced him that this wasn't so, Roberts caved in.[1]

The election would introduce into the vernacular the phrase, "the better element"—meaning those voting for progressive candidates and legislation, generally people with higher incomes, better education. The term's usage substantiates an emerging conscience, an acquiescence to the compromising demands of urbanization, and the growing intelligence of the Georgia body politic. It provides evidence that 1940 was mind miles ahead of 1930, that without the encumbrances of the cotton culture, the southern mind was susceptible to change. Not a lot of change, but change. Gene would not be known as "the better element's" man.

One Talmadge worker worried that the loose Talmadge organization was letting voters slip through its hands. In a letter to Carlton Mobley, he wrote, "Am afraid we are inclined to be a little confident about the outcome. . . . On the surface everything appears to be fine, but there is a light registration all over the state. . . . The farmers have been very busy with their crops and there was not enough interest taken to see about their qualifying." Mobley agreed there was not much interest, but he did not agree as to the cause.[2] Gene said he would build interest—with 15,000 pounds of fried fish for his July 4 opener.

Georgia was overcast on the fourth; rain swept over the state indiscriminately. It had never rained at an opening Talmadge speech. Arnall had talked so furiously before the day was over that he got a painful cramp in his arm; a nurse had to come onto the platform and knead his arm while he continued speaking. He accused Gene of being Georgia's answer to Hitler; the governor exercised "unwarranted, unprecedented and unbelieveable power." Arnall asked the people to "awaken to the dangerous trend in our state government"; it was a fight against "disgrace, disunity, dishonesty and shame." [3]

The platform Arnall presented was built around the school crisis. It also advocated weakening the office of governor by removing his ability to control departments of state and their employees. It would remove the Board of Regents from politics, by making that body a constitutional office. Arnall's ten-plank platform also promised support to FDR and the war effort. Perhaps the best thing Ellis Arnall had going for him politically was the campaign wizardry of the masterful Roy Harris. Harris was assigned to the counties, and from the headquarters at the Henry Grady, he worked tirelessly to line up county bosses.

Gene had driven down to Moultrie early on the morning of July 4, wearing a heavy overcoat. There were no motorcades this time, just Gene and his driver. As they neared Moultrie, Gene told the man to pull off at the next farmhouse for him to go to the outhouse. The driver protested, saying they were almost to town and Gene could go to a filling station. But using farmers' outhouses was a part of the Talmadge image, and he wouldn't hear of missing this chance to win another voter. The driver pulled up at the farm, and Gene disappeared around the house and down the tiny trail. When he returned, he was rubbing the seat of his pants and seemed in some pain.

"What's the matter?" the driver asked.

"A Goddamn black widow spider bit me on the ass!"

The driver roared off to Moultrie with Gene groaning in the back seat. A doctor was found; Gene was given medication and advised to forget the speech. He refused the advice.[4] His opening speech was to last an hour. Gene began in great pain, but was hardly into his talk when heavy clouds exploded in a drenching rain that sent the large crowd scattering off in all directions. Gene wouldn't quit, though only a handful now stood before him; the rest of those who stayed sat in their cars, fogging up their windows. The rain pelted Gene's lonely figure, slightly bent with pain, but he kept talking hard and loud so that those in their cars could hear. The water pounded the paper bunting, washing its fragile red, white, and blues over the pine planking in gashes of color. It drenched Gene's suit and plastered his hair against his head, but still he went on—wet to the bone, alone and hurting badly from the bite. After twenty-five minutes, he could give no more; he hobbled dejectedly from the platform to the applause of honking car horns. Only one prompter had remained with him, and when he asked, "What about the Negroes going to our schools, Gene?" Talmadge responded, "Before God, friend, the niggers will never go to a school which is white while I am governor." He blamed the whole mess on carpetbaggers, Communists, and newspapers. Hellbent Edwards took over for him, and then Hellbent's son, a young man whom university students had tried to get to throw eggs at Gene until they discovered he was a Talmadge supporter seeking sympathy for his man.

Even the band had arrived late for the speech. But the people did come out of their cars and trucks and yellow school buses long enough to eat the 15,000 pounds of fish and most of the 100 gallons of sweet pickles and to drink the 50 barrels of tea.

The Talmadge camp reported that "a slick young fellow" had written a "whopper" of a tune for Gene, but it must be said Arnall upstaged him with a song written to "Oh! Susannah:"

> Ole Gene Talmadge
> He's always up to tricks,
> Now he's put a pickaninny
> In his peanut politics.[5]

The Atlanta *Journal* noted that Gene's candidacy had soured because of too much racism, and he was in trouble on the county level because he had neglected the sheriffs and cut revenue to the counties by lowering their millage rate. Old friends seemed to be leaving him in droves, and it became a part of every Arnall speech to have ex-Talmadge people turn in their red suspenders. Students disrupted rallies chanting "To Hell with Talmadge," and at Statesboro, on July 29, a roughneck who drove Gene and guarded him on occasion got angry at the students and tossed a can of tear gas into their midst while Gene spoke. Although the incident was minor, news of it exploded through the state press and grew out of proportion through word of mouth. Gene was accused of allowing hoodlums to remain in his camp.[6]

This type of incident formed the basis for one of the most telling attacks Arnall made in the campaign. He said Gene was "carrying a bunch of strong-arm rats and pluguglies ready to use mustard gas on children. I am glad I do not associate with machine gun operators. . . . I am glad I do not live in fear of friends I have doublecrossed." [7] The Atlanta *Journal* followed this up with a summation of what Talmadge critics thought of him. It was an image that would be in their minds long after his death. In analyzing why violence followed a Talmadge campaign the paper said, "Talmadgism by its very nature tends to produce this sort of thing." It means "bullying, browbeating, dictatorship. Its reliance is not on reason but on arbitrary force. Its appropriate emblems are a gas bomb and a blackjack." [8]

In the same vein, the paper had earlier written that it is "the same old

Talmadge that has been hugging or haunting public office for 25 years." It said, "One looks in vain through his welter of words for a statesmanly idea or constructive purpose." But, "He turns his back on vital questions and urgent needs . . . to conjure up false issues and strut his demagogue stuff. The same old Talmadge seeking four more years of misrule and clownishness . . . four more years in which to daub" Georgia's symbolic arch "with a pair of red suspenders and a mop of rowdy hair. In all his 25 years of political showmanship, Eugene Talmadge has never represented the Georgia that lives in the heart and hopes of its people. . . . He has misrepresented those he has flattered most . . . the small farmers, tenants, sharecroppers . . . his candidacy is an insult to Georgia's intelligence." [9] The editorial was not completely accurate in assessing the Talmadge career, but it was an excellent portrayal of what a lot of people had come to think of him.

In a campaign that seemed characterized by blunders, Gene succeeded in making one more that could only have backfired. His old and loyal friend, Tom Linder, who was then agriculture commissioner, wanted to run against Russell for the senate. But Gene wanted Russell's support if possible; at the least, he wanted Russell to remain neutral in the governor's race. Gene feared that if Linder ran against Russell, his vast number of supporters would think Gene had put him up to it and would thus vote for Arnall. When he couldn't talk Linder out of running, Talmadge persuaded the Democratic Executive Committee to rule that an officeholder had to quit one office if he wanted to run for another. Linder had two years left in his term, and he refused to quit. Infuriated at Gene, he quit his camp and campaigned against him.[10] Critics said it was another example of how ruthless Talmadge could be.

Gene knew by late in the campaign that he had been established as a man against education, and he was having so hard a time shaking this stigma that he tried, in rural areas, where college was relatively meaningless, to downgrade education. In one cotton community, Porterdale, he said, "They talk about education. It ain't never taught a man how to plant cotton. It ain't never made your garden bloom. It ain't ever taught the experience necessary to raise cows and chickens. You gotta git out and do them things, and no school education is gonna help ya." [11] This kind of reasoning made sense to the farmer, who saw the Negro as the real issue anyway.

The complexity and the hypocrisy of the southern racial situation is clearly reflected in the 1942 race. It seems strange that Talmadge was called the racist candidate, while his opponents, men of liberality, education, and humanism, could utter statements similar to Gene's and yet not be cast in the same mold. In August, for instance, the president of the University of Georgia, Harmon Caldwell, announced that he was against "bringing racial charges" against his school, because he was going on record giving his "unqualified assurances" that "there has never been . . . during my administration any effort to promote, encourage, or suggest the coeducation of members of the white and colored races." He concluded in his circumlocutory, but unmistakable, way, saying his views "on race questions are similar to those held by any intelligent southern man." [12]

One week later, the friend of education, Ellis Arnall, said from the stump, "Why if a Negro ever tried to get in a white school in the section where I live, the sun would not set on his head." Despite these kinds of statements, the Atlanta *Constitution* felt no hyprocrisy in condemning Talmadge's campaign as "the most false and shameful in the history of the state." Clark Howell, Jr., had a vendetta against Gene, which was obviously prejudicing his paper's reporting.[13]

Gene kept the critics going by saying, "We in the South love the Negro in his place—but his place as at the back door." Talmadge supporters in Athens were so worried they didn't even want Gene in town: "I believe it will be best for you not to speak in Clarke County for reasons you and your friends know best . . . but to speak at surrounding towns." The chairman of the Clarke County Democratic Executive Committee advised: "It might be best to wait until after the closing of school," before making a speech in Athens. It seems odd, in view of a slip Arnall made over state radio, that he was not construed as a racist like Gene. Arnall, thinking his radio time had ended, was overheard saying, "Any nigger who tried to enter the university would not be in existence [the] next day. We don't need a governor [or] a sheriff to take care of that situation." [14]

On election night, Jim Peters ran into Gene in the crowded halls of the Henry Grady. Gene said, "Jim, it looks mighty good."

Peters answered, "Governor, it doesn't look that way to me."

"Why not?"

"All the counties coming in early are giving you votes by small numbers, and those are counties we felt we could win."

"Jim, you are right. Not a one they have reported will end up in my column." [15]

And he was right. Ellis Arnall drew 174,757 popular votes to Gene's 128,394. Arnall also beat Gene badly in the county-unit vote, winning

261 units to Gene's 149.[16] For all of its passion, the race failed to draw as many voters as did the rather dull 1940 election in which 355,068 votes were cast against the 305,151 in 1942. Obviously, many men of voting age were at war, but when compared with the 390,849 who voted in the senate race in 1936, the vote would still seem not as high as the passions of the day were supposed to have been—and certainly not as high as they had been when the people were faced with voting for or against the New Deal. It must also be said, however, that the war detracted to a degree from the state issues.

The morning after the defeat, Jim Peters was the first man in Talmadge's office. He found the governor quiet and dejected, but reflective and honest in the cool of the day after. "Jim, I can take what happened yesterday and come back to fight again, but I'm sorry for my friends."

"Governor, I was not greatly surprised at the results."

And in one of the rare times Gene admitted he was wrong: "Well, if I had listened to you early in June, all of this would not have happened, because it was the university issue that defeated me." [17]

Gene's defeat did not mean Georgians were ready to embrace Negroes or to allow integrated schools; but the vote was a significant statement which testified to the profound changes that had occurred in the white Georgians' minds. They had faced the racial issue and for the first time in history, they had blinked—thereby showing a flexibility, not much, but some. The voters did show that they valued something more than white supremacy. Probably few other issues would have caused such a vote, but the fact that one issue did cause the white reaction was historically significant. Gene had misread Georgians' willingness to reject the old way for a second time. He had shown again how his personality politics could not withstand a confrontation with great issues. Reality had again defeated idealism.

It was difficult to believe that only a decade had passed since Gene exploded into the governor's office touted as a savior and reformer. He had in a great sense entered state politics in the last year of its near-total capitulation to the old way. The people of Georgia had changed drastically in some respects, during the intervening ten years; but in many respects they had been changing since World War I, and in other respects, they strongly retained many of their old attitudes and much of their ancestors' consciousness. Few Georgians had actually changed in their attitude toward Negroes, for it must be remembered that Ellis Arnall promised little to blacks. What he did do was play down the black as an issue, while letting it be known that he was anti-Negro in a more quiet and polite manner than Gene. He allowed white Georgians to retain their consciences; retain their comfortable hypocrisy; to vote one way and believe another; to show some compromise which they did want to do, while knowing deep down they had lost nothing.

To supporters he didn't know, Gene wrote, "The tide was against us, and it seems we were unable to overcome it." To those he knew better, he wrote, "The newspapers were so unfair that we were unable to overcome it." [18]

Gene best characterized his image, and how, in that year, it was so out of place, when he asked a reporter if his enemies thought he were a damn fool.

The reporter answered: "Some think you're a damn fool, others think you're a dictator, some think you're just mean as hell."

Gene thought for a minute, then announced, "I am. I'm just as mean as hell." [19]

In 1942 Georgia, a lot of people agreed, and most of them voted for Ellis Arnall.

For the growing legions who said you had to keep a close eye on Old Gene, a juicy bit of underhandedness was disclosed in January, just before he turned the keys over to Arnall. It involved a once-a-month delivery of boxes heaped with all manner of vegetables and meats that had been grown and processed by the inmates at the state prison farm —since 1940. To make matters worse, the deliveries had also been made to the house in McRae. Confronted with the report of this, the governor had no excuses or apologies: "I didn't pay a penny for any of it. I'd advise the next governor to try the same plan. It helps to keep expenses down." [20]

Later in the year, columnist Ralph McGill sought to discredit Talmadge by reporting in two editorials that Gene had been seen at a Ku Klux Klan meeting. McGill received a long letter from his antagonist, saying he was not an evil man because he had attended the Klan banquet. "Ralph, I don't hate anyone. I know that hatred dwarfs the man who carries it in his soul, and does not effect the one whom he hates at all." With his typical simplicity he continued, "Everyone had a good time, and I wish, Ralph, that you could have been there." [21]

The two men, though admirers of each other, and both social segregationists, were miles apart on the worth of a group such as the Klan. Talmadge closed his eyes to its brutality; McGill faced it head on and rejected it loudly.

Talmadge's 1942 defeat pointed up the problem with his weak political organization. Gene *was* the organization. The machinery beyond him was so slapdash and unsophisticated that it must have ranked as one of the weakest structures of any major politician in Georgia history. In "issue" years like 1936, 1938, and 1942, Gene was beaten partly because he had no tight organization to hold the counties in line. Personality politics were invariably beaten by larger issues. Gene could not and did not dominate and defeat a major issue. He possibly could have with the right organization. But every man who ever worked a Talmadge campaign agreed they were run "out of Gene's hip pocket."

Herman explains, "Because of the county-unit system, you had 159 separate races. In each of those counties you had bosses or just plain politicians, each of whom wanted to be a deputy governor in his own little area. You can imagine the amount of trades and deals this could involve if a candidate wanted to set up a well-run machine. My father chose not to, but went straight to the people. Because of this, we never had much support with the county politicians. He was such an independent-minded man he didn't want to enter office with so many favors to pay off. We'd pick out some two-horse farmer, somebody you never heard of, and make him county manager. The only time we were strong in a county was when we overwhelmed it with supporters." [22]

Out of work, Gene moved further to the right, unrestrained by having to please a constituency. He became more and more vocal against Roosevelt and the war. He accused the government of taking advantage of the war to promote the cause of the black. He became so isolationist that he even jumped Churchill for meddling in the affairs of the United States Senate. And conversely, he said FDR was "dictating" to foreign lands by trying to spread the New Deal for "world regimentation." He said the New Dealers were working toward a "full-fledged police system over the world." In his hatred of Roosevelt, his *Statesman* carried such headlines as, "Election of Roosevelt Means Promoting Negroes in Georgia." [23]

He was so convinced that the war was destroying rural Georgia that he said farmers should not have to go into the army in large numbers and that married farmers should be released. [24] It must be said that during this period Talmadge became the total cultural isolationist. He was much more than a "nigger hater"; he was a man who saw the world war as a devastating follow-up to the New Deal in the changes it was wreaking upon conservatism and the traditions of his people. Nothing better represented these changes than the growing Negro liberation movements.

Gene's personal hatred for Roosevelt reached a peak during this period. Roosevelt "thought all politicians were crooks";[25] and since 1935, when Gene started his run for the presidency, Roosevelt had had the Internal Revenue Service trying to find irregularities in the Talmadge career. The investigators were known to have checked banks around the world for secret accounts, and they were even seen on the Talmadge farms counting pigs, cows, and chickens. In 1945, after ten years of exhaustive but fruitless searching they came to Gene's law office and "presented him a bill for $3,000 for all the work they had done." Gene exploded at the men: "Now you Goddamn sonofabitches have been after me for ten years. Now you go over to the federal court and get an indictment to make me pay, and I'll see you in court!" The men left and were not heard from again. Perhaps, if the news of this very thorough secret investigation had been publicized, the rumors of Talmadge's making money under the table would not have been so strong.

Gene's assets in 1945 were around $80,000. He owned the farm in McRae, the old family place at Forsyth, a farm at Lovejoy, and small property in Wheeler and Telfair counties. His primary interest was cattle, though he had a lot of land planted in pine. He had largely given up any notion of making money out of pure farming. He derived some income from his law practice, but never devoted enough time or energy to it to make much. Politics remained his life between 1942 and 1946, and into its discussion and acting went most of his energy.

Gene's weight had fluctuated through the years. His 5'9" frame was sturdy, but did not carry weight well. He weighed 130 when he was agriculture commissioner, 180 in 1932, but his weight was down in 1945. Cirrhosis of the liver was draining his body badly. It showed, and he felt it, but he rarely discussed it.

During the Arnall years, Talmadge haunted the Georgia scene—a ghost's voice hellbent on halting the future. But it was a frightened voice, scared that the wave of history had at last washed over the impregnable culture of his fathers. So easily had the people succumbed to the siren call of change that Gene found himself with only one hoary root left, one last undeniable link to yesterday—the black. He alone anchored the tenacious culture, the old consciousness. Gene Talmadge knew if this one last tie was uprooted, his world would be gone forever.

18

The Negro's Second Emancipation

Nineteen forty-six dawned with a lust for life. It was a time of rebirth for Europe and a time for returning to normality for most Americans, though not so much to the normality of the past. Discernible alterations had come to millions of people because of the war, the New Deal, technocracy, and the mass media. A productivity level unimagined before the war had added to the perceptible changes and to the personal-priority and value systems. The liberal thrusts of the late 1930s and early 1940s had also given impetus to the black movement. As in World War I, the Negro had swept out of the countryside and into industry and the service. Many southerners carefully noted these movements, though they could rarely have been construed as steps forward socially.

Like the nation, Georgia had also witnessed changes. The rural to urban migration had continued. Cotton production had fallen off, continuing a twentieth-century trend, and an industrial awareness had at last arrested the thinking of a large part of the citizenry. The New Deal, the depression, and the war had forced rural Georgia into a participatory relationship of physical involvement with the industrial economy of the nation.

The little new deal of E. D. Rivers and the liberalisms of Ellis Arnall had afforded Georgia needed reforms and showed a rare governmental conscientiousness regarding the people's needs. The social reforms that Rivers' and Arnall's administrations made were unprecedented in Georgia history and represented a profound new relationship between Georgia and the federal government. Their cooperative involvements marked a turning point in power relinquishment by the state. By the close of Arnall's tenure liberalism was heard to be wheezing. The way was becoming more difficult, and a hint of reaction to that movement seemed to move in with the close of the war. The people appeared to have been overwhelmed by events and changes. The consistency of ac-

215

tion and its concomitant tensions had created the desire for a halt and a silence of sorts.

The backlash to change, which was not universal in Georgia, brought many eyes back to the Negro. It appeared that only one vestige of the past remained fairly intact, and that happened to be the cornerstone of the old way, the Negro. The servile Negro remained, and his physical presence made him a tangible security symbol for Georgians.

Gene considered the Negro the vulnerable spot in the liberal's armor. His son Herman, now back from the navy, and a number of other astute advisers were in disagreement with Gene over the degree of emphasis that should be placed on the racial issue. Herman had seen his father ride race to defeat in 1942; and while Georgia was still very much racist, she had shown that a flexibility had entered her consciousness on that subject. She was not so dogmatic. She had allowed her attitudes toward the black to suffer erosion, not very much, but there had been movement.

The arguments in the inner circle in late 1945 were shadowed by the uncertainty of what Ellis Arnall would do. Early winter had seen a great deal of jockeying by a number of would-be candidates for the support of Arnall. Georgia law prevented him from succeeding himself, and his lieutenants had styled Arnall their kingmaker. Their intentions were based on the widely held feeling that Arnall's liberalism had become the politics of the future in Georgia. They felt he was so popular that he could name the next governor. The princes included Arnall's adjutant general, Marvin Griffin; his speaker of the house, Roy Harris; E. D. Rivers, the man who claimed to have "made" Arnall what he was; and assorted others who could not claim such close connections.

Probably no man could claim greater debts, or greater right to the term *kingmaker*, than Roy Harris, and he was letting it be known that this was his turn to run. Any rebuttal was given an angry, "Goddamnit! I've been kingmaker for three governors. Now it's my turn to be King!" [1] It was true. Gene and Ed and Ellis had all had their turns at the top, and all had owed a great deal of their success to the mastery of Roy Harris. Of the handful of major politicians of that day, Harris remained the only one who had not made it to the top. It is doubtful that there has been a more powerful or skillful legislator in this century in Georgia than Harris, and the voters knew it—which didn't mean they wanted him for governor, and the politicians felt they knew that. Perhaps he had been too visible, known for too much backroom maneuvering, too much bossism of Augusta politics. He was a machine man.

All preened themselves and strutted before the Arnall throne, and to a man they did not see the eye of Arnall looking inward. Ellis wanted to run again. He had gotten none of the national offices or cabinet posts he had reportedly wanted so badly. FDR was gone. Since there was no one left to take him out of Georgia politics, he decided to stay. Arnall's desire to run was not all ego. He knew his four years of reform could be severely damaged by an arch-conservative like Talmadge. But the camps of the aspirants reeled with shock and fury at Arnall's request that the legislature revoke the anti-succession amendment. Ed Rivers swore he would destroy Arnall, and the explosive Harris committed himself to the same plan, only he would not mask his attempts as Rivers would. He would take the fight to his personal battleground, the house floor. Griffin had neither the power nor the resources to do much, other than wait out the legislative decision.

Arnall had angered two very powerful allies by his decision, and he had incensed many rural-conservative legislators who were tired of his domination. Backing up this growing feeling against Arnall was the shadow of Talmadge. Rumors were everywhere that he was waiting in the wings, that Old Gene would make another run at it. He had done his share of feeding the rumors, jawing like an old war-horse to one friend in his excited manner, "There ain't another Goddamn sonofabitch that can get elected governor! I been sick and it might just kill me, but I'm a gonna do it."

When the friend asked Gene why risk his health when his son Herman could run, he snapped, "Naw, I'm the only Goddamn sonofabitch that can win!" [2] He refused to believe the Arnall liberals could withstand an all-out campaign against the black, and he knew of no man who could better carry out that campaign than himself.

The 1946 legislature had hardly opened before the skirmishing began, and Arnall started fishing for support. It appeared the amendment would pass easily when it flew through the senate on January 15.[3] The senate passage was the signal flare for Harris and the Talmadge-Rivers forces in the house to firm their lines, and the political year was off to a slam-bang start.

Arnall had no trouble finding willing ears in the house, but he was being confronted with embarrassing accusations of his being a scalawag, a sell-out to his state. He had accepted a $60,000 fee to tour the

North, speaking about his land and its promises and problems. Only the word got back that Ellis was being too frank in talking Georgia down, and this created a furor.

The second-term amendment came before the house on January 25, and to the profound disappointment of every southern liberal it was defeated by eleven votes.[4] Rivers was immediately notified that Arnall would never support him because of his part in the defeat, and Rivers grew even more bitter. Arnall's camp released a warning to the unannounced candidates: "We have no doubt that Ellis Arnall is still the strongest man in Georgia politics." Georgia's congressmen were vocally disappointed over Arnall's defeat; they predicted that a large field would result in a divided vote and a victory for Gene Talmadge. Gene's 100,000 core supporters assured him a healthy county-unit vote, and that was all Gene was banking on. What worried the congressmen was that the only man strong enough to beat Gene couldn't run.[5]

With the dust of battle still settling, a relatively new name was suddenly launched by liberals. From Marietta a small James V. Carmichael for Governor Club was formed by an unattached citizens' group. There were, however, old-time professionals guiding the group, trying to remain unnoticed by the accusing fingers of the other candidates.[6] Carmichael, a two-term legislator from Cobb County, had been the highly successful manager of Marietta's huge Bell aircraft plant. To many he typified the new southern businessman—progressive, hard working, intelligent, prosperous, adaptive to change, and somewhat liberal. He was physically attractive and a proven vote getter, but he was barely known by the state electorate. This did not keep the Atlanta *Constitution* from heralding his candidacy.

As suddenly as it had started, however, the Carmichael campaign fizzled out. He withdrew. His wife had applied tremendous pressure for him not to run; also, he was offered the presidency of the big Scripto ballpoint pen company, and since he was looking for an out, he took it.[7] The Arnall forces sank to a new low. They looked with horror at the growing Talmadge candidacy and its threat of liberal oblivion. Some thought they should back Rivers, but the majority felt the scandals and unprincipled directions of his administration made his brand of liberalism as uninviting as Gene's nineteenth-century conservatism. Besides offering a helter-skelter brand of New Dealism, Rivers had quietly been in on the defeat of the amendment. That, more than anything else, made him anathema.

The Talmadge camp was shocked on March 1 to hear that a straw

vote taken in Coffee County showed that the leading candidate for
governor was old Talmadge crony, Tom Linder. Gene was the second
choice. The frightening thing was that in the last three gubernatorial
elections Coffee had voted for the winner. Linder could wreak havoc
in Gene's ranks, and Gene immediately began figuring some way to
head off his old friend.

While the boys toe-danced all over the political stage, an event critical to all their futures occurred in a New Orleans federal court. The
court ruled that blacks must be allowed to vote in previously all-white
primaries. The news broke in Atlanta on March 8, and sent Roy Harris into a frenzy of activity. The decision also provided Gene with some
badly needed angles on the racial issue which needed some substantiation. It had generally been felt that the black had advanced, but there
had also been the comfort of knowing his advancement had been more
myth than reality. The court ruling changed all that and thrust the Negro into the foreground as an issue. It also sent a shudder through
Georgia's liberal establishment, for very few of them favored social
integration. It would have cost them their progressive credibility to
join the chorus against the black; but worse than that, they feared that
an outburst of white supremacy would obliterate them at the polls. Roy
Harris promised them that race would be an issue by calling for a special legislative session to save the white primary on the same day the
federal court ruled it illegal.

By March 18 Talmadge had announced a plan calling for a special
session that would abolish the state's primary laws altogether, thereby
leaving primary regulations up to the parties. After this law was passed
the Democratic party, meeting in executive session, would rule that the
Democrats would have a white primary and that its results would be
governed by the county-unit system. But Gene's plan displeased both
liberals and conservatives. Abolishment of the primary laws meant an
end to the county-unit system and an end to the laws that protected the
elections from fraud. Both groups were afraid that once the state's voting regulations and structure were abolished, the political foundation
of the state would be destroyed. It was too great a chance to take just
to protect the white primary.[8] The issue seemed in limbo.

"Politically speaking, to have been a black man in Georgia before
April 4, 1946, was to have been nothing," remembers Atlanta *Daily
World* publisher, C. A. Scott. "In 1944, I headed up a group of At-
lanta blacks who voted in a bloc and were actually responsible for a

candidate winning a primary election. She was eventually defeated, but the fact that we voted in large numbers and it had an effect was very exciting. I had been chomping at the bit for ten years. I just wanted to vote like an American." [9] But the real crack in the segregation system came in the middle of the gubernatorial maneuverings, in April, 1946, Scott recalled; and it came from a Texas court decision which ruled that blacks must be allowed to vote in the white primary. In other words, there could be no white Democratic primary. Arnall scoffed and said the Texas decision would have no effect on Georgia, but Gene Talmadge made determined plans to enter the race in a head-to-head fight against the black man.

"That decision was the Negro's second emancipation," said Scott. "And it scared Gene to death. You know, we never thought Talmadge was as bad as he sounded. It was the mobs he stirred up. He was just exploiting the race issue, and he was able to do it because of the one party system."

Herman Talmadge was an integral part of the 1946 campaign, pushing from the start for a more liberal approach and a dampening of the racial issue. Without his father's knowledge, he wrote the 1946 platform. Reportedly Gene exclaimed, "Good God Almighty! Who wrote this stuff!"

Herman answered quietly, "I wrote the platform. It's time for you to announce if you're going to run."

"You're carrying me pretty far, aren't you son?" Gene referred to the liberal planks.

"You've got to travel fast if you're going to win this one." [10]

Roy Harris opened the month of April by announcing that he had polled the legislators and 123 of them had said they favored a special session. So great was the pressure Harris and Gene were building that Arnall was forced to respond. In a statement that doomed his chances of a second term, in a moment of unprecedented courage, Arnall asked Georgians as "good people" to let the blacks vote in their primary. He said he would not call a session to circumvent the courts. He felt that even if the legislature met, it would not vote out the primary laws for fear of losing the county-unit system and the criminal laws. A strong coalition of liberals and conservatives had assured Arnall that they would concur in this decision.[11] By his stand Arnall had drawn the battle lines for the summer campaigns. Any man seeking his support would have to back this volatile position of allowing the white primary to die. Arnall, to the contrary, didn't think the issue so volatile. He felt Georgians were sick of racist politicians and hardly cared whether the black voted. Politically, his candidates would get the black vote because of his stand. He knew he had lost the staunch conservative vote to Gene and Roy, and thus felt he had little to lose by moving further to the left.

One of the stranger meetings in that year of growing bitterness occurred in late spring at the home of Tom Linder. Shortly after supper one evening, his reading was disturbed by a knock at the door; upon answering the door, Linder was startled to see Gene Talmadge standing alone in the night. His manner was strangely reticent; he seemed inwardly worried and very serious. There followed an awkward exchange, with Gene expressing his regrets over their splitting up and over the way Gene had treated Linder. Gene said he had heard his old friend was considering running for governor on the race issue. Linder said it was true, but that it was the last thing he wanted to do. He said he was so "damn scared" about the Negroes entering white society through the court ruling that he was desperate to do something to stop them. Gene agreed and said white supremacy was the one issue that could elect a governor and save the state. Talmadge said he was convinced that no other issue could defeat the Arnall forces. But Gene said the Arnall crowd was too strong to beat if the conservatives ran two strong candidates on the same platform and he was asking Linder to tell him then and there what his intentions were. If Linder was determined to run, Gene said he would withdraw. But Linder was delighted to hear that Gene would run on a white supremacy ticket and said that he would gladly forget the race. With that Gene thanked him, promised he would run a hard campaign, and left. Twenty years earlier, almost to the day, a much thinner Gene Talmadge had appeared at Linder's door asking if he could run for office. He did not look like the same warrior. His face now had a hawkish appearance. He was sixty-one years old and looked more; but Linder knew no man would wage a tougher campaign, and he was glad to place the burden on Gene's shoulders. Gene's visit was probably as much bluff as anything. He had committed himself to run, but he was worried over the votes Linder would pull from him, especially those precious county-unit votes. He figured Rivers would hurt enough.[12]

Many members of Gene's family and some of his friends had begged him not to run. Mitt had pleaded with him repeatedly. He was a sick man and he looked it. And the sickness was in the place he had neglected most of his life, his stomach. He still drank too much; he still ate sporadically, grabbing a meal when his schedule allowed it. And the pace that he kept, the tensions and anxieties, were ruinous. Mitt feared for his life.[13] On April 16 he announced he was a candidate for his fourth term as governor. His platform would be based on white supremacy.

Gene's announcement left little doubt that this was the old Talmadge. The extent to which he had regressed surprised even his friends. He tried to equate the 1946 postwar period with Reconstruction, saying that the South had now been occupied by the New Deal, as it had been by the Yankees following the Civil War. He reasoned that since the war on poverty was over, the federal government should disappear. He said, "Issues now prevailing in Georgia, and the chaotic aftermath of the war, rehabilitation of veterans and the period of conversion" make the campaign for governor "the most important one since carpetbagger days." He said this necessitated his major plank being white supremacy. It would insure a "Democratic white primary unfettered and unhampered by radical communist and alien influences."

The remainder of Gene's platform shocked his worst critics. Far-sighted, reformist, pragmatic—it stood in stark contradiction to the major plank. Herman was given full credit for the unprecedented progressivism of the 1946 platform. The platform included raising teachers' pay by 50 percent, providing a million dollars a year to the counties for rural medical facilities, paving every road over which a mail truck traveled, and giving a lifetime driver's license and a five-year ad valorem exemption to veterans. Gene even said that "social reforms must be protected and maintained." This was perhaps a little too much of a nod to the changing times, for he soon swerved back to plank number one. He said aliens were trying to get Negroes to vote. Paternalistically, he said, "We must protect the Negro from the communist . . . influence." Gene closed his contradictory announcement by exhorting, "We must go forward in Georgia to become the most progressive State in the Union." [14] Gene was trying to straddle both sides of the road, and it remained uncertain whether this new politically accommodating Talmadge would be allowed his let's-please-everybody platform.

While the state buzzed about "new" Old Gene, a race was shaping up in Richmond County, a race that was critical to Roy Harris and ultimately to the state of Georgia. Harris had been the intractable boss of Richmond County politics for longer than anyone could remember, but his cracker party was being challenged that spring for the post of county commissioner by a newly formed and more liberal independent party. The bitter rhetoric that emanated from the race was amplified by the Atlanta *Constitution*, whose management hoped that creating an aura of win-or-die for Harris would destroy Harris as a candidate for governor if he lost. Few were willing to bet, however, that Harris would lose a campaign based on the Negro.[15]

While Harris was marshaling the forces of segregation in Augusta, a dedicated group of liberals had been working on James Carmichael, trying to get him back in the state race. They were appealing to his sense of public-mindedness and holding out the promise of Arnall's support. Carmichael once again relented and announced for governor on April 15. His platform was plain and simple: to offer a choice "between good government and the old gang-type government" Georgians "rid themselves of four years ago." Carmichael thus positioned himself against Gene and Rivers and indicated that he was supporting the Arnall years. Arnall, reluctant to support anyone, said nothing, but the state's worried liberals breathed a sigh of relief that they now had a candidate.[16]

Ed Rivers was caught unawares by the quick succession of announcements, and in an almost comical fit of overreaction he announced from Omaha, Nebraska, that he too was a candidate. It noticeably lessened his impact, for state attention was centering on Augusta and the vitriolic, almost violent race the Harris forces were waging. Their voices reached a racist shrill that repelled even the conservative Augustans. On April 17 Roy Harris was defeated in what was considered a highly significant rejection of racism. Georgia liberals were elated; many thought this conservative reversal reflected a state trend. Harris was bitterly disappointed. No courthouse gang or professional politicians would back a man who could not carry his own county, and Roy Harris' dream of being king vanished. Gene, more than anyone else, breathed a sigh of relief, because the Harris candidacy would have hurt him.

On April 29, the *Constitution* began a blatant attempt to get Carmichael elected through exposure, with a front-page story of his life. A New South-type businessman, ultra-successful, straightlaced and moderate—this was the image the paper presented. Carmichael trivia continued to flood the paper.

In announcing his father's plans, Herman said that for the first time at a Talmadge opener no food would be served. The truth was that there wasn't enough food after the war to be heaping it out. Herman romanticized the situation, saying, "With people starving in Europe, we don't think it is right to feed people here to get them to vote."

On May 6, Gene paid his qualifying fee; he was accompanied by an entourage that sent reporters scurrying for their typewriters. Instead of the usual throng of wool-hatters, there appeared a neat, scrubbed, and serious-looking group of students. Unnoticed was the fact that they were all veterans. School boys had never been a part of Talmadge politics, and the only veterans he usually referred to were of Civil War vintage. Old Gene was now New Gene, showing off students for the education crowd and updated war heroes. Suddenly, the wool-hat boys and the Civil War crowd had been replaced. They were an old show that had been closed by the times. This was New Gene—with new stagehands, a few new acts, a new script (which he occasionally referred to), and a brand spanking, all-cleaned-up and educated new cast. The show would go. The snack bar was closed for want of food, and Fiddlin' John had vacated the orchestra pit; but Gene was back for one more curtain call, and his appearance was all that ever mattered anyway.

After supper one night in late spring, Mitt found Gene in their living room, looking unusually troubled, a newspaper in his lap. "What's the matter, Gene?"

"I'm really worried, Mitt. Things are going wrong in this country. Things are breaking down. I don't know what's going to happen to us." [17] To a man hopelessly stranded in a mental time vacuum, a prisoner of his heritage, a cultural isolationist, he was right.

On May 9, a new and chilling dimension came to the race. Out of the distant darkness that hung over Atlanta's Stone Mountain a giant bonfire glowed. It was a large Ku Klux Klan rally, proclaiming a "rebirth." Rumors of the affair swept the state, causing near hysteria and giving Gene most of the credit for bringing the Klan back to life with his demogoguery. The event itself was a comical rag-tag affair, which embarrassed its leaders because they kept running out of sheets to give new members. Many were forced to wrap themselves in paper and handkerchiefs.[18] They were the psychologically impoverished of the new age—the cultural laggers, the indebted, the uneducated, the scared, the have-nots in an age of haves. They grasped the Klan in desperation. It was the only club in town that invited them. Its mysterious-sounding rites and verbiage, its hoods and ornaments, and its history of resistance to the blacks and dedication to the past gave them a feeling of power and belonging. It was a sad lot that stood in paper and cloth wrappings against the night wind of Stone Mountain. They had been left behind by the glittering society below them, and it was high irony that society would look on these souls with such utter fear and dread, as though they were a well-disciplined horde that could sweep from the mountain and destroy at will.

In view of Carmichael's opening statement, it was again ironical that only Talmadge would be labeled the Klan's friend. The liberals' candidate said, "While I believe in helping the Negro . . . I will never . . . permit the mixing of the races in Georgia . . . in any . . . manner which violates our southern traditions." Here, in fact, was every Georgian. To be prejudiced was a cultural inheritance. The thing that differentiated a so-called racist from a "good man" was one's willingness to verbalize his feelings against blacks. Good white folks just didn't say much about the Negro. But they did less for him. In a state of racists, it was tragically funny how few people wanted to accept that label.

19

God Almighty,
Sears Roebuck, and
Gene Talmadge

Carmichael's awareness of the importance of the race issue was amplified by the embarrassment he suffered over some shenanigans pulled either by Talmadge's or Rivers' supporters. Someone in Atlanta had ordered thousands of leaflets printed that read: James V. Carmichael "invites all of his colored friends" to come and eat barbecue at his Moultrie speech. The leaflets were tacked up on trees in Moultrie's colored section. The Carmichael staff seemed to be in a state of hysteria trying to find the culprit. Vehement denials were sent to every newspaper, reiterating the candidate's segregationist stand; and a well-publicized investigation was started to find the guilty parties. Gene and Ed were no doubt amused. Carmichael was finding out fast that he was dealing with the oldest pros on the stump circuit, and there was nothing they loved better than a practical joke that made their opponent look like a fool, in a good-natured way of course. Carmichael's platform, strangely enough, lacked some of the depth the Talmadge platform had. The aura of "continuation" was apparently deemed more important than in-depth planks which could easily alienate the vague, but not mythical, transitional Georgia of 1946. Carmichael had done what no one thought should be done in January; he was moving right down the middle. Gene Talmadge had pulled him there with his effective racist rhetoric; and Ed Rivers had pushed him there because of the almost wildly liberal programs he had initiated as governor. The year 1946 was not supposed to have been the year for the middle-of-the-road candidate, but in a transitional period with voters finding appeals on both sides, Carmichael was lucky to have stumbled onto the path.

Gene started his race with a small disaster. After his 1942 fiasco with the university, he was remembered as the man who cost the school system its accreditation. He admitted that this had been his biggest political mistake; and his staff knew that if he was to bring those thousands back who left him over the issue, he would have to bring the situation to a head. He would go to the school and speak to the students, thereby showing that he was no bogeyman, no enemy after all.

Word of Gene's coming had excited the students far more than he had anticipated. If Georgia was undecided about its liberality, her students were feeling few restrictions, and many were ready to hoot this vestige of the past. His appearance in the Fine Arts Auditorium brought loud jeers and catcalls; in the words of the *Constitution*, Gene was "nearly laughed, booed, and heckled off the stage," by the raucous students.[1] This, however, is questionable. Even though they did throw barbed questions, they did boo, and they did laugh—it was almost impossible to heckle Gene off a stage. He was too quick with stinging retorts and knew too well how to handle himself in verbal combat. The students failed to pin him down, partly because his speech contained little they could argue with. Much of it dealt with veterans, and many of the students were vets of voting age. While Gene was speaking inside, a handful of students were busy hanging him in effigy from a dormitory window across the street. The figure was quickly torn down, however, and Gene did not see it when he left the auditorium.

Talmadge was furious the next morning when he read in the *Constitution* a headline story that sounded like he had practically been run off the campus. The story definitely made him look bad, so bad that he called a press conference to denounce the Atlanta papers as having "sold out" to the Negro, being "scalawags." [2] He said the *Constitution* "printed what they wanted to happen." He said he had never "addressed a more intelligent, courteous and polite audience." [3] Gene told his office staff that if the columnist who wrote the effigy story, M. L. St. John, ever came around his office again, he was to be "thrown out." [4] Gene's fury caused him to make an angry attempt to ruin the credibility of the papers. He hated their management, but respected reporters like McGill, whom he tried to get to write his biography. He said, "I don't hate you boys personally; I just don't like what you write." [5]

The big Talmadge show arrived in Lyons on May 18 for the campaign opener. And the star put it all together—prancing, shouting, cajoling; but somehow the crowd wasn't responding as it once had. Gene had been around for a long time; he had worn hard on some, and he had worn some on everybody. It was all on the radio now, and the day was blazing hot. There was no food, and it was May, too early. The wool-hat few who turned out did their parts—yelled, laughed, howled; but it was all like an old movie seen too many times. It was flat.

Gene felt the popular vote was too risky, and he built his effort around the county-unit vote. The master of that power structure, Roy Harris, was brought on. Having the support of Roy, considered even more racist that Gene, would mean complete forfeit of the city vote and anything else but the most conservative. Therefore, the small counties must be won. Harris' entry increased the volume of the hecklers who began hounding Gene. More disturbing was the embarrassing crowd of four hundred who turned out at Thomasville where once there had been thousands. There were no barbecues, no motorcades, no tree-climbing Haggards, no Fiddlin' John, no patriotic fist-fights, no little Genes being brought forth to be baptized, no surging masses clinging to his arms, trying to touch him, to see him; instead there was an electric air of tension, of apprehension about where this talk of hatred would lead. Something had gone out of it all.

Another part of the old Talmadge entourage had become scarce, the Atlanta reporters. Gene and the reporters had enjoyed an ironical relationship since the Atlanta press had turned on him. They had once whiled away the miles with Gene between speeches—laughing, telling ribald tales of women and politicians, coarse, often vulgar stories that gave color to politics and legend to Talmadge. They had drunk and slept together and knew more on one another than each dared tell, even though Gene would daily mount the stump to lambast their papers and they in turn would file their often-critical stories on his politics. Gene had needed them, and the papers, for circulation, had needed Gene. But it had all turned sour in 1946. The owners of the Atlanta press no longer thought of him as an amusing, muleheaded demagogue. He was now considered a threat to the safety and health of the state, and they turned on him with all the power at their disposal. Their opposition became so bitter that Gene's attacks on the papers helped create an air of hostility with Talmadge supporters that became so real the reporters started driving in unmarked cars, trying to hide their identities at speeches. Many received threatening phone calls and were cursed on the street.

M. L. St. John, the *Constitution*'s political editor and the man who had written the university effigy story, had been trailing Gene over the state, and one day found himself outside a tiny backwoods town at the back of a wool-hat crowd which, by the nature of its "weavin' and wavin' " was obviously feeling close to the man in front of them who kept slinging his finger at them and smacking his suspenders. It was a small crowd and Gene soon recognized St. John standing low at the rear. He suddenly tore into a ferocious attack on "them lying' Atlanta newspapers" and with a violent gesture that shook the reporter's frame, shouted, "Thar he is now!" The boys twirled in an instant, and the terrified reporter braced himself for a charge. Gene's face changed mercurially and he benevolently ordered, "Let him through, boys. Let him come up here on the platform and hear the truth. Then thar won't be no reason not to print the truth." The crowd reluctantly cleared the way and St. John walked gingerly through their menacing ranks. As he walked up to Gene, his tormenter leaned close to the reporter's ear and with elfish delight whispered, "I know you're a pretty good fellow, you just write that way." [6]

Not only was Talmadge drawing small crowds, the rest of the field was doing even worse. Crowd size, that great barometer for campaign success a decade before, died with the 1946 election—another victim of the times. The *Constitution* was moved to headline, "What Has Happened to Georgia's Political Crowds?" In what should have been one of the more closely followed races in years, there appeared to be scant public interest. A number of reasons were offered by the paper. Radio had entered the most remote homes in Georgia, and during the hot summer days it was easier to listen to the hookup of the speech than to stand sweltering in person. The ending of the big barbecues and fish frys and the festival atmosphere they created also affected crowd size. Prespeech music was now often blared out through loudspeakers instead of live, and this too killed much of the fun. Another reason for diminished crowds, a reason unarticulated by the paper, was the tinge of fear attached to this campaign. Many people felt there would be a race riot in Georgia that summer and they were afraid to go out. Changing times, that all-encompassing generality, were another factor. In the space of a decade and a war, the lives of Georgians had become busier, more complicated and sophisticated; people were involved with other things to do. There were more ways to have fun, other heroes to worship than the politician on the stump.

In Cartersville on June 5 many thought Gene's racist rhetoric reached its peak. The federal government had just ruled that a Negro had the right to sit anywhere he wished to sit on a bus that crossed state lines. Gene told the gathered reporters at Cartersville, "Now here's something that will burn your papers up." He said if he were elected there would be no interstate bus travel through Georgia. In order to come through his state, all passengers would have to disembark fifty feet within the state line and buy a ticket good only through Georgia; the traveler would do the same thing at the other end of the state, and this ticket would be good for the rest of his destination. Thus no one would ride into and out of Georgia; they would only ride within her. All Negroes would be ushered to the back of the bus while it traveled through the state.[7]

The next day Gene said from the stump, "I was raised among niggers and I understand them. I want to see them treated fairly and I want to see them have justice in the courts. But I want to deal with the nigger this way; he must come to my backdoor, take off his hat, and say, 'Yes, sir.' "[8] Gene's progressive planks could be heard to shatter under this kind of talk, and his constituency narrowed. Even the McRae *Enterprise* was prompted to come out for Carmichael, which didn't bother Gene; neither did the fact that he would get none of the growing Negro vote. He said it would be an "accident" if he got even one black vote.

On the basis of these May and June speeches, the Atlanta *Journal* launched the toughest attack it had made on the long Talmadge career, an attack reflecting the concern of the Atlanta liberal establishment. The June 9 paper said, "It is time this blatant demagogue, this fomenter of strife, this panderer of the passions of the ignorant . . . was exposed for what he is. That is a blatherskite, a cheap fraud and a menace to the security and welfare of all of us." The paper said he was a man insanely possessed with victory and that "in the clutch of the contest he becomes frenzied and in the fear of defeat will stop at nothing." It closed with a list of careful adjectives: "He is as sly as a coon, as slick as an eel. . . . Let's be done with this sorry charlatan."

The candidates rarely spoke in the same city at the same time that summer, but when they did it was pure entertainment. Rivers was probably the better speaker, Gene was the more electrifying, and Carmichael was the statesman of the three. At one Toombs County speech Gene and Ed were at their uninhibited best. Gene arrived late as usual, waiting for the introductions to end and the first speaker to start, then entering amid blowing horns and screaming supporters. On statewide radio, the response boomed over the airwaves like an avalanche. When it came his turn to speak Gene gave one of his "ass bustin', Goddamn sonofabitchin' " speeches that had the boys braying like hounds at the moon. But when he finished, instead of returning to his seat, he announced that he was leaving and that everyone in the crowd should go with him. With all the theatrics he could muster, Gene made a grand exit. But very few left, for Gene had gotten the boys so worked up they were ready to tear into Rivers. When he got up and started to speak, the boys began hooting and yelping so loud he was drowned out. Rivers, furious at what he knew was going out over the state, yelled, "You sorry wool-hat crumbs! Why don't you leave with Gene!" This really turned the boys on and their voices roared in unison. Rivers then tried to embarrass them into shutting up by taking the microphone and talking loudly into it. "Ladies and gentlemen of this state. Can you hear these south Georgia crumbs? They're trying to shut me up. This is the kind of people that vote for Gene Talmadge. They're crumbs! Come on boys, let's see how loud you can boo!" With great bravado he then stepped to the edge of the platform and started waving his arms like an orchestra leader, leading the boys in booing. Gene could see as he entered his car that "Old Black Bow Tie" had outfoxed him. Gene was getting old.[9]

Rivers continued to bear down on Gene. On June 26, he told what the Atlanta crowd already knew, but the country crowd had always refused to accept. He said Gene was no country boy; he was "a regular sheik in Atlanta and a redgallused hick when he gets out of town. You just ought to see him sliding across the polished ballroom floors in Atlanta hotels." Rivers said, "No Arabian sheik in all his pomp . . . was ever more dolled up than Talmadge . . . a carnation stuck in his coat, his fingernails polished, and his hair slicked down with goose grease, dancing the tango." [10]

On June 13 Arnall finally gave in to the tremendous pressure of Carmichael's behind-the-scenes men and publicly came out for their man. In fact he came out more than the public knew. Carmichael had been dealing from weakness with the courthouse crowd. He needed some chips and Arnall provided them. Agreeing that the county-unit vote was going down the drain as far as Carmichael was concerned, Arnall promised "to place the roads where they are needed" and offered a large sum of money out of existing state funds to back up his words.[11] With that, the Carmichael crowd hit the road with their fat bag full of trinkets.

The test of it all, the outcome of the liberal-conservative struggle for power in Georgia politics, came to a head on June 17 when the state voted in the Democratic primary. The forces of each candidate had gathered in the hotel headquarters to hear the votes come in that night. Telephone lines were loaded to county supporters at the polling places throughout the state, getting firsthand word. The crucial factor was the county-unit vote and one man would know that better than anyone, Roy Harris. Since Carmichael was getting poor information on the counties, his staff had a friend of Harris who had defected call Roy and disguise his voice talking through a rolled piece of paper. After reaching Harris at Gene's headquarters the man said he was from Augusta and had $10,000 he wanted to place on the winner. Who should he bet on? Harris answered without reservation, "I wouldn't bet on Carmichael." He then named off the counties that at that hour were certain for Gene. When the conversation ended, the Carmichael staff knew Gene Talmadge had been elected governor through the county-unit vote. The headquarters closed up as if the word of God had been received. No one doubted the authoritative account given by Harris. The defeat would be made even more crushing as the popular votes came in, showing that Carmichael had defeated Gene in that column. The voice of the present had been squelched by the voice of the past. The apparent disinterest of the electorate was not reflected in the final vote. An enormous turnout gave Carmichael 313,389 popular votes to Gene's 297,245 and Rivers' 69,489. But in the crucial county vote, Gene got 242 to Carmichael's 146 and Rivers' 22.[12]

Gene said in a state of near physical collapse, "I'm prouder of this victory than any race I ever won." There can be no doubt that race gave Gene that victory—race, and that incredibly complex description of social status, "place." This was the great qualifier in any discussion of the black: Gene had said that "place" was at the backdoor; Carmichael had said simply and vaguely that it was not in white society. Matters of degree only, and yet in 1946 in the state that was developing a conscience, the two degrees were miles apart. Gene's fault was his honesty. He was reaching down deep inside and tearing out for public viewing the brutal, ugly side of Georgia's heart, and the state's so-called liberals were repelled by what they saw of themselves. For the most part Carmichael kept the issue neatly under the rug. He allowed Georgians their racism and their conscience too, as Arnall had in 1942.

Perhaps no more telling definition of the postwar liberal's hypocritical stand on the Negro was ever given than the admission made by *Constitution* editor Ralph McGill, a great writer, courageous man, and a much-advertised liberal, in his column on May 31: "I have always opposed social equality or mixing of the races." And yet McGill honestly saw no inconsistency in calling Gene a racist. The difference that McGill saw as critical was in the degrees of opposition to Negro advancement he and Talmadge represented. Gene feared almost any progress, while McGill offered the black wide latitude in economic and educational advancement and opportunity. Gene's dogmatic approach afforded the Negro so little latitude in ascension that to move at all was excruciatingly difficult. His dogma was so unconciliatory that it offered violence as a viable alternative, though Gene did not practice violence. Gene addressed the problem, McGill did not. Gene verbalized his real feelings and they were often ugly; McGill did not. Their differences were real, but so much of the difference, for better or worse, appears to have been one of honesty. The best that could be said for McGill's brand of segregation was that it lacked a totality of conviction and thus held the possibility of change and compromise.

In late July, as the heat of the election was apparently wearing off, the festering boil of hatred burst, and the brutality of racism cast a long dark shadow over Georgia. In the rural farm community of Monroe a group of white men intercepted two young black men and their girl-friends out on a country road, dragged them from their car, broke the arms of the girls as they clung terrified to the car door, then system-matically, and for no reason, shot all four until they could hardly be recognized. News of the murders shocked the nation, and the South. Georgia was crucified in the nation's press. A reporter in Monroe the next day asked the sheriff what was being done about catching the kill-ers; he said that no one was talking, there were no clues or suspects, nothing could be done. Then with chilling indifference he said, "They hadn't ought to killed the two women." A large white man shuffled up and sneered, "This thing's got to be done to keep Mister Nigger in his place. Since the court said he could vote, there ain't been any holding him." [13]

These comments received full play across the country and cemented into many northern minds a generalization about southerners and the South. Typical of their reaction was an editorial written in Dunkirk, New York: "Have you ever travelled through Jo-Jah? Some of the cities are right nice. But the rest of the country area and the bulk of the inmates of that red-soiled desert of pine scrub, swamps, sandy land, mules, ram-shackle shacks, negroes and just plain white trash is a pretty poor section. Brother, you go out of that state thanking heaven you're Yankee!" [14]

Eugene Talmadge was given wide credit for having caused the inci-dent because of his inflammatory campaign. He didn't help matters when asked to respond to the murders: "Regrettable." Holding Gene fully responsible, the Charlotte *News* wrote on July 19: "The South will one day be rid of its Bilbos and Talmadges, but not until we have completed the long and painful process of purging ourselves of the sickness upon which they feed. We chase an illusion when we seek an overnight cure for the malady that has racked the South for more than eighty years."

20

"It Ain't Nothin' but a Little Ole Bleedin' Vein"

Although visibly weakened by the race, Gene "was a little restless and took some friends and went down to Mexico and stayed awhile, then traveled up to Wyoming." [1] After returning to McRae, "We were sitting out on the front porch of the Talmadge house," a family friend remembered. "Gene was rocking, and he looked worse than I had ever seen him. Mitt came out and he said, 'Mitt, I'm hungry.' There was something pathetic about the way he said it, and it really got under my skin when she snapped back, 'That's all you think I'm good for is standing around the damn kitchen. Well, I'm not gone do it!' And she walked around the side of the house. Mitt refused to cook for Gene a lot. It used to be regular gossip around town, about how Gene would literally have to go visit his friends at supper time if he wanted to eat. One thing for sure, Mitt was the only person Gene couldn't have his way with." [2] Mitt's reaction wasn't meanness; but it was indicative of the stubbornly independent nature of their relationship.

The next day he left with a friend for Jacksonville to rest. Mitt stayed home. That night around 9:00, while eating stew, he collapsed onto the table unconscious. He was rushed to St. Vincent's Hospital in shock with a ruptured vein in his stomach. Transfusions brought him off the danger list, and the visitors who rushed down from McRae to bring him pajamas and well wishers were surprised to see him jump out of bed and walk around like nothing had ever happened.[3] Herman was one of the first to arrive and he was told by doctors that Gene would be unable to attend the state convention. Herman then wrote his father's speech, which he would give.

A young Atlanta reporter, Celestine Sibley, was sent to Gene's bedside to get a story from the governor-elect. She had just returned from California, her child was sick, and she was angry with the paper for ordering her to go. She found Gene's entire floor in the hospital sealed off, but managed to sneak through the guards. She found Mitt sitting outside his door, told her that she was a reporter who had no choice but to be there, that her child was sick, and asked if she could please see Gene or write out some questions for him so that she could return to Atlanta. "Mrs. Talmadge was very nice and took some questions I scribbled down in to him. He sent her back out and told me to come inside for five minutes. He was lying up in the bed with a ten-gallon hat on and some loud pajamas. He good-naturedly fussed at me, 'Young lady, I'll see you for five minutes, then I want you to go home immediately and see about your sick child.' When I asked what was wrong with him, he shrugged and said, 'Aw, it ain't nothin' but a little ole bleedin' vein.' " [4]

Gene seemed to recover quickly, but the cirrhosis condition of his liver, and his sallow, sickly appearance created grave doubts among his advisers and family about his surviving a four-year term. With so much at stake, with the forces of liberalism routed and a chance to fight for the white primary, the Talmadge forces were thrown into intense debate over what to do in the event of Gene's death. The family did not feel he was in any imminent danger, and Mitt reacted angrily when asked if she thought Herman should be appointed governor-elect right then. "Gene ain't gone appoint nobody!" She snapped. "Herman can't make governor like Gene!" [5]

Oddly, enough, the solution came from a school superintendent from Jasper, Georgia, who discovered an old law which said the man with the second-most votes in the general election would become governor if the victor died before being sworn in. Herman knew there would be write-in votes for Carmichael, so he began spreading the word for a write-in vote on his own behalf. Loud publicity was avoided, because it would have looked inappropriate for son to be running against father. Of the events, Herman said, "I never had any idea he was dying until a week before his death. Nobody did. But we ran me as a write-in candidate for insurance. As it turned out Carmichael got a little over five hundred votes, and I got a little over five hundred, only it was a handful more than he got." [6]

Following the convention—which he did not attend—Gene returned to Atlanta where he conferred over the coming legislative session, hunted quail, and spent some time on the Lovejoy farm south of Atlanta which he was trying to build into a productive income center like the McRae and Forsyth farms. He seemed to have recovered. On Friday, November 30, he reported to Atlanta's Piedmont Hospital for a "routine checkup." Pronounced fit, he was rushed back on Monday hemorrhaging again. He climbed into bed with his hat on. He was now paying the price he had said he would. Soon after the votes had been counted in July, someone had shouted, "Gene, you've won!" He had answered, "Yes, I've won, but it's going to cost me ten years of my life." [7] In one of the most grueling races in Georgia politics, he had made 272 speeches and had completely ruined his health.

In the meantime, his programs were drafted out for the January legislature, and Roy Harris said he was completing plans for preserving the white primary. His plan would have disqualified every registered voter in the state. Gene stayed abreast of everything from his room, appearing fairly well and alert to most. But by mid-December his liver stopped responding to treatment, and he sensed he was dying. He phoned two friends, reporter Ed Bridges and adviser Lindley Camp, to his side and said, "Boys, I'm dying, but my doctors won't tell me so. I need somebody to pick up after I'm gone, and it oughta be Hummon. Hummon's a brilliant boy; he has a great future in politics. He could even be senator. Lindley, you know a lot of politics, and you can guide him there. Ed, you're a reporter and you can get him publicity. I want you boys to promise to help him in any way you can." [8] They did so and left.

On Wednesday and Thursday he received more transfusions. It was announced on December 20 that he had contracted acute hepatitis. His condition, though critical, was not considered hopeless. He was being fed intravenously, was conscious, and saw a steady stream of visitors. Late on Friday, Henry Spurlin received a call from the governor. Spurlin had been out buying cattle for Gene and had just gotten home when the call came through. Gene's voice was hardly audible. He whispered, "Spud, don't buy no more cows." Spurlin immediately called the family and said Gene was dying and they raced to his bedside. The doctors confirmed that he was slipping badly at 7:00 that evening. Asked how long he would live, his doctor said, "He will be gone by 7:00 in the morning." [9] Gene lapsed into a coma later that night and at precisely 7:00 the next morning, he abruptly breathed in and died.

During his illness, a rather morbid joke had circulated, saying that Gene Talmadge was the only man in Georgia who could have the whole state praying at once—one half that he would die, the other half that he would live. Such had been his impact that the Atlanta *Journal* wrote the next day: "The death of Eugene Talmadge closes one of the remarkable and colorful careers in the long annals of Georgia politics. . . . A vivid and compelling spirit has passed."

On the same day the *Constitution* carried this statement: "When this spectacular but puzzling and frequently contradictory personality ceased to be, he already was a legendary and almost fabulous character. The Georgia scene will seem strange and empty without him." [10]

Eugene Talmadge was an immovable object in a time of unprecedented motion. His rocklike stance attested roots that went very deep into the culture of his ancestors. His words had been their words. His footsteps trailed a well-worn path imprinted with the heelmark of his fathers. He was the last great Georgia disciple of their vanquished era, and his strength was drawn from the bonds he held with that time. To his eyes the future was not a license for change, but a body to hold the spirit and soul of the past. The old way was the only way, for its canons held the moral, spiritual, and economic fibres of the state and its society together. Though the lessons of that past were a bleak scenario of human desperation and failure, Talmadge was incapable of the intellectual detachment needed for an objective overview.

No one who ever heard him speak, or knew him, or lived in Georgia during the years he was in office, ever felt indifferent about Eugene Talmadge. He rose and rode on passions. His was a politics of crisis. Hard times had opened the door for him, and he had projected himself as frontiersman, lone gun-fighter, champion of the little man, a figure of heroic proportions and resolve. Hard times had demanded and allowed that he do and be that. And it was a mold and a role that he liked. It was one that he became obsessed with, stereotyped into, and finally one that he could not live out of. He became an actor who knew no other performance save the one that contained the swashbuckling entrance, the grand battle scene, and a thousand curtain calls. He was the last of his kind on the Georgia political stage, and one of the best performers of his kind that ever lived. His presence dominated Georgia politics for almost twenty years, and reverberations of his impact continued long after that. But what was his impact?

His basic appeal was to the businessman, because of his economic and governmental beliefs, and to that nebulous legion called "the little people," because of his cultural principles. The business community generally supported Talmadge because he said that government should leave them alone. They particularly approved of his hatred for taxes. In an era of prosperity, this might have been fine, but in the depressed thirties Talmadge's hands-off approach simply let the people wither and die alone. If the businessman supplied the money, the poorer farmer class supplied the core vote that gave Talmadge his power. He had no real solutions for these people. His solutions had all been proven wrong by the very past he revered. He served them as an emotional crutch when their consciousness was being shattered by the catastrophic depression and the subsequent radicalism of the New Deal. They clung to Gene as children cling to an old blanket. And while they gave him their hearts, they denied him their minds. As long as he played by their rules, they supported him; but when he tried to take the new fruits from them, or sought real power by running for the United States Senate, they denied him. They wanted him basically powerless, though they reveled in his power plays. Talmadge was a prisoner of history—a cultural isolationist lost in a time frame that he was unable to leave on his own and that his supporters finally refused to help him leave.

Gene Talmadge strode the decade when Georgia got up and went along—when she began to pull up stakes, learned to say "yes," became less preoccupied with self, and when, in looking beyond Me and Mine, she lost something and gained something. Her people had looked beyond the tall pines at the end of the field and realized for the first time that something better must be there; and in doing so they admitted defeat, admitted they could no longer go it on their own. They ceased to be the eternal frontiersmen out there alone, undefeatable, self-sustaining and reliant, certain of their place in the scope of things. Georgia, during Gene Talmadge's years, admitted she was fallible. But she did none of these things on her own. Nor did she do them because she necessarily wanted to, or had the foresight to, or because her leaders said they were the right things to do. The orders came from outside—from long ago when international markets began controlling cotton, from when the cycle of debt ushered in its numbing servility, when the insidious plague of the boll weevil came cancerously from the West, and when technology and industry offered the alternatives of a new age. The sledgehammer strokes had been applied by the Great Depression which smacked the mind into a pliable putty.

It's all in the facts—in the reams of statistics that say how many people did what and when they did it. Their ordeals and sufferings are inked in the book in the form of numbers; and the numbers do not lie, though they do not tell why, only who and when and where. They do not tell how the thing called tractor one day sputtered out between the rows and made the black and the poor-white fieldhand useless. They don't tell about the radio that thrust the outside world into the singular world of the farmer, vastly broadening his horizons overnight; or about the fantasylike cornucopia of goods and services that created a strange new gnawing, a desire to possess the new symbols of status, a desire so strong that a feeling of impoverishment drove the farmer to do what nothing else before had driven him to do. They don't tell about the growth of manufacturing that promised a paycheck at the end of each week—pluralities in a world that had known only singularities. The mind stretched, and it liked what it saw beyond the end of the field.

A new awareness, a crushing depression, a bug called boll weevil, uncertain prices, new things to own and to do, the emergence of the federal government, and particularly its alterative New Deal—they all seemed to converge at once in the early thirties, and they gave the reasons for the statistics that said who and how many.

The mind, only a handful of years removed from the circumstances, finds the simplicity of the times difficult to accept in light of today's pluralities. It seems almost incomprehensible, in the advanced year of 1940, that 262,699 of the 321,000 rural homes had outside toilets, 41,925 didn't even have that; and 83,422 urban homes had outside toilets. And of the 321,000 rural homes, an incredible 254,550 had no electricity, and 7,313 had neither electricity, nor gas, nor kerosene; they had no light source other than candles and a fireplace. These facts, to a degree, make us misinterpret the migration from farm to city, but only in forgetting that the migrations of mind and body occurred at different times. Migration did occur, but it was not an overnight re-establishment of lifestyles. The importance of the migration often lay in the fact of physical displacement—just getting the people off those farms, getting their hands away from those plows and that cotton seed. The fact of and the strength of that move is, again, in the figures. In 1910, 61 percent of all Georgians were termed rural farm dwellers. In 1920, the figure had dropped to 58 percent. And in 1930, for the first time in the state's history, that figure fell to less than half the population, 49 percent. By 1940, the figure had hit 44 percent. There is drama here. There is preparation for profound change. And the drama of a Gene Talmadge is that he arrived in the dead middle of this great physical and mental shift. The fact that he was elected to state office four times during this period does not indicate that shifts were meaningless. To the contrary, they illustrate the agony and the passion of the move. These were a people briefly awash, having pushed off from a safe shore and uncertain of the new ground they were testing. Eyes darted quickly back to the old place; hearts were touched instantly by its recollections; hands formed on the plow handles unconsciously grasped for worn grain. Gene was that shore they had left, and that was his ultimate loss.

Notes

CHAPTER 1
1. Tom Linder, interview, May 5, 1969.
2. Absalon H. Chappell, *Miscellanies of Georgia* (Columbus, Ga., 1928), 21.
3. Richard Hofstadter, *The Age of Reform* (New York, 1955), 45.
4. Monroe County Deed Book, A, 20, in Forsyth County Courthouse, Ga.; Talmadge bought land lot 73 in the Goggins district.
5. *Ibid.*, 71; he bought land lot 36 in the same district.
6. *Ibid.*, 293–95.
7. Monroe County Deed Book, C, 89.
8. James C. Corley, interview, August 10, 1971.
9. Old Deeds of Monroe County, in Forsyth County Courthouse, Ga.
10. Marylynne Talmadge, interview, May 1, 1970.
11. Monroe County Deed Book, Book 30, p. 488.
12. Corley, interview, August 10, 1971, and Marylynne Talmadge, interview, May 1, 1970.
13. Kimball Zelner, interview, November 14, 1970.
14. Hapeville (Ga.) *Statesman*, September 4, 1934.
15. Marylynne Talmadge, interview, May 1, 1970.
16. *Ibid.*
17. Zelner, interview, November 14, 1970.
18. Marylynne Talmadge, interview, May 1, 1970.
19. Henry Spurlin, interview, August 1, 1973.
20. C. Vann Woodward, *Tom Watson: Agrarian Rebel* (New York, 1938).
21. Mrs. John Monaghan, interview, May 25, 1970.
22. Ulrich Bonnell Phillips, *A History of Transportation in the Eastern Cotton Belt to 1860* (New York, 1908).

CHAPTER 2
1. Lawrence Wood Robert, interview, July 26, 1971.
2. Bethel Harbin, interview, February 8, 1971; Spurlin, interview, August 1, 1973.
3. Mrs. Eugene Talmadge, interview, February 8, 1971.
4. *Ibid.*
5. C. B. Abt, interview, May 31, 1971.
6. William Kitchens, interview, May 31, 1971.
7. Mrs. Eugene Talmadge, interview, August 1, 1973.
8. *Ibid.*, February 8, 1971.
9. Corley, interview, August 10, 1971.

10. Mrs. Eugene Talmadge, interview, August 1, 1973.
11. Spurlin, interview, August 1, 1973.

CHAPTER 3

1. Albert B. Saye, *Georgia's County Unit System of Election* (Athens, Ga., n.d.); John M. Greybeal, "The Georgia Primary Election System" (M.A. thesis, Emory University, 1932); Lynwood M. Holland, "The Conduct of Elections in Georgia" (M.A. thesis, Emory University, 1933); Alice Owens, "The County Unit System as an Integral Part of the Georgia Primary Election System" (M.A. thesis, Emory University, 1934).
2. Frank Lawson to John Helm Maclean, November 29, 1942, and J. Thomas Askew to Maclean, October 28, 1942, both in John Helm Maclean Collection, Georgia Historical Society, Savannah, Box 2.
3. Duncan Clegg, interview, February 8, 1971.
4. Harbin, interview, February 8, 1971.
5. Confidential interview; see "The Governor of Georgia Remembers that He Was Once a Flogger Himself," *Life* (December 8, 1941), 40–41.
6. Harbin, interview, February 8, 1971.
7. Atlanta *Constitution*, May 12, 1946.
8. Lamar Murdaugh, interview, December 31, 1971; John A. Whitley, interview, August 29, 1971.
9. Spurlin, interview, June 23, 1973; Rufus Jarmin, "Wool Hat Dictator," *Saturday Evening Post* (June 27, 1942), 19.
10. Harbin, interview, February 8, 1971.
11. Whitley, interview, August 29, 1971.
12. Harbin, interview, February 8, 1971; Murdaugh, interview, December 31, 1971; Jarmin, "Wool Hat Dictator," 19.
13. Telfair (Ga.) *Enterprise*, May 27, 1920.
14. Clegg, interview, February 8, 1971.
15. Telfair (Ga.) *Enterprise*, August 5, 1920.
16. Clegg, interview, February 8, 1971.
17. George Brown Tindall, *The Emergence of the New South, 1913–1945* (Baton Rouge, 1967), 1.
18. *Georgia Statistical Abstract* (Athens, Ga., 1927).
19. C. Vann Woodward, *The Burden of Southern History* (Rev. ed.; Baton Rouge, 1968), 27.
20. Murdaugh, interview, December 31, 1971.
21. Confidential interview.

CHAPTER 4

1. Spurlin, interview, August 1, 1973.
2. James Peters, interview, June 12, 1970.
3. Murdaugh, interview, December 31, 1971.
4. *Ibid.*
5. *Ibid.*; Linder, interview, April 20, 1970.
6. Murdaugh, interview, December 31, 1971; Linder, interview, April 20, 1970.
7. Murdaugh, interview, December 31, 1971; Linder, interview, April 20, 1970.
8. Mrs. Eugene Talmadge, interview, February 8, 1971.
9. Spurlin, interview, August 1, 1973.
10. Murdaugh, interview, December 31, 1971.
11. Peters, interview, June 12, 1970.

12. Corley, interview, August 10, 1971.
13. Atlanta *Constitution*, July 4, 23, 25, 28, August 4, 13, 1932.
14. *Ibid.*, July 24, 25, 30, 1926; Murdaugh, interview, December 31, 1971.
15. Clegg, interview, February 8, 1971; Murdaugh, interview, December 31, 1971.
16. Mrs. Eugene Talmadge, interview, August 1, 1973; Murdaugh, interview, December 31, 1971.
17. Clegg, interview, February 8, 1971; Atlanta *Constitution*, August 4, 1926; Savannah *Morning News*, August 4, 1926.
18. Atlanta *Constitution*, August 13, 1926; Murdaugh, interview, December 31, 1971.
19. B. Tarver Woodall, interview, January 26, 1972.
20. Jarmin, "Wool Hat Dictator," 21.
21. *Georgia Official and Statistical Register* (Atlanta, 1927), 326–29.
22. Hapeville (Ga.) *Statesman*, September 23, 1941.
23. Georgia, Office of the Comptroller General, Campaign Expenses, 1926, in State of Georgia Archives, Atlanta.
24. Murdaugh, interview, December 31, 1971.

CHAPTER 5

1. Hugh Howell, interview, January 17, 1970.
2. Georgia, Department of Agriculture, *Biennial Report* (1927–28), 11–12; *Report of the Comptroller-General of the State of Georgia* (Atlanta, 1929), 165–81; Georgia, Legislative Papers (1927), Senate Bill 271 and House Bill 241, in State of Georgia Archives, Atlanta.
3. Atlanta *Constitution*, July 29, 1928.
4. *Ibid.*, August 2, 1928.
5. Cobb County (Ga.) *Times*, August 16, 1928.
6. *Georgia Official and Statistical Register* (Atlanta, 1929), 381.
7. Atlanta *Market Bulletin*, October 2, 1930.
8. *Georgia Statistical Abstract* (Athens, 1969), 128, 136, 138, 144, 223. Willard Range, *A Century of Georgia Agriculture, 1850–1950* (Athens, 1954), 172–74, 271; Citizens' Fact-Finding Movement in Georgia, *Georgia Facts in Figures* (Athens, 1946), 17, 19, 21.
9. *Georgia Official and Statistical Register* (Atlanta, 1931), 636.
10. Atlanta *Market Bulletin*, April 9, 1931.
11. Murdaugh, interview, December 31, 1971.
12. Georgia, Legislative Papers (1931), Senate Report 40, Senate Report 46; Georgia, *Senate Journal* (1931), 449, 499, 758–63; Georgia, Department of Agriculture, Biennial Report (1929–30), 55, 64.
13. Georgia, *Senate Journal* (1931), 449, 499.
14. *Ibid.*, 758, 763.
15. *Ibid.*, 800–801.
16. Georgia, *House Journal* (1931), 1295–99.
17. Georgia, *Senate Journal* (1931), 1303.
18. Georgia, Department of Agriculture, Market Bureau Acts, Section 3, Paragraph 8.
19. Georgia, *Executive Minutes* (1932), 64, 65, in State of Georgia Archives, Atlanta.
20. Atlanta *Constitution*, August 11, 16, 18, 1931, October 18, 1931.
21. Georgia, *House Journal* (1931), 1295–1303.
22. Georgia, Legislative Papers (1931), House Record 122.

23. Ralph E. McGill Collection.
24. *Georgia Laws* (1931), Pt. I, Title II, No. 297., pp. 53–54.
25. Atlanta *Market Bulletin*, December 24, 1931.
26. Atlanta *Constitution*, February 3, 1931.
27. *Ibid.*, May 10, 1931.

CHAPTER 6

1. Atlanta *Constitution*, April 10, 1932.
2. Macon *Telegraph*, February 28, 1932.
3. Murdaugh, interview, December 31, 1971.
4. Confidential interview.
5. Peters, interview, June 12, 1970.
6. Spurlin, interview, August 1, 1973.
7. Telfair (Ga.) *Enterprise*, July 4, 7, 1932.
8. Clegg, interview, February 8, 1971.
9. Atlanta *Constitution*, July 5, 1932; Telfair (Ga.) *Enterprise*, July 7, 1932;
   Howell, interview, January 17, 1970; A. Dixon Adair, III, "Eugene Talmadge of Georgia" (M.A. thesis, Princeton University, 1936), 23.
10. Atlanta *Constitution*, July 22, 1932.
11. Telfair (Ga.) *Enterprise*, July 14, 1932.
12. *Ibid.*, August 5, 1932.
13. Jarmin, "Wool Hat Dictator," 111.
14. *Ibid.*, 21.
15. Telfair (Ga.) *Enterprise*, August 11, 1932.
16. Jarmin, "Wool Hat Dictator," 111.
17. Adair, "Eugene Talmadge of Georgia," 26–27.
18. *Georgia Official and Statistical Register* (Atlanta, 1932), 545.
19. Hapeville (Ga.) *Statesman*, September 15, 1932; Telfair (Ga.) *Enterprise*,
    September 15, 1932.
20. Hapeville (Ga.) *Statesman*, September 15, 1932; Telfair (Ga.) *Enterprise*,
    September 15, 1932.
21. Atlanta *Constitution*, October 7, 1932.
22. Howell, interview, January 17, 1970.

CHAPTER 7

1. Mrs. Eugene Talmadge, interview, February 8, 1971.
2. Georgia, *House Journal* (1933), 183–95.
3. *Ibid.*, 204–10, 465, 971.
4. Savannah *Morning News*, April 10, 1933; Georgia, *Attorney General Opinions* (1933–1934), 230–31; Georgia, *Executive Minutes* (1933), 13, 15, 17.
5. Georgia, *Senate Journal* (1933), 81, 84.
6. Atlanta *Constitution*, January 18, April 12, 1933.
7. *Ibid.*, January 23, 1933; Sarah McCulloh Lemmon, "The Public Career of
   Eugene Talmadge: 1926–1936" (M.A. thesis, University of North Carolina,
   1936), 155.
8. V. O. Key, *Southern Politics in State and Nation* (New York, 1949).
9. Georgia, *Senate Journal* (1933), 724–26.
10. *Ibid.*, 970, 965, 966.
11. *Ibid.*, 971.
12. *Ibid.*, 1440; Georgia, *House Journal* (1933), 872–80.
13. Georgia, *Senate Journal* (1933), 973, 1197; Georgia, *House Journal* (1933),
    2325.

14. Georgia, *Senate Journal* (1933), 1127.
15. New York *Times*, March 2, 1933.
16. Atlanta *Constitution*, March 2, 1933.
17. *Ibid.*, March 22, 1933.
18. Macon (Ga.) *Telegraph*, April 1, 1933.
19. Atlanta *Constitution*, February 18, 1933; New York *Times*, February 26, 1933; Columbus (Ga.) *Inquirer*, March 22, 1933; Savannah *Morning News*, March 20, 1933.
20. *Georgia Laws* (1821), 49.
21. Atlanta *Constitution*, March 20, 21, 1933.
22. Savannah *Morning News*, June 20, 1933.
23. Atlanta *Constitution*, May 2, 1933.
24. Atlanta *Journal*, May 5, June 1, 1933.
25. *Ibid.*, June 6, 1933.
26. *Ibid.*, June 14, 1933.
27. Georgia, *Executive Minutes* (1933), 189–93.
28. George B. Hamilton, interview, September 8, 1971.
29. Atlanta *Journal*, June 20, 1933.
30. Atlanta *Constitution*, June 24, 1933; Atlanta *Journal*, June 24, 1933; Savannah *Morning News*, June 30, 1933.
31. Atlanta *Journal*, June 26, 1933; Howell, interview, January 17, 1970.
32. Savannah *Morning News*, July 5, 1933.
33. *Ibid.*, June 30, 1933.
34. Atlanta *Journal*, July 29, 1933.
35. Savannah *Morning News*, July 30, 1933.
36. Hapeville (Ga.) *Statesman*, quoted in Oglethorpe (Ga.) *Echo*, August 11, 1933.
37. Key, *Southern Politics*, 128, 110.

CHAPTER 8

1. Corley, interview, August 10, 1971.
2. Howell, interview, January 17, 1970.
3. W. O. Brooks, interview, November 18, 1972.
4. Ed Bridges, interview, October 8, 1970.
5. Spurlin, interview, May 16, 1972.
6. Confidential interview.
7. *Ibid.*
8. Carlton Mobley, interview, October 16, 1970.
9. Mrs. Eugene Talmadge, interview, August 1, 1973.
10. John Whitley, interview, February 18, 1970.
11. Spurlin, interview, August 1, 1973.
12. Mrs. John Monaghan, interview, May 25, 1970; Corley, interview, August 10, 1971; Spurlin, interview, August 1, 1973.
13. Lawson to Maclean, November 25, 1942, in Maclean Collection.
14. Lawson to Maclean, November 29, 1942, *ibid.*
15. Bridges, interview, October 8, 1970.
16. Confidential interview.
17. Bridges, interview, October 8, 1970.

CHAPTER 9

1. Georgia, *Executive Minutes* (1933), 67.
2. Calhoun (Ga.) *Times*, March 22, 1934.

3. Randall Evans, interview, June 8, 1970.
4. Hamilton, interview, September 8, 1971.
5. John and Wanda Whitley, interview, February 18, 1970.
6. Macon (Ga.) *Telegraph*, July 6, 1936.
7. Atlanta *Constitution*, July 5, 1936; Athens (Ga.) *Banner Herald*, July 4, 1934.
8. Herman Talmadge, interview, September 2, 1972.
9. Macon (Ga.) *Telegraph*, September 4, 1934.
10. Atlanta *Constitution*, July 5, 1934.
11. Eugene Talmadge, Memorandum for the President, November 30, 1934, in Official File 1535, Eugene Talmadge, 1933–1943, Franklin D. Roosevelt Library, Hyde Park, N.Y.
12. *Georgia Official and Statistical Register* (Atlanta, 1933, 1935, 1937); Atlanta *Constitution*, September 12, 1934.
13. Athens (Ga.) *Banner Herald*, September 13, 1934.
14. Adair, "Eugene Talmadge of Georgia," 64.
15. Atlanta *Journal*, August 5, 1934.
16. Bridges, interview, October 8, 1970.
17. *Ibid.*
18. Spurlin, interview, August 1, 1973; William Kimbrough, interview, March 4, 1973; Brooks, interview, November 18, 1972.
19. Hapeville (Ga.) *Statesman*, November 20, 1934.
20. Peters, interview, June 12, 1970.
21. Atlanta *Constitution*, November 24, 1934.
22. Peters, interview, June 12, 1970; Herman Talmadge, interview, September 2, 1972; Bridges, interview, October 8, 1970.
23. Hamilton, interview, September 8, 1971.

CHAPTER 10

1. Georgia, *Senate Journal* (1935), 53.
2. *Ibid.*, 54.
3. *Ibid.*, 55, 60, 61.
4. *Ibid.*, 60, 61.
5. Randall Evans to William Anderson, June 9, 1969, in possession of the author.
6. Atlanta *Journal*, July 5, 1936.
7. Howell, interview, January 17, 1970; John Whitley, interview, February 18, 1970.
8. Lamar Ball, interview, September 20, 1970.
9. Atlanta *Constitution*, February 6, 1935; T. Harry Williams, *Huey Long* (New York, 1970), 814.
10. Mark Dunahoe, interview, October 18, 1970.
11. Thomas Elkins Taylor, "Ellis Arnall" (M.A. thesis, Emory University, 1954), 212.
12. Eastman (Ga.) *Times Journal*, February 5, 1935.
13. James T. Patterson, *The New Deal and the States: Federalism in Transition* (Princeton, N.J., 1969), 75.
14. Georgia, *House Journal* (1935), 1838; Atlanta *Constitution*, March 27, 1935.
15. Peters, interview, June 12, 1970.
16. Roy Harris, interview, April 12, 1968.
17. *Ibid.*
18. Georgia, *Senate Journal* (1935), 1963–64.
19. Columbus (Ga.) *Inquirer*, April 1, 1935; Georgia, *House Journal* (1935),

489, 912, 1146, 1302, 1700, 1592–96, 2904–2905, 2015; Atlanta *Journal*, March 24, 1935; Taylor, "Ellis Arnall," 212.

20. Atlanta *Journal*, March 24, 1935.
21. Atlanta *Constitution*, March 26, 1935.
22. Hamilton, interview, September 8, 1971.
23. Peters, interview, June 12, 1970.
24. Atlanta *Journal*, March 25, 1935 .
25. Peters, interview, June 12, 1970.
26. Atlanta *Journal*, March 27, 28, 29, 1935.

CHAPTER 11

1. John and Wanda Whitley, interview, February 18, 1970.
2. *Ibid.*
3. *Ibid.*
4. *Ibid.*
5. Mrs. Herman Talmadge, interview, September 2, 1972.
6. Hapeville (Ga.) *Statesman*, April 2, 1935.
7. New York *Times*, April 19, 1935.
8. Robert, interview, November 2, 1971; Howell, interview, January 17, 1970; Linder, interview, April 20, 1970; John Whitley, interview, February 18, 1972.
9. Hapeville (Ga.) *Statesman*, July 2, August 20, 1935.
10. Lemmon, "The Public Career of Eugene Talmadge," 243.
11. Harlee Branch to Stephen T. Early, October 10, 1934, in President's Personal File 216, FDR Library, Hyde Park, N.Y.
12. Marvin McIntyre to Franklin D. Roosevelt, November 11, 1934, in Official File 1535, FDR Library.
13. Eugene Talmadge to Franklin D. Roosevelt, December 11, 1934, in President's Personal File 216, FDR Library.
14. Eugene Talmadge to Franklin D. Roosevelt, March 26, 1935, in President's Secretary File, Box 184, FDR Library.
15. Ralph McGill to Franklin D. Roosevelt, April 18, 1935, in Official File 1535, FDR Library.
16. George Creel to Franklin D. Roosevelt, May 5, 1935, in Official File 1535, FDR Library.
17. Printed copy of Eugene Talmadge speech, in Official File 1535, FDR Library.
18. Harlee Branch to Marvin H. McIntyre, July 11, 1935, in Official File 1535, FDR Library.
19. Eugene Talmadge, Memorandum to the President, July 15, 1935, in Official File 1535, FDR Library.
20. Memo from Harlee Branch to Marvin McIntyre, July 18, 1935, in Official File 1535, FDR Library.
21. Letter from eight of Georgia's representatives to the president, July 22, 1935, *ibid.*
22. H. T. McIntosh to Harlee Branch, July 11, 1935, in President's Personal File 216, FDR Library.
23. Clark Howell to Marvin H. McIntyre, July 30, 1935, in Official File 1535, FDR Library.
24. L. Edmondson to Lawrence W. Roberts, Jr., August 21, 1935, in President's Personal File 216, FDR Library.
25. Harlee Branch to Marvin McIntyre, August 5, 1935, in Official File 1535, FDR Library.
26. Letters from Georgia representatives, August 15, 1935, *ibid.*

27. Arthur M. Schlesinger, Jr., *The Age of Roosevelt: The Coming of the New Deal* (3 vols.; Boston, 1959), II, 274n.
28. New York *Times*, January 30, 1936.
29. U. S. *Senate Documents*, 7th Cong., 1st Sess., 1957ff., 1981ff.
30. Atlanta *Journal*, December 29, 1935.
31. *Ibid.*, January 2, 3, 4, 1936.
32. "Poker Players," *Time* (January 20, 1936), 18.
33. Atlanta *Journal*, January 3, 1936; Macon *Telegraph*, May 10, 1936.
34. New York *Times*, January 28, 1936.
35. *Ibid.*, January 30, 1936.
36. Howell, interview, January 17, 1970; Linder, interview, January 21, 1970; Atlanta *Journal*, January 29, 1936.
37. New York *Times*, January 31, 1936.
38. Hapeville (Ga.) *Statesman*, February 4, 1936.
39. Woodward, *The Burden of Southern History*, 20.
40. Benjamin Stolberg, "Buzz Windrip, Governor of Georgia," *Nation* (March 4, 11, 1936), 271, 316–18; Johnathan Daniels, "Witch Hunt in Georgia," *Nation* (August 5, 1941), 94.

CHAPTER 12

1. Georgia, *Executive Minutes* (1936), 9, in State of Georgia Archives, Atlanta.
2. *Ibid.*, 12.
3. *Ibid.*, 13.
4. Hamilton, interview, September 8, 1971.
5. Mobley, interview, April 28, 1969; Hamilton, interview, September 8, 1971; Atlanta *Journal*, February 20, 1936; Atlanta *Constitution*, February 20, 1936.
6. Georgia, *Executive Minutes* (1936), 15.
7. Spurlin, interview, August 1, 1973.
8. Hamilton, interview, September 8, 1971.
9. *Ibid.*
10. Mobley, interview, April 28, 1969.
11. John Whitley, interview, February 18, 1970; Georgia, *Executive Minutes* (1936), 18.
12. Atlanta *Journal*, February 28, 1936.
13. *Ibid.*
14. Atlanta *Constitution*, February 28, 1936.
15. *Ibid.*, March 2, 1936; Atlanta *Journal*, March 1, 1936.
16. Hamilton, interview, September 8, 1971.
17. Atlanta *Journal*, March 4, 1936.
18. *Ibid.*; Atlanta *Constitution*, March 4, 1936.
19. Atlanta *Journal*, March 5, 1936.
20. Howell, interview, January 17, 1970; Atlanta *Constitution*, March 5, 6, 13, 1936.
21. Atlanta *Constitution*, March 7, 1936.
22. Atlanta *Journal*, March 14, 1936; Atlanta *Constitution*, March 15, 1936.
23. Atlanta *Constitution*, March 15, 1936.
24. Atlanta *Journal*, March 18, 1936.
25. *Ibid.*, March 24, 1936.
26. *Ibid.*, May 9, 1936.
27. Mobley, interview, October 16, 1970.

CHAPTER 13

1. Telfair *Enterprise*, May 28, 1936.

2. Atlanta *Journal*, May 12, 1936.
3. Hapeville (Ga.) *Statesman*, June 23, 1936.
4. Atlanta *Journal*, June 17, 1936.
5. *Ibid.*, June 22, 1936.
6. *Ibid.*, June 21, 1936.
7. Howell, interview, January 17, 1970.
8. Peters, interview, June 12, 1970.
9. Murdaugh, interview, December 31, 1971.
10. Telfair *Enterprise*, July 5, 1936; Clegg, interview, February 8, 1971.
11. Atlanta *Journal*, July 7, 1936.
12. *Richard Russell, Georgia Giant*, Cox Broadcasting Co. Television Film, Atlanta, 1970.
13. Dunahoe, interview, November 2, 1972.
14. *Richard Russell, Georgia Giant*.
15. Atlanta *Journal*, July 22, 1936.
16. Atlanta *Constitution*, August 5, 1936.
17. John Whitley, interview, August 29, 1971.
18. Atlanta *Constitution*, August 28, 1936.
19. Atlanta *Journal*, August 21, 1936.
20. Howell, interview, October 17, 1970.
21. Atlanta *Constitution*, August 27, 1936.
22. Dunahoe, interview, October 18, 1970.
23. Atlanta *Journal*, August 26, 1936.
24. Dunahoe, interview, October 18, 1970.
25. Atlanta *Constitution*, September 9, 1936.
26. Hamilton, interview, June 19, 1970; *Georgia Official and Statistical Register* (Atlanta, 1936).
27. Atlanta *Journal*, September 9, 1936.
28. Dunahoe, interview, October 18, 1970.
29. Joseph L. Bernd, "Grass Roots Politics in Georgia" (Emory University Research Committee, Atlanta, 1960), 7.
30. Dunahoe, interview, October 18, 1970.

CHAPTER 14

1. Murdaugh, interview, December 31, 1971.
2. Atlanta *Market Bulletin*, October 17, 1929.
3. Confidential interview.
4. Hapeville (Ga.) *Statesman*, May 7, 1938; Atlanta *Journal*, May 13, 1938.
5. Jasper B. Shannon, "Presidential Politics in the South, 1938," *Journal of Politics*, I (1939), 146–49.
6. Robert, interview, July 26, 1971.
7. Atlanta *Journal*, June 16, 1938.
8. *Ibid.*
9. *Ibid.*
10. Atlanta *Constitution*, July 22, 1938.
11. *Ibid.*, August 2 and July 24, 1938.
12. Atlanta *Journal*, August 9, 1938.
13. Atlanta *Constitution*, August 11, 12, 1938.
14. Atlanta *Journal*, August 12, 1938.
15. *Ibid.*, August 11, 12, 1938; Atlanta *Constitution*, August 12, 1938; James McGregor Burns, *Roosevelt: The Lion and the Fox* (New York, 1958), 324.
16. Atlanta *Journal*, August 13, 14, 1938.
17. *Ibid.*, August 15, 1938.
18. *Ibid.*, September 12, 1938.

19. Atlanta *Constitution*, September 13, 1938.
20. *Ibid.*, September 15, 1938.
21. *Georgia Official and Statistical Register* (Atlanta, 1938), 504.
22. Peters, interview, June 12, 1970.
23. Talmadge Campaign Correspondence, 1938, Appling County File.
24. Howell, interview, October 17, 1970; Corley, interview, January 25, 1970; Murdaugh, interview, December 31, 1971.
25. Eugene Talmadge to R. C. Grace, September 21, 1938, in Talmadge Campaign Correspondence.
26. Atlanta *Journal*, October 1, 1938.
27. Corley, interview, January 25, 1970.
28. Eugene Talmadge to J. R. Corkle, April 23, 1938, in possession of Hugh Howell.
29. Atlanta *Journal*, October 7, 1938.
30. Eugene Talmadge to Mrs. M. W. Gonzales, April 23, 1938, in Talmadge Campaign Correspondence.

CHAPTER 15

1. Corley, interview, August 10, 1971.
2. Peters, interview, June 12, 1970.
3. *Ibid.*
4. Confidential interview.
5. *Ibid.*; Atlanta *Journal*, June 9, 1940.
6. Atlanta *Constitution*, June 13, 1940.
7. Atlanta *Journal*, June 3, 1940.
8. *Ibid.*, July 3, 1940.
9. Atlanta *Constitution*, September 12, 1940.
10. Atlanta *Journal*, July 11, 1940.
11. *Ibid.*, September 12, 1940.
12. *Georgia Official and Statistical Register* (Atlanta, 1939, 1940, 1941), 501.
13. Atlanta *Constitution*, September 13, October 3, 1940.
14. Evans, interview, June 8, 1970.
15. Atlanta *Journal*, October 1, 1940.
16. Atlanta *Constitution*, October 3, 1940.
17. Atlanta *Journal*, October 3, 4, 1940; Private Papers of Governors, Eugene Talmadge, Group Record 51, Series 67, State of Georgia Archives, Atlanta.
18. Atlanta *Journal*, December 22, 1940.
19. *Collier's*, quoted in Atlanta *Journal*, January 12, 1940.
20. Clipping in Governor's Unofficial Papers, State of Georgia Archives, Atlanta.
21. Atlanta *Journal*, May 2, 1942.
22. Jarmin, "Wool Hat Dictator," 111.

CHAPTER 16

1. Walter D. Cocking, "Report of the Study of Higher Education of Negroes in Georgia," in Special Collections, University of Georgia Libraries, Athens, Ga., 1938.
2. "The Present Program of Teacher Education at the University of Georgia and Its Future Development," typescript in Special Collections of Stanton J. Singleton Papers, University of Georgia, Athens, Ga., 1936.
3. William Tate, "Memo on Cocking," typescript in Special Collections, University of Georgia Libraries, Athens, Ga., 1970.
4. R. J. H. DeLoach Papers, Special Collections, Georgia Southern College Libraries, Statesboro, Ga.

5. *Minutes of the Board of Regents of the University of Georgia* (Georgia State Archives, Atlanta, 1941), 213, 216.
6. M. C. Huntley, "Report on Charges of Political Interference in the University System of Georgia," typescript in Special Collections, University of Georgia Libraries, Athens, Ga., 1941.
7. *Board of Regents Minutes*, 228; Atlanta *Constitution*, June 17, 1941; Hapeville (Ga.) *Statesman*, June 17, 1941.
8. Hapeville (Ga.) *Statesman*, June 17, 1941.
9. Bulloch (Ga.) *Times*, September 3, 1942; James F. Cook, "Politics and Education in the Talmadge Era: The Controversy Over the University System of Georgia, 1941–1942" (M.A. thesis, University of Georgia, 1972), *passim*.
10. Atlanta *Constitution*, June 20, 1941.
11. Lucian Goodrich to Eugene Talmadge, in Eugene Talmadge Correspondence, 1941.
12. Peters, interview, June 12, 1970.
13. Mrs. Eugene Talmadge, interview, August 1, 1973.
14. *Board of Regents Minutes*, 7; Peters, interview, June 12, 1970; Daniels, "Witch Hunt in Georgia," 93; Atlanta *Journal*, July 15, 16, 1941; Eugene Talmadge Correspondence, State of Georgia Archives, 1941; M. L. Brittain, *The Story of Georgia Tech* (Chapel Hill, N.C., 1948), 292–95; Zell Bryan Miller, "The Administration of E. D. Rivers as Governor of Georgia" (M.A. thesis, University of Georgia, 1958), *passim*; Marvin S. Pittman, "Political Interference of Governor Eugene Talmadge with the Georgia Teacher's College," typescript in Special Collections, University of Georgia Libraries, 1941, pp. 69–72.
15. Eugene Talmadge to unknown, July 17, 1941, in Eugene Talmadge Correspondence.
16. E. Merton Coulter, interview, December 24, 1973.
17. Atlanta *Constitution*, July 17, 1941; Eugene Talmadge to unknown, July 18, August 21, 1941, in Eugene Talmadge Correspondence.
18. Hapeville (Ga.) *Statesman*, July 29, 1941.
19. Ellis Arnall, interview, November 14, 1972.
20. Spurlin, interview, August 1, 1973.
21. Atlanta *Journal*, September 1, 1941.
22. *Board of Regents Minutes*, November 1, 1941.
23. Sandy Beavers to Eugene Talmadge, November 25, 1941, in Eugene Talmadge Correspondence.
24. Eugene Talmadge to Sandy Beavers, November 26, 1941, *ibid.*
25. Sandy Beavers to Eugene Talmadge, November 26, 1941, *ibid.*
26. Atlanta *Journal*, August 26, 1941.
27. Sandy Beavers to all Board of Regents members, November 27, 1941, in Eugene Talmadge Correspondence.
28. Clipping in Ralph E. McGill Collection, Special Collections, Box N-2, Emory University.

CHAPTER 17

1. Harris, interview, April 12, 1968.
2. Edgar Dyal to Eugene Talmadge, July 7, 1942, Carlton Mobley to Edgar Dyal, July 10, 1941, both in Talmadge Campaign Correspondence, Appling County File.
3. Atlanta *Constitution*, July 5, 1941; Atlanta *Journal*, July 4, 1942.
4. Evans, interview, June 8, 1970; Linder, interview, May 5, 1969; Murdaugh, interview, December 31, 1970.

5. Atlanta *Journal*, July 19, 1942.
6. *Ibid.*, July 19, 1942.
7. *Ibid.*, July 30, 1942.
8. *Ibid.*, July 29, 1942; Atlanta *Constitution*, July 29, 1942.
9. Atlanta *Journal*, July 30, 19, 25, 1942.
10. Linder, interview, May 5, 1969.
11. J. C. Johnson, interview, August 1, 1972.
12. Atlanta *Journal*, August 2, 1942; Atlanta *Constitution*, August 2, 1942.
13. Atlanta *Journal*, August 10, 1942; Atlanta *Constitution*, August 2, 1942.
14. Atlanta *Journal*, September 4, 8, 1942. See also E. K. Lumpkin to Eugene Talmadge, August 7, 1942, William T. Ray to Eugene Talmadge, August 18, 1942, and H. J. Rowe to Eugene Talmadge, August 8, 1942, all in Eugene Talmadge Campaign Correspondence, Clarke County File.
15. Peters, interview, June 12, 1970.
16. *Georgia Official and Statistical Register* (Atlanta, 1939, 1941, 1943), 653.
17. Peters, interview, June 12, 1970.
18. Eugene Talmadge to Alvin V. Seller, and Eugene Talmadge to John A. Lawrence, September 17, 1942, both in Talmadge Campaign Correspondence, Appling County File.
19. Jarmin, "Wool Hat Dictator," 20, 21, 109.
20. Typed sheet on Talmadge life, in Ralph E. McGill Collection, Box N-2.
21. Eugene Talmadge to Ralph McGill, December 20, 1943 in Ralph E. McGill Collection.
22. Herman Talmadge, interview, September 2, 1972.
23. Hapeville (Ga.) *Statesman*, January 6, August 17, 1944.
24. *Ibid.*, December 25, 1945, March 16, 1944.
25. Herman Talmadge, interview, September 2, 1972.

CHAPTER 18

1. M. L. St. John, interview, June 16, 1971.
2. Dunahoe, interview, October 18, 1970.
3. Atlanta *Constitution*, January 10, 16, 1946.
4. *Ibid.*, January 26, 1946.
5. *Ibid.*, January 27, 1946.
6. Bridges, interview, October 8, 1970.
7. *Ibid.*
8. Atlanta *Constitution*, April 13, May 16, 1946.
9. C. A. Scott, interview, February 28, 1974.
10. Herman Talmadge, interview, September 2, 1972; Peters, interview, June 12, 1970.
11. Atlanta *Constitution*, April 15, 1946.
12. Linder, interview, May 5, 1969.
13. Mrs. Eugene Talmadge, interview, August 1, 1973.
14. Atlanta *Constitution*, April 6, 1946.
15. *Ibid.*, May 10, 1946.
16. James V. Carmichael, interview, August 12, 1972; Bridges, interview, October 8, 1970.
17. Mrs. Eugene Talmadge, interview, August 1, 1973.
18. Atlanta *Constitution*, May 9, 1946.

CHAPTER 19

1. Atlanta *Constitution*, May 17, 1946; Athens *Banner Herald*, May 17, 1946.

2. Atlanta *Journal*, May 17, 1946.
3. Atlanta *Constitution*, May 18, 1946.
4. St. John, interview, June 16, 1971.
5. Ball, interview, September 20, 1970; St. John, interview, June 16, 1971.
6. St. John, interview, June 16, 1971.
7. Athens *Banner Herald*, June 5, 1946.
8. Evans, interview, June 8, 1970.
9. St. John, interview, June 16, 1971.
10. Athens *Banner Herald*, June 26, 1946.
11. Bridges, interview, October 8, 1970.
12. *Georgia Official and Statistical Register* (Atlanta, 1946), 493.
13. Louisville *Courier Journal* July 28, 1946, clipping in Ralph E. McGill Collection, Box N-2.
14. Dunkirk (N.Y.) *Evening Observer* clipping, *ibid.*

CHAPTER 20

1. Spurlin, interview, August 1, 1973.
2. Confidential interview.
3. Spurlin, interview, August 1, 1973.
4. Sibley, interview, October 10, 1972.
5. Bridges, interview, October 8, 1970.
6. Herman Talmadge, interview, September 2, 1972.
7. *Ibid.*
8. Bridges, interview, October 8, 1970.
9. Spurlin, interview, August 1, 1973.
10. Atlanta *Journal*, December 22, 23, 24, 1946; Atlanta *Constitution*, December 22, 23, 1946.

Bibliography

A Note on the Sources

Gene Talmadge lives in this book primarily because of oral interviews. The book, therefore, is as strong and as weak as the veracity of those interviews. For some sort of verification, contradictory statements were continually sought from other associates who would have had access to similar information. Assertions were also checked against newspaper and book information, and most individuals were called or visited twice for the purpose of double-checking. These attempts at determining the truth, however, still cannot guarantee absolute authenticity. The memory is often the servant of the conscience and the victim of individual perceptions, likes and dislikes, beliefs and attitudes. There were some contradictions, mostly of detail, but none affected the conclusions or appraisals in the book. There was, in fact, broad substantiation throughout most of the interviews.

The disappointment of bringing Talmadge back is the almost total lack of unofficial or even official papers. Most were summarily burned whenever he left office. Apparently a great number of his papers were piled in the basement of the McRae home, only to be slowly ruined by seeping groundwater, and then thrown out. Such has been the misfortune of the archives of so many of Georgia's leaders.

INTERVIEWS

Abt, C. B., May 31, 1971
Almand, Bond, May 12, 1971
Anderson, H. B., July 18, 1972
Arnall, Ellis, November 14, 1972
Ball, Lamar, September 20, 1970
Bridges, Ed, October 8, 1970
Brooks, W. O., November 18, 1972
Cameron, Mrs. Lucy, May 6, 1973
Carmichael, James V., August 12, 1972
Clegg, Duncan, February 8, 1971
Corley, James C., January 25, 1970, August 10, 1971
Coulter, E. Merton, December 24, 1973
Dunahoe, Mark, October 18, 1970

Evans, Randall, June 8, 1970
Hamilton, George, June 19, 1970, September 8, 1971
Hand, Fred, May 18, 1970
Harbin, Bethel, February 8, 1971
Harris, Roy, April 12, 1968
Howell, Hugh, January 17, 1970, October 17, 1970
Jackson, Mrs. Harriet B., January 17, 1971
Johnson, J. C., August 1, 1972
Kimbrough, William, March 4, 1973
Kitchens, Remer, May 5, 1971
Linder, Tom, May 5, 1969, April 20, 1970
Mobley, Carlton, April 28, 1969, October 16, 1970
Monaghan, Mrs. John, May 25, 1969
Murdaugh, Lamar, December 31, 1971
Pace, James, April 10, 1972
Peters, James, June 12, 1970
Ray, Elsie, July 10, 1972
Robert, Lawrence W., July 26, 1971
St. John, M. L., June 16, 1971
Scott, C. A., February 28, 1974
Sibley, Celestine, October 10, 1972
Spurlin, Henry, May 16, 1972, August 1, 1973
Talmadge, Mrs. Eugene, February 8, 1971, August 1, 1973
Talmadge, Herman, September 2, 1973
Talmadge, Mrs. Herman, September 2, 1973
Talmadge, Marylynne (Mrs. Horace Clark), May 1, 1970
Whitley, John A., February 18, 1970, August 29, 1971
Whitley, Mrs. John (Wanda), February 18, 1970, August 29, 1971
Woodall, B. Tarver, January 26, 1972
Zelner, Kimball, November 14, 1970

GOVERNMENT DOCUMENTS

FEDERAL

United States Senate, Special Committee to Investigate Lobby Activities, Hearings. *Senate Documents*, 74th Cong., 1st Sess., 1957 ff.

STATE OF GEORGIA

Attorney General Opinions, 1933–34. Georgia State Archives, Atlanta.
Comptroller General's Office. Campaign Expenses, 1926. Georgia State Archives, Atlanta.
Department of Agriculture. *Biennial Report*, 1929, 1931. Georgia State Archives, Atlanta.
———. *Georgia: Her Resources and Possibilities*. Atlanta: Georgia State Archives, 1895.
Executive Minutes (1931, 1933, 1934, 1935, 1936). Georgia State Archives, Atlanta.

Georgia Laws (1931), Part 1, Title II, No. 297, and Article II. Georgia State Archives, Atlanta.
Georgia Official and Statistical Register (1925, 1927, 1929, 1931, 1933, 1935, 1937). Georgia State Archives, Atlanta.
House Journal (1931, 1933, 1935, 1941). Georgia State Archives, Atlanta.
Legislative Papers, 1927. Georgia State Archives, Atlanta,
Minutes of the Board of Regents of the University of Georgia, 1941. Georgia State Archives, Atlanta.
Private Papers of Governors: Eugene Talmadge. Record Group 51, Series 67, including Senate Race Expenses and Talmadge 1938 Bank Deposit Book. Georgia State Archives, Atlanta.
Ray, Elsie. Scrapbook, in Governor's Unofficial Papers: Eugene Talmadge. Georgia State Archives, Atlanta.
Report of the Comptroller General of the State of Georgia (1929). Georgia State Archives, Atlanta.
Senate Journal (1931, 1933, 1935, 1941). Georgia State Archives, Atlanta.

COUNTY (Georgia)

Monroe County Deed Book A, C, H, 30, 46, 47, and "Old Deeds." Forsyth, Ga., Monroe County Courthouse.
Telfair County Superior Court Minutes (1922), Nos. 4, 5. McRae, Ga., Telfair County Courthouse.

CORRESPONDENCE

FROM EUGENE TALMADGE TO:

Beavers, Sandy, November 26, 1941. In Eugene Talmadge Correspondence (1941). Georgia State Archives, Atlanta.
Burger, D. N., August 15, 1942. In Talmadge Campaign Correspondence, Appling County File. Georgia State Archives, Atlanta.
Cape, O. C., September 3, 1942. In Talmadge Campaign Correspondence, Oconee Countee File. Georgia State Archives, Atlanta.
Gonzalez, Mrs. M. W., October 8, 1938. In Private Papers of Governors: Eugene Talmadge. Georgia State Archives, Atlanta.
Grace, R. C., September 21, 1938. In Private Papers of Governors: Eugene Talmadge. Georgia State Archives, Atlanta.
Lawrence, John A., September 17, 1942. In Talmadge Campaign Correspondence, Appling County File. Georgia State Archives, Atlanta.
McCorkle, J. R., April 23, 1938. In possession of Hugh Howell.
McCravey, E. L., April 30, 1942. In Talmadge Campaign Correspondence, Appling County File. Georgia State Archives, Atlanta.
Seller, Alvin V., September 25, 1942. In Talmadge Campaign Correspondence, Appling County File. Georgia State Archives, Atlanta.
Unknown, July 18, 1941. In Eugene Talmadge Correspondence (1941). Georgia State Archives, Atlanta.

TO EUGENE TALMADGE FROM:

Arnold, James W., August 17, 1942. In Talmadge Campaign Correspondence, Oconee County File. Georgia State Archives, Atlanta.
Beavers, Sandy, November 25, 26, 1941. In Eugene Talmadge Correspondence (1941). Georgia State Archives, Atlanta.
Burger, D. N., August 17, 1942. In Talmadge Campaign Correspondence, Oconee County File. Georgia State Archives, Atlanta.
Carter, R. C., August 13, 1942. In Talmadge Campaign Correspondence, Appling County File. Georgia State Archives, Atlanta.
Cummings, John J., November 19, 1941. In Eugene Talmadge Correspondence (1941). Georgia State Archives, Atlanta.
DeLoach, John, January 23, 1941. In Eugene Talmadge Correspondence (1941). Georgia State Archives, Atlanta.
Lumpkin, E. K., August 7, September 25, 1942. In Talmadge Campaign Correspondence, Oconee County File. Georgia State Archives, Atlanta.
Morris, J. G., September 18, 1938. In Private Papers of Governors: Eugene Talmadge. Georgia State Archives, Atlanta.
Poindexter, C. H., May 19, 1942. In Talmadge Campaign Correspondence, Appling County File. Georgia State Archives, Atlanta.
Ray, William T., August 18, 1942. In Talmadge Campaign Correspondence, Oconee County File. Georgia State Archives, Atlanta.
Rowe, H. R., August 8, 1942. In Talmadge Campaign Correspondence, Oconee County File. Georgia State Archives, Atlanta.
Tindall, J. D., September 19, 1938. In Private Papers of Governors: Eugene Talmadge. Georgia State Archives, Atlanta.
Welch, R. D., July 14, 1942. In Talmadge Campaign Correspondence, Appling County File. Georgia State Archives, Atlanta.

OTHER CORRESPONDENCE

Edgar Dyal to Carlton Mobley, June 7, 1942. In Talmadge Campaign Correspondence, Oconee County File. Georgia State Archives, Atlanta.
Randall Evans to the author, June 9, 1969; Mrs. John Monaghan to the author, January 25, 1971; and Mrs. Harriet B. Jackson to the author, May 17, July 27, 1969, all in possession of the author.
Frank Lawson to John Helm Maclean, November 25, 29, 1942, both in John Helm Maclean Collection, Georgia Historical Society, Savannah, Box 2.

ARTICLES

Arnall, Ellis (as told to Walter Davenport). "Revolution Down South." *Collier's* (July 28, 1945), 17ff.
Bailes, Sue. "Eugene Talmadge and the Board of Regents Controversy." *Georgia Historical Quarterly*, LIII (December, 1969), 409–23.
Basso, Hamilton. "Our Gene." *New Republic* (February 19, 1936), 35–37.
Belvin, W. L. "Georgia Gubernatorial Primary of 1946." *Georgia Historical Quarterly*, V (1917), 50, 37, 53.

Creel, George. "Wild Man from Sugar Creek." *Collier's* (December 21, 1935). 31ff.

Daniels, Jonathan. "Witch Hunt in Georgia." *Nation* (August 2, 1941), 93–94.

Davenport, Walter. "The Shouting Dies." *Collier's* (May 2, 1936), 12–13ff.

"Death of the Wild Man." *Time* (December 30, 1946), 18.

"Exit Gene Talmadge." *Time* (September 21, 1942).

Gaillard, Peyre. "Georgia At Last Has a Good Governor." *American Mercury* (May, 1934).

"Gene and Junior." *Time* (September 7, 1936), 11.

"Georgia's Kingfish Cut All Budgets But His Own." *Newsweek* (June 15, 1935), 14.

"Georgia's Negro Vote." *Nation* (July 6, 1946), 12ff.

Huie, William Bradford. "Talmadge: White Man's Governor." *American Mercury* (February, 1942), 181–90.

Jarmin, Rufus. "Wool Hat Dictator." *Saturday Evening Post* (June 27, 1947), 20ff.

McGill, Ralph. "How It Happened Down in Georgia." *New Republic* (January 27, 1947), 13–14.

"Poker Players." *Time* (January 20, 1936), 18.

"Portrait: Arnall and Talmadge." *Newsweek* (September 21, 1942), 30.

"Red Galluses Gene." *Life* (July 29, 1946), 32, 33.

Shannon, Jasper. "Presidential Politics in the South: 1938." *Journal of Politics*, I (1939), 146–70.

Steed, Hal. "Talmadge Takes His Issue to the Nation." *New York Times Magazine* (May 12, 1935), 6ff.

Stolberg, Benjamin. "Buzz Windrip." *Nation* (March 4, 1936), 269, 271; Article continued in March 11 issue, 316, 318.

"Talmadge on Warpath." *Newsweek* (July 28, 1941), 50.

"Talmadge Threatens Book Burning." *Publisher's Weekly* (August 16, 1941), 460.

"The Governor of Georgia Remembers He was Once a Flogger Himself." *Life* (December 8, 1941), 40, 41.

NEWSPAPERS

Athens *Banner Herald*, 1932–1946.
Atlanta *Constitution*, 1926–1946.
Atlanta *Journal*, 1926–1946.
Calhoun *Times*, 1932–1938.
Columbus *Inquirer*, 1932–1946.
Macon *News*, 1928–1946.
Macon *Telegraph*, 1928–1946.
Market Bulletin, 1926–1931.
New York *Times*, 1933, 1936, 1941.
Oglethorpe *Echo*, 1933.
Savannah *Morning News*, 1932–1946.

Hapeville (Ga.) *Statesman*, 1933–1946.
Telfair (Ga.) *Enterprise*, 1920–1946.

BOOKS AND MONOGRAPHS

Arnall, Ellis. *The Shore Dimly Seen*. New York: Lippincott, 1946.
Arnett, Alex Mathews. *The Populist Movement in Georgia*. New York: Columbia University Press, 1922.
Banks, Enoch Marvin. *The Economics of Land Tenure in Georgia*. New York: Columbia University Press, 1905.
Brittian, M. L. *The Story of Georgia Tech*. Chapel Hill: University of North Carolina Press, 1948.
Brooks, Robert Preston. *The Agrarian Revolution in Georgia, 1865–1912*. Madison: Bulletin of the University of Wisconsin, 1914. No. 639, History Series, Vol. III, No. 3.
Burns, James McGregor. *Roosevelt: The Lion and the Fox*. New York: Harcourt, Brace, Jovanovich, 1958.
Cash, W. J. *The Mind of the South*. New York: Random House, 1941.
Chappell, Absalon H. *Miscellanies of Georgia*. Columbus, Ga. n.p. 1928.
Citizens' Fact-Finding Movement in Georgia. *Georgia Facts in Figures*. Athens: University of Georgia Press, 1946.
Coulter, E. Merton. *Georgia: A Short History*. Chapel Hill: University of North Carolina Press, 1960.
Evans, Chandler. *Cyclopedia of Georgia*. Atlanta: n.p., 1906.
Georgia Department of Agriculture. *Georgia: Historical and Agricultural*. Athens, Ga.: Franklin Printing and Publishing Company, 1901.
Gosnell, Cullen B. *Government and Politics in Georgia*. New York: Thomas Nelson and Sons, 1936.
Harper, Roland M. *Development of Agriculture in Georgia from 1850 to 1920*. University, Alabama: Privately published, 1923.
Henson, Allen Lumpkin. *Red Galluses*. Boston: House of Edinboro, 1945.
Hofstadter, Richard. *Age of Reform*. New York: Random House, 1955.
Johnson, Amanda. *Georgia as Colony and State*. Atlanta: Walter W. Brown, 1938.
Key, V. O. *Southern Politics in State and Nation*. New York: Alfred A. Knopf, 1949.
Odum, Howard W. *Southern Regions of the United States*. Chapel Hill: University of North Carolina Press, 1936.
Patterson, James T. *The New Deal and the States: Federalism in Transition*. Princeton, N.J.: Princeton University Press, 1969.
Phillips, Ulrich Bonnell. *Life and Labor in the Old South*. New York: Little Brown and Company, 1929.
Range, Willard. *A Century of Georgia Agriculture*. Athens: University of Georgia Press, 1954.
Rauch, Basis. *The History of the New Deal, 1933–1938*. New York: Creative Age Press, Inc., 1944.
Saye, Albert. *Georgia's County Unit System of Election*. Athens: University of Georgia Monograph, n.d.

Schlesinger, Arthur M., Jr. *The Age of Roosevelt: The Coming of the New Deal*. 3 vols.; Boston: Houghton Mifflin, 1959. Vol. II.

Steed, Hal. *Georgia: Unfinished State*. New York: Alfred A. Knopf, 1942.

Thompson, Holland. *The New South: A Chronicle of Social and Industrial Evolution*. New Haven, Conn.: Yale University Press, 1921.

Tindall, George B. *The Emergence of the New South, 1913–1945*. Baton Rouge: Louisiana State University Press, 1967.

University of Georgia Bureau of Business and Economic Research. *Georgia Statistical Abstract*. Athens, Ga., 1968.

White, George. *Statistics of the State of Georgia*. Savannah, Ga.: W. Thome Williams, 1849.

Williams, T. Harry. *Huey Long*. New York: Alfred A. Knopf, 1970.

Woodward, C. Vann. *The Burden of Southern History*. Baton Rouge: Louisiana State University Press, 1969.

————. *Tom Watson: Agrarian Rebel*. New York: Macmillan, 1938.

THESES AND OTHER UNPUBLISHED PAPERS

Adair, A. Dixon, III. "Eugene Talmadge of Georgia." M.A. thesis, Princeton University, 1936.

Cocking, Walter Dewey. "Report of the Study on Higher Education of Negroes in Georgia." Special Collections, 1938, University of Georgia Libraries.

Cook, James F. "Politics and Education in the Talmadge Era: The Controversy over the University System of Georgia, 1941–1942." Ph.D. dissertation, University of Georgia, 1972.

Crooks, Mary Glass. "The Platform Pledges of Governor Eugene Talmadge and Resulting Statutes." M.A. thesis, University of Georgia, 1953.

DeLoach, R. H. J., Papers. Special Collections, Georgia Southern College Libraries, Statesboro, Ga.

Gibson, Chester James. "Eugene Talmadge: A Case Study in the Use of Common Ground during the 1936 Gubernatorial Campaign in Georgia." M.A. thesis, University of Georgia, 1967.

Greybeal, John M. "The Georgia Primary Election System." M.A. thesis, Emory University, 1952.

Holland, Lynwood. "The Conduct of Elections in Georgia." M.A. thesis, Emory University, 1933.

Howell, Clark, Collection. Emory University, Atlanta, Ga.

Huntly, M. C. "Report on Charges of Political Interference in the University System of Georgia." Typescript in Special Collections, 1941, University of Georgia Libraries.

Lemmon, Sarah McCulloh. "The Public Career of Eugene Talmadge: 1926–1936." M.A. thesis, University of North Carolina, 1952.

McGill, Ralph E., Collection. Special Collections, Emory University, Atlanta, Ga.

Maclean, John M. "The Rise of Eugene Talmadge, 1884–1934." Manuscript on file with Georgia Historical Society, Savannah, Ga.

Miller, Zell Bryan. "The Administration of E. D. Rivers as Governor of Georgia." M.A. thesis, University of Georgia, 1958.

Pittman, Marvin S. "Political Interference of Governor Eugene Talmadge with the Georgia Teacher's College." Typescript in Special Collections, 1970, University of Georgia Libraries.

Roosevelt, Franklin D. Presidential Papers. FDR Library, Hyde Park, N.Y.

Singleton, Stanton J., Papers, 1936. University of Georgia, Athens, Ga.

Southern Association of Colleges and Schools. "Investigation by the Committee Appointed by the Southern Association of Colleges and Secondary Schools, Held at the Ansley Hotel in Atlanta, Georgia, on November 3 and 4, 1941: In re: University System of Georgia." Special Collections, 1941, University of Georgia Libraries.

Tate, William. "Memo on Cocking." Special Collections, 1970, University of Georgia Libraries.

Taylor, Elkin. "A Political Biography of Ellis Arnall." M.A. thesis, Emory University, 1959.

Index

263